THE PLANTAGENETS

The Plantagenets

History of a Dynasty

J S Hamilton

continuum

Continuum UK, The Tower Building, 11 York Road, London SE1 7NX
Continuum US, 80 Maiden Lane, Suite 704, New York, NY 10038

www.continuumbooks.com

First published 2010

British Library Cataloguing-in-Publication Data
A catalogue record for this book is available from the British Library.

ISBN 978 1441 15712 6

Typeset by Pindar NZ, Auckland, New Zealand
Printed and bound by MPG Books Ltd, Cornwall, Great Britain

Contents

For Helen, Isla and Ewan,
in gratitude for their enduring patience,
encouragement and faith.

Acknowledgements

I am very grateful to a number of people for their support throughout the overly long period involved in the production of this book. First of all, thanks to Professor Nigel Saul for initially approaching me to undertake the Plantagenet volume in this series. His continuing encouragement and sage advice has been invaluable. I am also grateful to Martin Shepherd and Tony Morris, under whose editorial guidance the book was begun for London Books. In the later stage of production for Continuum, Ben Hayes was instrumental in pushing me forward to the finish line at long last. Along the way, several colleagues read and commented on earlier drafts of chapters, and I am particularly grateful to James R. King of Midwestern State University and George B. Stow of LaSalle University for their observations and advice. I am indebted to the written work of a great number of scholars of thirteenth- and fourteenth-century England, as will be clear from the bibliography at the end of the volume. Special thanks are also due to Chris Given-Wilson, Mark Ormrod, Seymour Phillips, Philip Morgan and Michael Bennett, each of whom provided suggestions, comments and encouragement at various stages of the project. Finally, I must thank Baylor University. Support for this project was provided by a University Research Grant, and I could not have completed the book without the extraordinary efforts of the research librarians and interlibrary loan specialists in Moody Library. My final thanks go to my wife and children, to whom this book is dedicated.

JSH
Waco, Texas, October 2009

A Simplified Genealogy of the Plantagenet Dynasty, 1216–1399

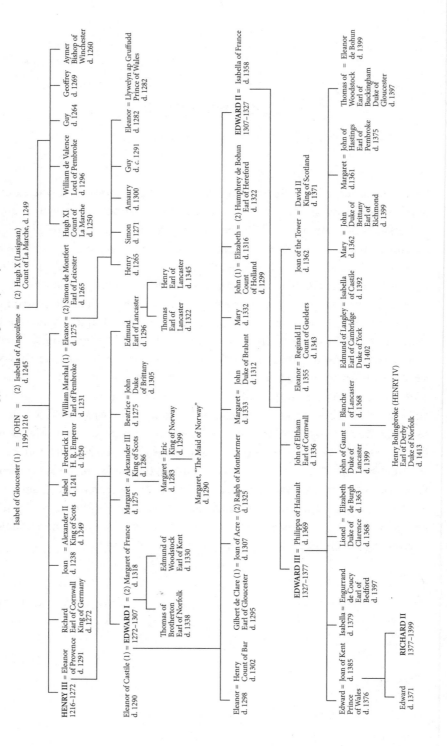

Map 1 Plantagenet Britain

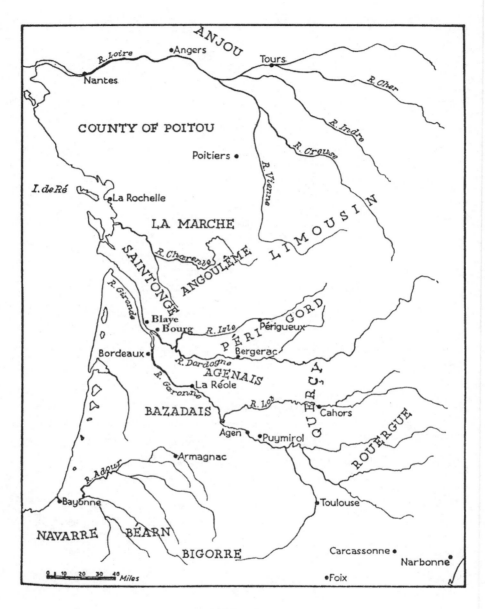

ANJOU

•Angers

R. Loire

Tours

Nantes

R. Cher

COUNTY OF POITOU

R. Indre

R. Creuse

R. Vienne

Poitiers •

I. de Ré

La Rochelle

LA MARCHE

LIMOUSIN

SAINTONGE

R. Charente

ANGOULÊME

R. Gironde

PÉRIGORD

Blaye
Bourg

R. Isle

Périgueux

Bordeaux •

R. Dordogne

Bergerac

AGENAIS

QUERCY

La Réole

R. Garonne

R. Lot

BAZADAIS

Cahors

ROUERGUE

Agen

•Puymirol

•Armagnac

R. Adour

Bayonne

Toulouse

NAVARRE

BÉARN

BIGORRE

Carcassonne •

Narbonne •

0 10 20 30 40 Miles

•Foix

Map 2 Medieval Aquitaine

Introduction

The Plantagenet dynasty derives its name from the *Planta genesta*, the broom plant that Geoffrey, count of Anjou, apparently used as a personal emblem. Geoffrey's son Henry II may be considered the first Plantagenet king. He and his sons Richard I and John, however, are more commonly referred to as the Angevins, as they continued to control a cross-channel empire that stretched from the Pyrenees to the borders of Scotland. For the purposes of this study, the Plantagenet dynasty will be taken to refer to the five kings from Henry III to Richard II who ruled England from 1216 until 1399, when Richard II was deposed by his cousin Henry Bolingbroke, who established the Lancastrian dynasty as Henry IV. Each of the Plantagenet kings was faced with his own challenges and opportunities, yet there is a surprising degree of continuity to be found in the outlooks, attitudes and concerns of each of these kings, not least their concern for the Plantagenet dynasty itself.

Remarkably, three of the five Plantagenets came to the throne as minors: Henry III succeeded John at 9 years of age; Edward III was 14 years old when his father was deposed by his mother Isabella; and Richard II succeeded his grandfather Edward III at 10 years of age. All three of these Plantagenets would have to overcome a variety of obstacles before they were able to assert their royal authority and articulate a vision of kingship that resonated with the political elites of their day. Henry III would be assisted by such able councillors as William Marshal, Hubert de Burgh and the papal legates Guala and Pandulf. Edward III would find himself more overshadowed initially than any other of the dynasty, faced as he was by the dominating presence of Roger Mortimer, first earl of March; it required a daring coup led personally by the king and a small group of his intimate companions to liberate himself from this unwanted tutelage. Richard II would find himself in a constant struggle with members of his own family, particularly his uncles, the younger sons of Edward III, and his cousin Bolingbroke.

Every one of the Plantagenet kings would face political crises of the first order.

The political history of the thirteenth and fourteenth centuries can be regarded as a commentary on the Magna Carta, the great charter of liberties that King John had been forced to accept in 1215. This was particularly obvious in the case of Henry III, who came to the throne with a French army entrenched on English soil and many of his magnates in open revolt. His repeated confirmation of the Magna Carta transformed it into a fundamental element in the English constitution. Throughout his reign, Henry faced baronial opposition – from the 1250s, led by the mercurial Simon de Montfort – and in the interplay between the king and his baronial foes, parliament began to emerge as a significant representative institution (at least in theory, if not yet always in practice).

Henry's son, Edward I, is generally regarded as a powerful, indeed masterful, king, yet he too faced a grave political crisis in 1297, when the marshal and constable – the earls of Norfolk and Hereford, respectively – refused to serve overseas separately from the king's own army. Edward was forced to confirm Magna Carta and the Charter of the Forest in 1297, and again in 1300, in order to restore domestic harmony, but even that might not have been enough had not the Scottish victory at Stirling Bridge shocked the aristocracy into a more cooperative frame of mind. As part of his effort to find broad-based support for taxation to fund his wars, in 1295 he summoned knights of the shire, burgesses and lower clergy to what has become known as the Model Parliament, even though such inclusiveness would not become the norm for many years to come.

Edward II, certainly the least talented of the Plantagenets, was faced with a seemingly endless series of crises from the outset of his reign. Early on, he was forced to accept the Ordinances of 1311, every bit as great a constraint on his royal prerogative and power as the Provisions of Oxford that Simon de Montfort had imposed on Henry III. The struggle for the enforcement of the Ordinances dominated the politics of the following decade. Finally liberating himself from baronial control after his defeat and destruction of the earl of Lancaster in 1322, Edward II had himself been toppled from the throne by his wife Isabella and her lover Roger Mortimer within 5 years, shortly thereafter to be deposed and almost certainly murdered.

Coming to the throne under such circumstances, the young Edward III trod cautiously for much of his reign. Having organized a successful coup against Mortimer in 1330, Edward III struggled to find his balance through the next decade, facing a political crisis largely of his own making in 1340–1341. It is a measure of Edward's greatness that he managed to learn from this debacle, adjusting his expectations of the ability of both his ministers and his people to raise never-ending tax revenues for his wars. For the better part of three decades after 1340, before age and circumstances finally caught up with him, Edward would rule in cooperation with his magnates, and the increasingly prominent parliament. Nevertheless, the crisis of the Good Parliament of 1376 indicated the growing confidence and assertiveness of the parliamentary commons.

Richard II faced many of the same problems that his forebears had encountered with both the magnates and the increasingly vocal gentry now sitting in parliament. His reign was a rollercoaster of highs and lows. That parliament was now a fully mature institution is indicated by the fact that the pivotal events of his reign were played out in the Wonderful Parliament of 1386, the Merciless Parliament of 1388 and the Revenge Parliament of 1397. Controlled by conciliar councils both in his minority and later in the reign, Richard sought to articulate a vision of kingship, perhaps more consciously than any of his predecessors. The language of majesty developed at his court, and his artistic patronage of works such as the Wilton Diptych resonate with his sense of his own regality. In the end, however, like Edward II, Richard too was cast down from his throne, soon to be deposed and done away with, but unlike Edward he had no son to whom the crown could pass. His failure to produce an heir spelled the end of the Plantagenet dynasty.

Each of the Plantagenet kings faced complex diplomatic challenges. Henry III spent his entire life dreaming of recovering the French lands that his father John had lost, but his military resources and leadership were unequal to the task. Beyond that, he developed a grand vision of a Plantagenet empire stretching from the Mediterranean to the Scottish highlands. His catastrophic involvement in the so-called Sicilian Business of 1258 in which he agreed to buy the Hohenstaufen throne in Sicily from the pope for his younger son Edmund was only the most dramatic manifestation of this vision. His lavish patronage of his wife's Savoyard uncles and his own Poitevin half-siblings was an equally misguided course of action. Despite the retention of a diminished Aquitaine (or Gascony),[1] unlike the Norman and Angevin kings before him, Henry III was an English king, without great lands and revenues beyond the sea. Whereas the Norman kings had routinely spent more than half of their reigns overseas, Henry III spent only 4.5 years in a reign of 56 years on the continent. The great tragedy of the reign is his failure to understand and embrace this new reality.

Edward I's interests were more obviously British. At the same time as his Capetian rival Philip IV (1285–1314) narrowed his own focus to France itself, Edward aggressively pursued what might be termed an 'English Empire.' He was largely successful in securing control over Wales, as physically embodied in the magnificent castles with which he ringed the country. If, in the end, he was less successful in Scotland, it was not for want of effort, as he essentially conquered the northern kingdom on two separate occasions. Meanwhile, he dedicated himself to consolidating his grip on the remaining Plantagenet territory on the continent, the duchy of Aquitaine. The costs involved were enormous, some £750,000 between 1294 and 1298 alone, as he struggled both to conquer Scotland and save Gascony at the same time. But, in the course of his reign, he developed an administrative machinery that rivalled that of Capetian France and, if it could not produce all of the funds required, it was at least capable of managing and accounting for the resources available with previously unheard-of efficiency. The parliament that met at Westminster in February 1305 heard petitions not only from England, but from Wales, Scotland, Ireland, the Channel Islands and Gascony.

Edward II may well have shared the Plantagenet vision of kingship passed down from his father, in which the English crown was to dominate its British neighbours, but he was unable to bring it to realization. Although he campaigned frequently and at great expense in Scotland, most of his efforts were misdirected against an enemy who had no intention to engage in battle; on the one occasion when a major battle did take place, Edward suffered a devastating defeat at Bannockburn. Edward's penchant to rely on a small number of favourites rather than the broader political community had devastating consequences. Not only did this have an impact on domestic politics; it also influenced international affairs. For instance, Edward's response to the suppression of the Templars was shaped by his need to garner support from both the pope and the king of France in order to achieve Piers Gaveston's recall from exile. Although his relations with France were generally cordial, in no small part due to the diplomatic skills of his French wife Isabella, the final crisis of the reign was occasioned by his attachment to the younger Hugh Despenser, a circumstance which led him to send his eldest son and heir Edward to France to perform homage in his stead in 1325 – with profound consequences. Isabella would eventually return with a small army of English political exiles supplemented by mercenaries from Hainault with which she would quickly overthrow her husband and the Despenser regime, demonstrating the isolation of the king and his court both domestically and internationally.

Edward III, and along with him his eldest son, the Black Prince, still evoke the image of chivalric warfare that was so central to medieval culture. At the outset of his reign, however, Edward faced seemingly insurmountable problems. Initially, he had no choice but to acquiesce in the recognition of the claims of Robert Bruce in Scotland and Philip of Valois in France, but after he liberated himself from Roger Mortimer in 1330, he was free to pursue a different course. He turned first to Scotland, where he took advantage of Edward Balliol's claim to the throne to destabilize the Bruce regime. The bigger prize, however, was France. Like his father and grandfather before him, Edward III was primarily concerned with maintaining English rule in Aquitaine. His initial efforts to form a grand coalition on the continent with which to challenge Philip VI proved both enormously expensive and essentially ineffective, leading to the political crisis at home in 1340–1341. By the mid-1340s, however, Edward was pursuing a new policy based on mobility and English resources, and he was to enjoy a series of stunning successes at Crécy in 1346 and at Poitiers in 1356, where his son Edward, the Black Prince, captured King John II of France. The subsequent treaty of Brétigny restored an enlarged Aquitaine to Edward in full sovereignty. Ultimately, however, the combination of the fragmented nature of his new principality of Aquitaine, along with the greatly superior resources of the Capetians, made Edward's conquests untenable, and they began to slip away after the renewal of war in 1369.

In his handling of diplomacy and international affairs, the last Plantagenet reveals himself as something of a paradox. Richard II was a capable soldier, as he demonstrated in Ireland in 1394 and foolishly tried to replicate in 1399. But in the broader scheme of things, and particularly with regard to France, Richard pursued a policy of peace, a policy that was very unpopular with his nobility. At the same time, however, like the first Plantagenet, Henry III, Richard II appears to have had a broader imperial vision. He almost certainly considered himself a serious candidate to become Holy Roman Emperor, yet his subjects failed to share this vision, and may even have stood in its way. It is possible that this more universal rather than insular vision accounts not only for Richard's first marriage to Anne of Bohemia, but also his second marriage to the very young Isabella of France. Heirs of his body were a lesser consideration to Richard, yet his failure to produce such heirs played a significant role in his ultimate deposition and death.

Finally, we must consider the Plantagenet dynasty as just that – a living, breathing family enterprise. Henry III found himself essentially orphaned in 1215 following the death of his father and the return of his mother to her native Angoulême. Not surprisingly, he turned to a number of father figures in his youth, men such as William Marshal, Peter des Roches and Hubert de Burgh.

Even more important in the history of the reign would be his marriage to Eleanor of Provence, whose uncles William, Peter and Boniface of Savoy would soon come to dominate affairs. Henry's inordinate generosity to these foreign-born kinsmen, first the Savoyards and then the Poitevins, was out of step with the times. These people were 'foreigners' in the eyes of an increasingly 'English' political class. Henry's failure to understand this was a major contributing factor to the crises of the reign. Another family relationship with dire consequences was the marriage of Henry's sister Eleanor to Simon de Montfort. Henry's inability or unwillingness to provide Eleanor's full marriage portion was a crucial factor in Montfort's drift into opposition. On the other hand, Henry's cordial relationship with his brother-in-law Louis IX of France provided him with invaluable support at a number of critical points in the reign. More than that, the friendship and rivalry that developed between Henry and Louis certainly influenced Henry's own conception of kingship. This is seen most clearly in the rebuilding of Westminster Abbey as the Plantagenet royal church, but is also apparent in the king's personal piety and devotion to his family.

Edward I had come to the throne in circumstances very different to those that his father had faced as a boy of 9 years old half a century earlier. Edward had played an active role in the political upheavals that had marked the reign of Henry III. He had seen his own position as heir to the throne threatened by Simon de Montfort following the battle of Lewes in 1264; as king, he worked assiduously to strengthen both his sovereignty and the position of the royal family within the kingdom. Edward had married Eleanor of Castile in 1254 and she had already given birth to 7 of her 14 children prior to Edward's coronation (of the four males, however, only the future Edward II survived childhood). Although Eleanor developed something of a reputation for avarice, she did not bring a great following of Castilians with her to court, and she does not seem to have inspired the sort of resentment that Eleanor of Provence had sometimes occasioned. Eleanor is best remembered today for the memorial crosses that Edward constructed along the route of her funeral cortege in 1290, celebrating both his beloved consort and his dynasty. In 1299, Edward married for a second time to Margaret of France, youngest daughter of Philip III. Although much younger than the king, she quickly gave birth to two sons and a daughter. The boys, Thomas of Brotherton and Edmund of Woodstock, would play significant roles in the reign of their half-brother, Edward II. The fact that he passed over both of them in awarding the hitherto royal earldom of Cornwall to his favourite, Piers Gaveston, was among the first controversial acts of his reign. It is perhaps unsurprising that both ended the reign supporting Queen Isabella against their brother, the king.

Edward II's family relations were troubled. His mother died when he was 6 years old and most of his sisters left court while he was still a boy. His relationship with his father was difficult, with several well-documented confrontations taking place in the later years of the reign of Edward I. On the other hand, for much of the reign, his marriage to Isabella of France may have been happier than is sometimes suggested. Certainly, as a 12-year-old girl she was overlooked in the early years of the reign at a time when the king's undivided attention was focused on Piers Gaveston. But between 1312 and 1321, Isabella gave birth to four children and played a prominent role in diplomacy. The crises of the middle years of the reign were largely unconnected to the queen, but her marginalization by the younger Despenser in the 1320s ultimately led to a revolution of sorts when she returned from France in 1326 at the head of an army, accompanied by Roger Mortimer. Edward II also faced difficulties with the broader royal family. As already mentioned, his half-brothers eventually turned against him, but it was his cousin, Thomas of Lancaster, who proved his nemesis throughout much of the reign. Here, the policy of Edward I in reducing the number of earls and concentrating power in the main line of the royal family, came back to pose serious problems for his son.

The deposition of Edward II was portrayed by contemporaries as an act of abdication in favour of his son, maintaining thereby the integrity of the Plantagenet dynasty. Nevertheless, Edward III would need to restore the image of the royal house both at home and abroad. Edward III's early marriage to Philippa of Hainault, despite the irregular circumstances in which it was arranged, proved successful in every way. The queen was an invaluable companion and confidante to her young husband during the difficult first years of the reign. She would go on to fulfill the primary duty of any medieval queen by producing seven sons and five daughters, seven of whom survived into adulthood. Philippa also succeeded in integrating members of her Hainault affinity into the court without causing unnecessary conflict with the English nobility. Edward, for his part, devoted a great deal of his energy in providing for these children, but significantly he looked beyond England itself in identifying prospects and resources with which to settle them. In some cases, this meant within Britain, including Wales and Ireland, whereas in other cases it meant foreign marriages and titles. Edward was also careful to respect and reward the broader royal family, most notably Henry of Grosmont, earl and later duke of Lancaster. Unfortunately, a central aspect of

Edward's vision for a cooperative royal family was undermined by the prolonged illness and premature death of the Black Prince in 1376. This led to yet another Plantagenet minority for his grandson Richard II, and the almost inevitable internal conflict that comes with a regency.

Richard II must surely have been shaped by the heroic image of his father and grandfather, and yet both were ill and declining in the years to his accession. Buffeted by the chaotic conditions of his minority, in Anne of Bohemia Richard found a refuge. Richard and Anne appear to have had a genuinely warm and affectionate relationship, and yet there were no children of their union. It is possible that Anne was barren or that Richard was infertile. It is also possible that they entered into a chaste marriage as a matter of religious conviction, although such an undertaking would have been remarkable for a royal couple. Richard's lack of concern to produce an heir seems apparent from his decision to marry Isabella, the 7-year-old daughter of Charles VI of France in 1396. Yet, not surprisingly, the question of the succession was of paramount importance throughout the reign, not least of all to Richard's eldest uncle, John of Gaunt. By the terms of the entail of Edward III, Gaunt was Richard's heir, to be followed by his own son, Henry Bolingbroke, the future Henry IV. Richard's suggestion at various times in the reign that he would designate an heir, such as the earl of Aumerle, was threatening to the house of Lancaster and surely played its part in Bolingbroke's decision to seize not just his inheritance in 1399, but the crown, bringing the Plantagenet dynasty to a sudden end.

The story of the Plantagenet dynasty is compelling. The two centuries during which they ruled saw the last foreign invasion of England, three different outbreaks of civil war, as well as a popular uprising of unprecedented scale, and the initiation of a century-long war with France. During this same period, the quintessentially English institution of parliament was born and took shape. Meanwhile, a new sense of English identity was being embraced both at the top and bottom ends of society, an identity formed in relation both to a broader British identity and the continent. The Plantagenet kings played a crucial role in all of these developments, recasting England in fundamental and enduring ways.

1

Henry III (1216–1272)

The reign of King Henry III (1216–1272) was as long as it was eventful, and remains controversial today. With hindsight, it is possible to say that the most important date in the reign occurred well before the king's birth and more than a decade before his accession. This date was 24 June 1204 and it was when Rouen surrendered and with it the duchy of Normandy, to Philip II 'Augustus' of France. War with France had been provoked by the precipitate marriage of King John to Henry's mother, Isabella of Angoulême, on 24 August 1200, and John proved unable to recover his patrimony. The devastating defeat of his allies at the battle of Bouvines on 27 July 1214 confirmed the loss of Normandy and threatened the rest of the Plantagenet inheritance; upon this, everything else in the reign of Henry III would turn. This may not, however, have been obvious to Henry when his father unexpectedly died at Newark during the night of 27–28 October 1216. At the time, King John was confronted by widespread revolt among his own English subjects, as well as the presence of a French army that was solidly entrenched on English soil. As heir to the throne, John left a 9-year-old son. The fate of the Plantagenet dynasty hung by a slender thread. The reign of Henry III would prove to be a watershed in the development of English notions of kingship. For the supporters of the boy-king in 1216, however, the articulation of idealized visions of kingship would have to wait: for the moment, survival would be enough.

Henry III had been born in Winchester on 1 October 1207, the eldest of five children born to King John and his second wife, Isabella of Angoulême. Although his mother would survive well into the reign of Henry III (she died on 4 June 1246), and the children by her second marriage (in 1220) to Hugh de Lusignan, count of La Marche, would ultimately play a pivotal part in Henry's reign, Isabella herself appears to have played a very limited role in the dramatic events of the first year of the reign. Balked of any meaningful role in the regency council that formed around her son after the defeat of Louis of France, in 1218 she chose to return to Angoulême. In the early years of the reign, therefore, Henry III looked

not to his immediate family so much as to the broader *familia* of his father, to
men such as William Marshal and Peter des Roches, and to the many castellans
and captains, more of them French than English, whose loyalty was Henry's
greatest initial strength. Henry's quasi-orphanage may also have drawn him to a
closer bond with mystical parents, embodied in his lifelong devotion to the cults
of Edward the Confessor and the Virgin Mary.

On his deathbed, John reputedly had begged his executors to make sure that
William Marshal, earl of Pembroke, would assume the guardianship of his young
heir. This the Marshal did, but only with grave misgivings about the likelihood of
success, and only after receiving the endorsement of all those around the young
king, including the only other likely candidate for the guardianship, Ranulf, earl
of Chester. In the words of *The History of William Marshal*, evocative not only of
the chivalric ethos of the day but also of St Christopher and the Christ child, the
Marshal promised that if necessary he would 'carry [the king] on my shoulders
step by step, from island to island, from country to country, and I would not fail
him, not even if it meant begging my bread'.[1] Fortunately, he would not have to
carry the boy alone. In consequence of John having resigned the kingdom to
Pope Innocent III in 1213, the papal legate, Cardinal Guala Bicchieri, was already
in residence in England at the accession of Henry III, and his support for the boy
provided a degree of legitimization that no rival could hope to match. Another
crucially important figure in these early days of the reign was Peter des Roches,
bishop of Winchester, who probably exercised more personal influence over the
young king than anyone else, acting as Henry's tutor until his fourteenth birthday
in October 1221.

The hastily arranged coronation of Henry III on 28 October 1216 at Gloucester
can have had little positive impact on Henry's vision of kingship. Being denied
access to Westminster, which was in the hands of Philip Augustus's son and heir,
Louis, count of Artois, he was without the royal regalia. Furthermore, the archbishop of Canterbury, Stephen Langton, was absent at the papal court in Rome.
Guala therefore called upon the bishop of Winchester, assisted by the bishops
of Worcester and Exeter, to place the makeshift crown – a simple lady's chaplet
– on the young king's head. Nevertheless, the ceremony gave Henry a patina of
legitimacy that Louis lacked in the eyes of the English church, and increasingly
among the lay aristocracy as well. The coronation reinforced what was probably
Henry's single greatest advantage: unlike Louis who claimed election as king of
England, Henry was the rightful heir of his father and, for a feudal audience with
their own lands and sons to consider, this was an unassailable argument. It was

an argument further reinforced on 12 November by the reissue of a new version of the Magna Carta – a document that both King John and Pope Innocent III had repudiated, but which both King Henry III and Pope Honorius III (in the person of the legate Guala) now embraced.

The Battle of Lincoln on 20 May 1217 and the subsequent naval battle off Sandwich on 24 August of that year consolidated Henry's position. At Lincoln, William Marshal, that great paladin of the age, now in his 70s, performed his last great feat of arms, thoroughly routing the forces of the future Louis VIII of France. His bold decision to risk everything on a frontal assault against the rebel troops besieging Lincoln Castle led to the death of the French commander, and the capture of many of the leading English rebels. It was a truly decisive victory. Meanwhile, another great figure of the minority, Hubert de Burgh, also emerged as a war hero. His defiant defence of Dover Castle in the face of a siege by Prince Louis had, in part, been responsible for the victory at Lincoln, having compelled Louis to divide his forces. De Burgh's naval victory over the infamous pirate, Eustache the Monk, off Sandwich prevented reinforcements and supplies from reaching the French and virtually guaranteed the final victory for Henry III. Accordingly, in September, Louis agreed to the Treaty of Kingston-Lambeth, withdrawing his claim to the English throne. The excommunication of his followers was withdrawn by the papal legate, and their lands were restored to the *status quo ante bellum*, allowing for a lasting settlement. In November, the rapprochement of the king and his subjects was further consolidated by another re-issuance, at a great council in Westminster, of the Magna Carta, along with a wholly new Charter of the Forest that was drafted to address some of the most common and resented abuses perpetrated by Henry's royal ancestors.

Throughout 1218, William Marshal continued to lead the king's government, but only with the consent and counsel of the political community. As the Marshal lay dying in 1219, he returned the young king to the protection of the papacy in the person of the new papal legate Pandulf Verraccio, who had replaced Guala in 1218, and who would remain in England until the return of Archbishop Langton in 1221. Yet, despite the endorsement of the legate by the 'common consent and provision of all the kingdom', the day-to-day affairs of state were ultimately entrusted to Hubert de Burgh, the justiciar, in preference to Henry's tutor, Peter des Roches, bishop of Winchester. The choice of de Burgh rather than des Roches was highly significant. Des Roches, one of the detested 'Poitevins' of King John's reign (although, in reality, he was from Touraine), personified the evils of the previous reign, having served John as justiciar in the run-up to the civil war, from

1213 to 1215. Wealthy, powerful and an alien to boot, he was considered unlikely to follow the Marshal's moderate course. Hubert de Burgh, on the other hand, was an Englishman of modest background and means, a man more likely to be amenable to the will of the baronage than the powerful bishop of Winchester.

The greatest problem facing the minority government was the recovery of crown lands and the more general re-establishment of the king's authority. To achieve this, it was necessary to replace many of the sheriffs and castellans who had held their positions since the previous reign, and who, in truth, had been among those most loyal to Henry during the civil war. Further complicating matters, these men argued that their appointments could not be terminated until the king had come of age. Pandulf urged the justiciar to proceed along an aggressive course, but de Burgh acted with deliberation and caution. He was right to do so, for it was not only 'aliens' such as Faukes de Bréauté and the Poitevin count of Aumale, William de Forz, who resisted the reassertion of royal authority. In 1219, the Sheriff of Northumberland considered it useless to travel south to meet with the justiciar prior to the assembly of a great council, while in the following year the earl of Salisbury, William Longespée, wrote to Hubert concerning a royal order for the dismantling of Harbottle Castle in Northumberland, asserting that only the 'chief council of the king' could take such a decision. Between 1220 and 1223 – at which time the pope declared the king to be of age – the struggle to reassert royal authority moved forward slowly, but began to gain momentum.

The second coronation of Henry III at Westminster on 17 May 1220, appropriately the feast of Pentecost, was a decidedly different affair than the makeshift ceremony of 1216. The regalia, most if not all of it new, was splendid. A bejewelled golden crown was paired with a golden sceptre and a silver staff, while the king was richly robed in a tunic surmounted with a dalmatic of red samite decorated with gold orphreys and jewels, along with matching stockings and shoes. The coronation ceremony culminated in one sense with Archbishop Langton placing the crown of St Edward the Confessor on the king's head. In another sense, the repetition of the king's coronation oath, with its emphasis on the king's duty to preserve and recover the rights of the crown, signalled a renewed determination to do just that, to take possession of crown lands and castles in the name of the newly recrowned king. Indeed, on the following day, an oath was taken by the barons in which they reportedly swore to restore royal castles and wards into the king's hand, as well as to make faithful account for their farms at the exchequer. Over the next few years, considerable progress was made, with the king's administration, increasingly led by de Burgh, trading concessions in some areas – such as the discontinuation of a forest eyre in 1222, and a reaffirmation of the Charters in 1223 – for the recovery of royal rights in others, such as the resumption of the royal demesne.

In 1223, Pope Honorius III declared the 16-year-old Henry ready to rule in his own right. Almost at once, he faced a crisis. His former adversary, now King Louis VIII, invaded Poitou in 1224 and quickly overran it. At the same time, Hugh de Lusignan, second husband to Henry's mother, launched an attack on Gascony. The English response was both swift and forceful, an army being dispatched in 1225 under the earl of Salisbury and the king's 16-year-old brother Richard. They were quickly able to drive Lusignan out of Gascony, but Poitou remained in the hands of the king of France. The funding for this war had been made available by a tax on movables agreed to by a great council. In return, in February 1225, the king had reissued both the Magna Carta and the Charter of the Forest, sealed with the king's own seal. This third version of the charters became definitive: although Henry and later kings would reconfirm the charters, there would be no further amending of their content. The 1225 version of the Magna Carta did not greatly differ from its predecessors of 1215 and 1217, yet its importance should not be underrated. The repeated reissue of the charters established them as law, mandating standards for royal government. Additionally, the linkage between the political concessions made in great councils (and later parliaments) and grants of taxation became an increasingly important factor in royal government, one of the most significant developments of the reign.

On 8 January 1227 in Oxford, 'by common counsel', Henry III declared himself fully of age. In fact, however, for the next 5 years it was Hubert de Burgh, now elevated to the peerage as earl of Kent and in 1228 named justiciar for life, who dominated political life. The king meanwhile built up a large military retinue in his own household, and turned his thoughts to recovery of the Plantagenet lands in France. The prospect of such a recovery was enhanced by the unexpected death of Louis VIII in November 1226, leaving a 12-year-old boy, another Louis, as his heir. Henry was further encouraged by representations from the nobles of Normandy and Poitou seeking English intervention; in 1229, he collected the necessary funds through the imposition of a scutage and prepared to invade. In the end, however, his troops were mustered too late and his fleet proved inadequate; the expedition had to be postponed. Although Henry's military plans do not appear to have had the full support of the justiciar, another scutage was collected in 1230, and this time the king did set sail, landing at St Mâlo in May. Fighting was desultory and without a clear objective, and Henry proved unable to raise the Normans in rebellion against Louis IX and his iron-willed mother Blanche of Castile. Although the English force did probe as far south as Bordeaux, in the end little was achieved beyond the accumulation of debt. The recovery of his ancestral lands would continue to be a central concern for Henry, yet increasingly his hopes would appear unrealistic.

In the wake of his return from France in October 1230, Henry found himself at odds with de Burgh, who seemed not to share his vision for a Plantagenet revanche on the continent. In the spring of 1231, the Welsh prince Llewelyn ap Iorwerth (Llewelyn the Great) saw the death of the earl of Pembroke as an opportunity to raise a rebellion in Wales. Henry's efforts to suppress this were undermined by a separate dispute over the succession to the earldom of Pembroke led by Richard Marshal and the king's own brother, Richard of Cornwall. At that already tense moment, Peter des Roches returned to England and was quickly restored to prominence in Henry's court. Des Roches had been long absent from the realm on a pilgrimage that had taken him to Jerusalem with the Holy Roman Emperor Frederick II in 1229, and had seen him flourish as a diplomat, negotiating settlements between Frederick II and Pope Gregory IX in 1230 and between Henry III and Louis IX in 1231. He seemed the perfect foil to de Burgh.

Throughout the first half of 1232, Henry vacillated between the guidance of his two erstwhile mentors. In the spring, he travelled west with de Burgh to negotiate a settlement with Llywelyn, but at the same time he appointed Peter de Rivaux, a kinsman and close associate of des Roches, as treasurer of the king's household for life. Finally, on 29 July 1232, a violent quarrel broke out between Henry and de Burgh at Woodstock, following which Henry dismissed de Burgh as justiciar. De Burgh was subsequently charged with a wide variety of crimes, both professional and personal – he was even alleged to have poisoned both the earl of Salisbury and the earl of Pembroke. The former justiciar was forced to seek sanctuary – unsuccessfully as it turned out, being removed by force and imprisoned in Devizes Castle – and was stripped of all the lands and wealth he had accumulated since his initial appointment as justiciar by John in 1215. He would eventually be reconciled with the king prior to his death in 1243, but de Burgh nevertheless died a broken man, having spent his later years 'in melancholy retirement', to use Powicke's evocative phrase.[2]

The fall of Hubert de Burgh, however, led merely to the elevation of Peter des Roches. In 1233, Pope Gregory IX confirmed Henry's authority to recover crown rights, which allowed the king to cancel more than 50 grants that had been made to de Burgh's supporters. Most of these lands and resources immediately found their way into the hands of des Roches' supporters, including notorious figures from the previous reign such as Engelard de Cigogné, Peter de Mauley and Robert Passelewe. Henry also replaced all of the sheriffs, assigning 21 counties to Peter de Rivaux alone, and manned castles throughout the kingdom with foreign mercenaries, popularly, if inaccurately, described as Poitevins. This aggressive reassertion of royal authority quickly resulted in baronial complaints, and ultimately in a revolt led by Richard Marshal. Although he had little English support, Marshal made common cause with Llywelyn in the summer of 1233 and caused Henry some embarrassment in the ensuing campaign. Under increasing pressure to reform his government, Henry authorized negotiations with Llywelyn in March 1234. In May, he ordered des Roches to leave the royal court and return to his diocese of Winchester, while at the same time dismissing de Rivaux and his associates from office. At long last, Henry III was able to embark upon his kingship out from under the shadow of his two great, but polarizing, mentors.

At this point, it is necessary to assess the personality and character of Henry III. Henry was not an imposing figure physically. Like his father John, he appears to have stood approximately five feet six inches tall. He is reputed to have had a drooping eyelid, but otherwise his appearance is not remarked upon by contemporary chroniclers. The tomb effigy in Westminster Abbey sculpted by William Torel suggests his features to have been regular and not unattractive. In a number of chronicles, Henry III is described as *simplex*, yet even as a boy he was said to speak with '*gravitas et dignitas*'. Almost universally he is described as pious, but this piety has nevertheless tended to be undervalued, with Henry being overshadowed by his Capetian contemporary Louis IX. Henry's devotion to the cult of Edward the Confessor is well known, and its physical manifestation in the rebuilding of Westminster Abbey is perhaps Henry's greatest legacy. Less well known, but of considerable importance in assessing Henry's character, is his devotion to the Virgin Mary. Recent scholarship has convincingly demonstrated that Henry was no less devoted than his brother-in-law Louis to the Marian cult. He made no fewer than 11 pilgrimages to the shrine of Our Lady at Walsingham, frequently timed to coincide with the feast of the Annunciation. Indeed, it was from the shrine at Walsingham on the vigil of the feast of the Annunciation (24 March) in 1242 that Henry would issue the summons for knight service in support of his grand expedition to recover Poitou. Even when he was unable to be present personally, the king was attentive to the shrine, ordering thousands of tapers to be burned on the feasts of the Assumption, the Virgin's Conception and the Annunciation. Like Louis IX, Henry was devoted to the Lady Mass, which he celebrated not only on feast days of the Virgin, but also quite frequently on Saturday, the day of the week associated with her in contemporary thought. Even at Westminster, so closely associated with the Confessor, Henry himself laid the foundation stone for the Lady Chapel on the eve of his second coronation in 1220, and in 1256 he ordered the demolition of the upper levels of this chapel so that it might be rebuilt in harmony with the rest of the ongoing reconstruction of the abbey.

Henry's profound piety is also apparent in his involvement with a relic of the Holy Blood. On 13 October 1247, the king processed barefoot and dressed in a simple cloak from St Paul's Cathedral to Westminster Abbey carrying a crystal phial, sent to him by the Patriarch of Jerusalem and said to contain a portion of the most precious blood of Jesus Christ. This priceless relic was duly presented to the monks of Westminster and their patron saints, St Peter and St Edward, the latter being the king's own special patron. Mass was celebrated, and the sermon preached by the bishop of Norwich made specific, and favorable, comparison of this relic to the many relics of Christ's Passion recently collected in Paris by the king's brother-in-law, Louis IX. The service was followed by a knighting ceremony in which the king's Poitevin half-brother, William de Valence, was dubbed a knight. This was clearly meant to be a spectacular celebration of church and state, designed to enhance the prestige of both Henry III and Westminster Abbey. Unfortunately for Henry, from the outset there seems to have been considerable doubt about the authenticity of the relic. The cult of the Holy Blood was already widespread in thirteenth-century Europe, but the provenance of the various relics was often contentious. The donor in this case, the Patriarch of Jerusalem, had not previously been associated with the Holy Blood. Not only that, but many theologians, especially Dominicans including the great Thomas Aquinas himself, had considerable theological doubts about the possibility of the survival of physical relics of Christ after His Resurrection. The cult of the Holy Blood did succeed elsewhere in England, particularly at Hailes, Ashridge and Glastonbury, yet the Westminster relic quietly fell into obscurity. Here, as in other contexts, Henry's genuine piety cannot be doubted, yet circumstances conspired against him to diminish the impact of his gesture.

Finally, something should be said about the almsgiving of Henry III. Like all medieval kings, Henry was generous in his gifts to the various religious houses and shrines that he visited. His generosity was largely responsible for the building of houses for the Carmelites at Oxford, the Dominicans at Canterbury and the Franciscans at Norwich, Reading, Shrewsbury and York. Even more impressive, however, as an indicator of the king's piety, was his practice of feeding the poor (*fraters et pauperes*) on a daily basis. The basic number fed per day was 100 (150 if the queen was also in attendance), at a cost of 1–1½ *d.* per head, a figure equivalent to the daily wages of a labourer. Greater numbers were regularly fed when Henry arrived in a new location. For instance, in April 1260, when the king entered London he fed some 344 paupers, and in August of that year when he entered Winchester he fed another 282. On feast days, the king could be even more generous to the poor. Earlier in 1260, on the anniversary of the death of Edward the Confessor (5 January), Henry had provided meals for an extraordinary 1,500 paupers, whereas the vigil and anniversary of the translation of the Confessor (12–13 October) saw provision for no less than 5,000! That this almsgiving was motivated by genuine piety is clearly suggested by the fact that Henry had the parable of Dives and Lazarus painted on the walls opposite the king's dais – directly in his gaze as he dined – in the great halls at Ludgershall, Northampton and Guildford, a vivid reminder of the obligation of the rich to care for the poor at peril of eternal damnation. Giving was central to Henry's sense of self and kingship. He had a royal motto, painted on the walls of the royal residences at both Westminster and Woodstock: '*qui non dat quod amat non accipit ille quod optat*': 'He who does not give what he loves, does not receive what he desires.'[3]

Turning from his piety to his character more generally, Henry III has tended to receive even less favorable treatment. His dependency on father figures early in the reign and on members of his extended family later on has led to the depiction of a weak and fatuous ruler. It has been remarked that 'the king had objectives without expertise and ambition without energy'.[4] This is probably a fair assessment. One of Henry's greatest failings was his inability to reconcile his ambitious foreign policy with his restricted resources and his own shortcomings as a leader. If modern observers can discern an overarching strategic vision in Henry's policies, his contemporaries were repeatedly baffled and frustrated by his inability to attain one prize before fixing his gaze upon the next. This inconsistency and lack of resolve was also seen in domestic affairs. Although generous, as a medieval king was meant to be, his patronage was a source of considerable and highly consequential conflict throughout the reign. Not only was he too lavish in his gifts to Savoyard and later Lusignan relatives, he frequently made promises he could not keep, often substituting cash payments in lieu of future grants of land. His inability to make good on these promises, particularly to Simon de Montfort, was to have disastrous results. Moreover, Henry's government, increasingly short of money, repeatedly resorted to financial expedients that undermined his frequently professed support for the Magna Carta and the provision of order and justice throughout the realm.

Henry seems to have possessed to a lesser degree the Plantagenet temper for which his son, Edward I, is much better known. The prominent position of *Debonereté* in the king's bedchamber was perhaps monitory for the king as much as a challenge to his audience. Henry's fiery confrontations with Simon de Montfort on numerous occasions are well known and will be discussed below. But, that Henry's temper could be frayed not only by the earl of Leicester is indicated by a pair of incidents involving court jesters. On one occasion, Henry is said to have torn the clothes off one of his jesters, while another time he is reported to have thrown one into the Thames! There is a certain sense of wit and irony – and perhaps an element of bitterness – in the king's order in 1256 to have his lavatory at Westminster painted with a picture of the king of the Garamontes being rescued by his faithful hounds 'from the sedition plotted against him by his own men'.[5]

Nevertheless, Henry seems to have sought harmony in his relationships with family, friends and magnates. His devotion to his queen, Eleanor of Provence, will be considered below, but Henry also demonstrated paternal concern for his children throughout his life, being particularly distressed by the early death of his daughter Katherine in 1257. If his relations with his magnates did not always prove to be harmonious, his idealized vision of these relations is revealed to us by a painting he commissioned in 1243 for Dublin Castle in which he and the queen were depicted sitting with the baronage. This was to be located above the dais in the Great Hall, visible to all present. If Henry III was not a great king, he was a good man.

Henry is also described as having had an artistic temperament, and this is certainly true. Although Henry III is most closely associated with his building programme at Westminster, and rightly so, his involvement at the Tower of London should not be overlooked. Henry's concern for security, coupled with his aesthetic taste, combined here to result in major building works. Although the decision to build two new towers – one for the king and another for the future queen – was taken during the regency as early as 1220, it was only in the aftermath of the crisis of 1238 that major work was undertaken on the King's Hall between 1238 and 1241 at a cost of more than £5,000. At the height of his enthusiasm for the Crusade, in 1251 the king ordered the chamber of the king's chaplain at the Tower of London to be painted with the story of Antiochus the Great. In 1259, during another period of crisis, further construction was undertaken, a curtain wall being built to connect the new domestic apartments with the Coldharbour Gate, completing a walled circuit around the inmost ward. Henry's building campaign at the Tower demonstrates a keen awareness of symmetry, and serves as a good reflection of his aesthetic sense. Nevertheless, as has been convincingly argued, Henry III should be remembered not so much for transforming the Tower into a favoured royal residence, which it never was for him, as for transforming it into a state-of-the-art fortress with which to intimidate the city of London as well as the king's baronial opponents.[6]

But Henry's interest in domestic architecture was not limited to the Tower. At Westminster Palace, he was responsible for transforming the Great Hall into the 'Painted Chamber'. This room presented a powerful statement of his vision of kingship. Entering from the west, furthest from the royal bed that could and did function like its French counterparts as a *lit de justice* where serious legal and political concerns could be resolved, the visitor first encountered the royal motto (*Ke ne dune ke ne tine ne prent ke desire*). This injunction to charity was reinforced by images of the Virtues, which occupied the spaces between the windows. *Largesce* (treading upon *Covoitise*) and *Debonereté* (treading upon *Ira*) both faced west towards the audience.[7] Angels holding crowns hovered above the Virtues. Behind the king's bed was a painting of the coronation of Edward the Confessor, whereas on the opposite wall were St Edmund with his ring and St John dressed as a pilgrim. All of this was repainted in the aftermath of the great fire of 1263 during the period of greatest civil unrest in the reign, making this expression of Henry's ideals all the more remarkable.

It is Westminster Abbey, of course, with which Henry's artistic ideals and ambitions are most closely associated, and with good reason. In July 1245, Henry ordered the Confessor's church to be demolished to make way for a more magnificent set of buildings. Under the guidance first of Henry of Reyns and later of John of Gloucester, the Abbey was reconstructed to be a truly royal church. It is true that the design of Henry's Westminster had its roots in contemporary France, with Reims and Royaumont (in particular) being models. What is most important about the new church is not so much its form as its function. Westminster had long been recognized as the English coronation church, and its association with royalty pre-dated the Conquest and even the Confessor, as Edgar had built a royal residence there in the 960s. This association was reinforced with the canonization of St Edward in 1161 and his translation in 1163. However, by the mid-thirteenth century, Westminster had become more than a royal residence.

The settlement of the exchequer, the treasury and the law courts in Westminster over the course of the twelfth and thirteenth centuries, in close proximity to both Westminster Palace and Westminster Abbey, transformed the area into the political capital of England. Henry's lavish spending on both the Palace and the Abbey reflects this. Henry spent more than the equivalent of 2 years' revenues, between £40,000 and £50,000, on the construction and decoration of the abbey. The church was to contain a new shrine for Edward the Confessor and so, like the Painted Chamber, it associated Henry with his patron's 'conciliatory vision of kingship'.[8] Here, English kings would not only be crowned, but married and buried. Here, too, they would hold councils and parliaments. Here, would royal majesty be enthroned. The magnificent Cosmati marble pavement before the high altar speaks to this majesty on a cosmic scale.

Let us now return to events as they unfolded with Henry truly his own master at last. Beginning in 1234, 18 years into his reign, the composition of the court was finally of the king's own choosing. One of his closest associates was a young Frenchman who had arrived in England in 1230 seeking his fortune, Simon de Montfort. Third son of the great warrior who had led the Albigensian Crusade, Montfort sought to recover the earldom of Leicester to which his family had briefly made claim under John. Initially, Henry was much taken with this witty and self-assured companion, who did in fact receive a share in the Leicester estates within a year, and the title (if not the substance) of earl in 1236. After all, on his mother's side, Simon was the great-great-great grandson of William the Conqueror. In January 1238, Simon would also become the king's brother-in-law through his marriage to Henry's sister Eleanor, the widow of William (II) Marshal, the late earl of Pembroke. In the long term, this marriage would cause greater discord than harmony between the two men, but this could not have been foreseen at the time. In 1238, it seemed to bode well for the futures of both men.

By the time of Montfort's wedding to Eleanor, the king himself had also wed. The marriage of Henry III to Eleanor of Provence in January 1236 was to have far-reaching implications for his reign. His choice of a bride has been questioned since his own day. Despite their difference in age, the 12-year-old daughter of Count Raymond-Berenguer V might have been seen as a suitable match for the 28-year-old Henry had she been an heiress. However, as the second of four daughters, Eleanor was unlikely to inherit more than a modest portion of her father's holdings, especially since her older sister Margaret had married Louis IX of France some 2 years previously. Yet her family connections were still of considerable value from Henry's point of view, if not that of his critics, both contemporary and modern. Her so-called Savoyard uncles became powerful figures in English politics, but it would be wrong to describe them as favourites, as they were never really subservient to Henry's will or dependent upon his favour. It would also be wrong to dismiss them as parasites at the king's court, although they certainly received lavish patronage from the king. They were talented, had useful connections, and they quickly integrated themselves into English political society with little initial opposition. The picture of Henry's court awash in 'aliens', so prominent in the writing of the St Albans chronicler Matthew Paris, is an extreme exaggeration in the decade following the royal marriage.

The wedding took place on 14 January 1236 at Canterbury, and 6 days later Eleanor was crowned Queen of England at Westminster. London was decorated with silk banners and garlands of flowers, and various royal officials were charged with keeping the enormous crowd under control. A procession of mounted worthies from the City of London rode to Westminster, preceded by the king's trumpeters, where they presented hundreds of gold and silver cups to be used at the coronation banquet. At the coronation itself, the king in his full coronation regalia processed from Westminster Palace to the Abbey across a blue-rayed carpet under a canopy of purple silk supported on silver lances by the barons of the Cinque Ports. He was preceded by three earls bearing the ceremonial swords of state and by the treasurer and chancellor carrying the paten and chalice to be used in the coronation mass. Eleanor followed Henry under a similar canopy, escorted by two bishops, one on each side. Following a prayer at the church door celebrating the Virgin and child-bearing, Eleanor proceeded to the steps before the high altar where the archbishop of Canterbury anointed her with holy oil before placing a crown on her head. On the day of her coronation, Eleanor acted for the first time in the expected queenly role of intercessor, seeking pardon for one William de Panchehall. The importance of another queenly duty, to provide the king with heirs – and the importance of dynastic continuity – was soon vividly impressed upon her as well, when Henry commissioned a stained-glass Jesse window for the queen's bedchamber in Winchester.

Eleanor had been exposed to a variety of influences in her native Provence, ranging from troubadour poetry to the preaching of the first generation of the Franciscans. Henry apparently took Eleanor to Glastonbury in the summer of 1236 to see the site of King Arthur's burial, perhaps in recognition of her familiarity with Arthurian romance. From the outset of the marriage, Henry appears to have been genuinely pleased with his bride, to whom he remained faithful throughout his long life. Although royal records are generally impersonal, mediated as they are by the clerk transcribing them, we should perhaps give some credence to the formal language of the Curia Regis rolls where the queen is described as *karissima concors* and *dilecta concors* (dearest and beloved consort). An interesting personal note is found in the Close Rolls for 1240 when the king seems to have forgotten to order his wife's Christmas gift until the last minute, ordering an expensive golden, footed cup on 19 December.[9] There is a charming quality to the immediacy of Henry's order, speaking perhaps to two of his fundamental characteristics – a lack of foresight and a basic goodness of heart.

Henry took care to provide his queen with a welcoming environment. Eleanor was given a number of English companions such as her physician/tutor Nicholas Farnham and her steward Robert de Mucegros, as well as ladies of the chamber including the redoubtable Margaret Bisset who would personally foil an attempt on Henry's life in 1238. Soon, Eleanor would also have the company of her Savoyard uncles and a goodly number of Savoyard immigrants, including even a Provençal gardener. With the queen's comfort in mind, Henry undertook work at no less than nine royal residences. Along with the Jesse window at Winchester, he had the Queen's Tower at the Tower of London, on the site of the present Lanthorn Tower, whitewashed and decorated with painted roses. At Havering, her chamber was decorated with 20 glass windows containing heraldic shields. Charmingly, her chamber at Westminster was painted with a figure of winter 'to be portrayed with such sad looks and miserable appearance that he may be truly likened to winter'.[10] Having been raised in the warm Mediterranean sun, Eleanor would have suffered in the long English winters, and Henry must have recognized this in this painting. An English spring, however, can be as gentle as the winter is harsh and, at Everswell, Henry had 100 pear trees planted to further enhance an already idyllic setting.

The marriage to Eleanor of Provence introduced a new diplomatic element into English politics. If Eleanor brought little to her marriage in terms of dowry, she brought powerful connections of another kind. She was accompanied to England by her uncle William, bishop-elect of Savoy. Henry was greatly taken with William, who was soon described by a contemporary chronicler as the king's 'chief counsellor', and whom Henry rewarded with the lands, if not the title, of the earldom of Richmond. Soon the king was also promoting him – both aggressively and unsuccessfully – as a candidate to fill the vacant see of Winchester. William, however, left England in May 1238, never to return: he died prematurely in Viterbo in the following year. William's greatest impact during his brief sojourn in England was probably the intense dislike he inspired in Matthew Paris and, through that chronicler, the perceived linkage of the queen to aliens in general and Savoyards in particular.

Another of Eleanor's uncles, Peter of Savoy, arrived in England in December 1240. He was knighted by the king in January 1241, and in May of that year he received the honour of Richmond, which his brother William had previously held. He would be one of Henry's staunchest supporters and most trusted advisors throughout the reign, and would be particularly closely associated with his niece, the queen. A month later, yet another uncle, Boniface of Savoy, was elected archbishop of Canterbury, although he did not actually take up residence in England until 3 years later. Finally, Thomas of Savoy, count of Flanders in right of his wife Joan, became a pivotal figure in English affairs not only because the circumstance of a debt owed to him by Simon de Montfort proved to be a flashpoint in the deterioration of relations between Montfort and the king, but also because Flanders, as always, was crucial to English military and diplomatic schemes on the continent.

Eleanor's Savoyard uncles were, of course, high-profile visitors to England, but they were not the only newcomers to follow the queen from the continent. Of the approximately 170 recipients of royal patronage who can be identified as Savoyards, roughly half of whom settled in England, two-thirds were clerics and one-third knights. Along with the queen's relations, other prominent Savoyards also found a place in the king's inner circle, most notably Pierre d'Aigueblanche, who became bishop of Hereford, and Imbert Pugeis, who served as steward of the king's household. They, in turn, became magnets for other of their countrymen, who found places in their own households. A considerable number also found their way into the queen's service and were recipients of her patronage. Eleanor played an influential role in arranging marriages to wealthy Englishwomen for these newly arrived Savoyards, such as Peter and Ebulo of Geneva, Geoffrey de Joinville and Ebulo de Montibus. Similarly, Savoyard wives were provided for English heirs. In 1247, Alice of Saluzzo, granddaughter of Count Amadeus of Savoy, married Edmund de Lacy, heir to the earldom of Lincoln. In 1253, William de Vescy agreed to the marriage of his heir to whatever Savoyard bride 'the queen and [Peter of Savoy] shall provide',[11] while in 1257 Thomas of Savoy's own daughter Margaret was married to Baldwin, heir to the earldom of Devon. The queen's role in all this matchmaking was neither unnoticed nor widely approved of. In the Petition of the Barons in 1258, it was specifically requested that no woman whose marriage was in the king's gift be given to a foreigner. But during Eleanor's first decade or more in England, opposition to the Savoyards was generally muted and they were smoothly assimilated into English society.

Following the marriage of Henry and Eleanor and the emergence of William of Savoy at the centre of the royal court, Richard of Cornwall withdrew from court in indignation at his diminished stature there, and soon took the cross as a means to distance himself further, while yet retaining his honour. But otherwise there was little initial discontent with Henry's new circle of advisors. Indeed, this was a period of considerable harmony and cooperation. Along with the royal marriage, 1236 saw the publication of the Statute of Merton, which addressed a number of pressing legal concerns, and in 1237 the king reissued the Magna Carta and the Charter of the Forest. In return, the Westminster parliament of January 1237 awarded a tax of a thirtieth on movables, worth in excess of £20,000. As it turned out, this was to be last parliamentary subsidy granted to the king for three decades, but for the present it provided Henry with some much-needed cash.

The marriage of Simon de Montfort to Henry III's widowed sister, Eleanor Marshal, caused a brief but sharp crisis in 1238. Henry himself arranged the marriage of the couple, which took place on 7 January 1238 in his chamber chapel at Westminster. As Eleanor had previously taken a vow of celibacy before the archbishop of Canterbury following the death of her first husband, the younger William Marshal, the marriage was controversial. That the ceremony was conducted in secret and without the consultation of the magnates was contrary to the Magna Carta. Thus, the marriage provoked a rebellion led by Richard of Cornwall, Richard Marshal, earl of Pembroke (brother of Eleanor's late husband) and the earl of Winchester. The rebels confronted the king in arms at Stratford-le-Bow in late February, with Henry retreating to the security of the Tower at the beginning of March. William of Savoy was able to negotiate a settlement, in which the king's brother settled for a cash contribution of 16,000 marks toward the cost of his proposed crusade. The settlement may have been hastened by the impending death of Joan, Queen of Scotland, as both Henry and Richard were present at their sister's death at Havering on 4 March. From this point forward, Richard of Cornwall was unwavering in his loyalty to his brother, the king, and often served as a mediator in defusing later crises. As to Henry and Simon, their friendship was still strong at this point. The king was present at the baptism of Montfort's first son, significantly named Henry, in November 1238.

On 17/18 June 1239, Eleanor of Provence gave birth to her own first child, a son named Edward, after the king's patron saint, the Confessor. This event was important not only because Eleanor hereby fulfilled the most fundamental role of medieval queenship, but also because, in the aftermath of the birth, Henry III and Simon de Montfort had a serious falling out. The purification ceremony for Eleanor on 9 August 1239 was meant to be a joyous occasion. Some 500 tapers burned before the shrine of Edward the Confessor in Westminster Abbey, and the *Laudes Reginae* was sung in the queen's honour. In the midst of all this, however, the king confronted his erstwhile friend over a debt of 2,000 marks owed to Thomas of Savoy, for which Simon had apparently used the king as a guarantor without either Henry's knowledge or consent. In the heated exchange that ensued, in the presence of the archbishop of Canterbury, Henry went beyond the present question of the nature of the debt to Thomas, and accused Montfort of having seduced his sister Eleanor, despite her vows of chastity. He went on to suggest that Simon had secured a papal dispensation allowing the marriage only by means of bribery. Whether or not any of these charges was true remains uncertain, yet there are numerous reports in the chronicles of Montfort's continuing struggle with a troubled conscience over the violation of Eleanor's vows, so that Henry's accusations would have certainly struck home. In any case, humiliated and disgraced, Simon and his wife soon left England for France, where he was to remain until the following spring before returning to England to join Richard of Cornwall on his crusade. Henry and Simon would subsequently reconcile and fall out several more times, but this initial wound to Montfort's pride probably never healed.

Although the marriage of his sister Isabella to the Emperor Frederick II in 1235 had provided no more tangible benefit to Henry than his own marriage to Eleanor – indeed, it cost him a dowry of £20,000 – it did point to his interest in continental affairs. Henry developed increasingly close diplomatic ties with the Emperor, of whom he had certainly gained earlier knowledge through the personal experiences of Peter des Roches. The Plantagenets and Hohenstaufen shared a common adversary in the Capetians, and particularly following Henry's marriage to Eleanor, a common interest in Italian affairs. Henry also hoped for imperial support in his ultimate goal, the recovery of the lost English lands in France, although it is unlikely that Frederick, who attempted to broker a peace between England and France in 1236, shared Henry's vision. Regardless of his interests in the international stage, however, given his lack of resources, Henry III was in no position to go to war in the latter half of the 1230s, and during these years truces were arranged or extended with Llywelyn in Wales, Louis IX in France and Thibault I in Navarre.

In 1242, a golden opportunity to recover the Plantagenet holdings on the continent appeared to present itself. The transformation of Poitou into an appanage for Louis IX's younger brother, Alphonse of Poitiers, alienated Hugh de Lusignan and Henry's mother Isabella, who now, belatedly, looked to the English king for support. Henry only too readily responded to the call. Although parliament declined to offer the king any taxes beyond a scutage, Henry enthusiastically set about raising an army. In the end, the core of this force was no more than 200 knights, half of them drawn from the king's own household. Nevertheless, Henry landed in France in May and advanced as far as Saintes. But when Louis IX led his army across the Charente at Taillebourg, Henry rushed to its defence and headlong into a trap. He was lucky to escape, and was forced to retreat south to Bordeaux without offering battle. Indeed, the only reason why Henry was able to extricate himself from Taillebourg at all was the presence there of his brother, Richard. He, rather than the king, was accorded a truce of just one day on account of his status as a crusader, and this truce allowed the English withdrawal. Following this debacle, Simon de Montfort famously berated Henry for his lack of generalship, telling the king 'You should be taken and locked up like Charles the Simple', a reference to the unfortunate Carolingian king who had ceded Normandy to the Vikings in the tenth century. Bowing to the inevitable, in August, Hugh de Lusignan and Isabella returned their allegiance to Louis IX, ending the Poitevin revolt. Whether or not Henry III recognized it, the failure of his campaign in 1242 put paid to the Plantagenets' loss of all territories north of the Garonne for a century to come. Only Gascony remained of the once-great Angevin Empire.

In the immediate aftermath of the failed campaign, Henry had promised Gascony to his brother, Richard of Cornwall, out of gratitude for the escape from Taillebourg. Queen Eleanor, however, insisted that this must remain part of the inheritance of her son, Edward, and Henry acquiesced. In order to compensate his brother for this loss, as well as to enhance further the diplomatic position of the Plantagenet family, a marriage was arranged. Henry's relationship with the house of Savoy was further solidified as Richard married Queen Eleanor's younger sister Sanchia amid magnificent festivities at Westminster on 23 November 1243. Although it was unlikely that Henry would ever change his mind and 'confer Gascony upon him again of his mere liberality', Richard did receive the county of Cornwall, and the honours of Wallingford and Eye, along with additional lands valued at £500 per year. It is interesting to note that the fourth and youngest daughter of Raymond-Berenguer of Provence and Beatrice of Savoy, another Beatrice, would subsequently marry the brother of Louis IX of France, Charles of Anjou, in 1246, completing the remarkable advance of the house of Savoy.

Henry had returned from the Poitou campaign some £15,000 in debt, but through a combination of peace and particularly heavy taxation on the Jews of the kingdom, his financial situation soon recovered. During the 1240s, he sought to avoid conflict with the magnates and in this he was largely successful, often as a result of forgiving their debts and extending their liberties. He was also lavish in his hospitality and his patronage. His architectural patronage during this period reflected his vision of kingship, even if he could never fully realize this vision in practice. As we have seen, vast sums were committed to the rebuilding of Westminster Abbey at this time, but despite his taste for splendid royal display, Henry could hardly be described as autocratic or absolutist. Constraints upon his kingship had been a part of his life since boyhood, and if he sometimes bridled against infringement upon his prerogatives, nevertheless he repeatedly affirmed his commitment to the charters and genuinely meant it. Indeed, one of his failings as a king was his desire to please everyone and his tendency to listen to the advice of the last person to whom he had spoken, leading to frustrating inconsistency in virtually every aspect of his rule.

In December 1244, Louis IX of France took the Cross and announced his intention to go on crusade. Over the next 3 years, the French king accumulated a massive war-chest of one million *livres*, constructed a purpose-built Mediterranean port at Aigues Mortes to serve as the point of embarkation for his expedition, and stockpiled food and weapons on Cyprus in anticipation of his arrival there en route to the Holy Land. On the one hand, the prospect of Louis's absence abroad appeared to present Henry III with another opportunity to recover the lost Plantagenet lands. On the other, Henry himself was genuinely tempted to go on crusade with his brother-in-law. He had first taken the cross as long ago as 1216 at the time of his first coronation, and he would renew his vow in 1250. Meanwhile, if he could not go in person, he at least wanted to be represented in this great enterprise, suggesting that his Lusignan half-brother, Guy, lead one of the contingents in the crusading army, an offer rebuffed by the French king. And yet, regardless of whatever Henry's inclination might have been, matters closer to home proved more pressing than the relief of the Holy Land.

The last Plantagenet holding in France was Gascony, and by the late 1240s Henry III's grip here too seemed to be failing. Gascony was, of course, a notoriously difficult region to rule – or even to define. In an administrative sense, the region was usually referred to as the duchy of Aquitaine, a territorial entity whose history reached all the way back to Julius Caesar. In the course of Roman expansion and settlement, Aquitaine had at one point stretched as far as the Loire in the north and the Massif Central in the east with the Pyrenees as its southern boundary. This, more or less, was the territory inherited by the Plantagenets in the twelfth century through the marriage of Eleanor of Aquitaine to Henry II. But, by the time of Henry III, the duchy had shrunk back more nearly to the dimensions of Caesar's original province, bounded by the Atlantic in the west, the Garonne in the east and the Pyrenees in the south. This smaller Aquitaine (or Guyenne, as it was known in French sources) more closely approximated to Gascony, a region defined by its language and culture.

The difficulty in ruling Gascony resulted from several different factors, apart from the fact that it was so distant from the centre of English government. First of all, it was only partially feudalized. Along with largely independent commercial towns such as Bordeaux and Bayonne, there was also a good deal of allodial land held by headstrong local lords who claimed to owe little, if any, obedience to the duke. Moreover, the complex and contradictory customary law of the region enshrined the local lords' legal right to make private war on each other, further destabilizing the region. Finally, Gascony was regularly threatened by its many neighbours, not only the kingdom of France, but also by the Pyrenean kingdom of Navarre and the Spanish kingdoms of Castile and Aragon, whose rulers were themselves descendants of Eleanor, daughter of Eleanor of Aquitaine and Henry II, and at least in their view, legitimate claimants to the duchy. The policy initiated by Henry III when he had first travelled to Gascony in 1242–1243 involved concessions to the towns and the payment of fees and pensions to the nobles. Not only was this policy expensive, it also proved to have only limited success.

Henry now turned to his brother-in-law Simon de Montfort to pacify the turbulent duchy, appointing him as king's lieutenant in Aquitaine for a period of 7 years in May 1248. The appointment must have been somewhat unexpected. As recently as Christmas 1247, Montfort, who had previously accompanied Richard of Cornwall on crusade in 1240, had again taken the cross, planning to join Louis IX in his proposed expedition to the Holy Land. Between 1244 and 1248, Montfort had been virtually invisible in England, his withdrawal from court appearing somewhat peevish. Yet Montfort was a deeply religious man, and among his most important associations were his friendships with some of the greatest churchmen of his day: the Oxford Franciscan Adam Marsh (d. 1259);

Robert Grosseteste, bishop of Lincoln (d. 1253); Walter de Cantilupe, bishop of Worcester (d. 1266); Richard of Gravesend, Grosseteste's successor as bishop of Lincoln (d. 1279); and the Franciscan Eudes Rigaud, archbishop of Rouen (d. 1274). His surviving correspondence with these clerical leaders indicates the complexity of his character, a mixture of pride and self-interest with profound piety and sophisticated theological understanding. Despite his crusading zeal, however, Simon accepted the Gascon appointment, the king having promised him extensive resources, including full disposal of all duchy revenues not specifically owed elsewhere, as well as reimbursement for any expenses incurred in restoring or building castles and fortifications. Montfort was promised 2,000 marks in cash and the service of 50 knights for the first year of his lieutenancy; he probably arrived in the duchy with an even larger force than that.

Simon travelled first to Paris where he convinced Blanche of Castile, acting as regent for her son Louis IX, to extend the truce between France and England, which was about to expire. He then visited King Thibault I of Navarre, who agreed to submit his disputes with Henry III to arbitration. Finally, Simon paid a visit to the Countess of Bigorre, ruler of the small but strategically important county to the southeast of Gascony, who named him guardian of her county in return for an annual rent of 7,000 shillings in the money of Morlaas.[12] Having settled at least some of the external threats to the duchy, Simon now turned to Gascony itself, where he faced a chaotic situation at best.

Of the many Gascon nobles whose independence posed difficulties for whoever would rule the duchy, none was more troublesome than Gaston VII de Béarn. To say that the viscount of Béarn was volatile would be an understatement. During his remarkably long tenure of the county from 1229 until his death in 1290, Gaston revolted against his English overlords on at least three occasions, and repeatedly avoided performing homage for Béarn *per se*. In 1248, he was to be found ravaging the area around Dax, illustrating the ongoing conflict between towns and regional lords in the duchy. Other local lords were engaged in similar campaigns. The towns themselves, despite numerous privileges and concessions from Henry III, were generally divided by factional strife and provided only limited support to the king or his lieutenant. Although Simon immediately toured the duchy and its various administrative centres, he refused to recognize customary privileges. Moreover, armed with his mandate from Henry III, he seized possession of important castles and began construction of entirely new fortifications. All of these actions were viewed as provocative by the restless nobles and burgesses of Gascony.

In June 1249, Bordeaux was the scene of bloody faction fighting between the Colom and Soler families. Simon suppressed this urban violence with violence of his own. When confronted with resistance, as in Bordeaux, the lieutenant was ruthless. Lands and buildings were confiscated and destroyed, and Montfort even cut vines, an unforgivable act here in the heart of the wine country. By December 1249, representatives of the Soler clan had arrived in London to lay their protests before the king himself. They were soon followed by the current mayor of Bordeaux, William Raymond Colom, who presented the other side of the story. Although Henry referred the matter back to Bordeaux for trial – before Simon – he also wrote to his lieutenant, urging a less militant style of governance. The king's willingness to hear these complaints in the first place was a worrisome development from Simon's point of view. Inevitably, complaints about the earl's conduct continued to reach the ear of the king in London. Gaston de Béarn himself, having been placed under arrest by the lieutenant, travelled to England in person to plead his case, and to Montfort's dismay the viscount was pardoned and restored to his rights and lands. Gaston was, after all, the cousin of Queen Eleanor, and Henry may have thought that in receiving Gaston's homage he had gone a long way toward stabilizing the duchy. At the same time, however, he had both undercut his lieutenant's authority and insulted his honour, both of which proved to be counter-productive. Writing from Paris while representing the duchy at the French king's *Parlement* in March 1250, Montfort complained of the difficulty of his task, which required him to fight a guerrilla war without the commitment of his royal master, either financial or political. Henry's dispatch of commissioners to hear and settle disputes between Montfort and the Gascons in May 1251 confirms the legitimacy of Simon's complaints.

At the end of the year, in December 1251 while in York for the marriage of Henry III's daughter Margaret to Alexander III of Scotland, the king and earl confronted each other over the situation in Gascony. In Montfort's absence, Gascony had once again risen in revolt against his oppressive rule. Montfort sought leave to return and quell the uprisings, but Henry forbade this, blaming the earl's harsh rule for the duchy's unsettled conditions. Balked of his authority as lieutenant, Simon then demanded compensation for his expenses in accordance with the terms of his letters of appointment. Henry demurred. Only the intervention of Queen Eleanor prevented a complete impasse, and by March at least some of their financial disagreements had been settled. Meanwhile, Gaston de Béarn – his recent homage to Henry III notwithstanding – was busy besieging La Réole, and he would soon swear allegiance to Alphonso X of Castile, encouraging the Spanish king to revive his own claim to the duchy.

In January 1252, Henry sent a commission including his half-brother, Geoffrey de Lusignan, to investigate the state of affairs in the duchy. A truce was arranged, but the Gascon nobles refused to travel to London for hearings unless Montfort was also in England, not Gascony. Montfort did return to England, and in May 1252 Henry held a 'trial' of his lieutenant before his council. The charges against Montfort, many of which have survived, were delivered by Géraud de Malemont, the longtime archbishop of Bordeaux. Montfort was dismissive of the allegations levelled against him, repeatedly pointing to the terms of his appointment in justification of his actions. It is difficult to accept the characterization of the hearings provided by Montfort's friend Adam Marsh, who wrote that Simon acted throughout the hearings with 'the moderation of gentleness and the fullness of magnanimity.' Matthew Paris paints a very different picture, recording an exchange between the earl and King Henry that rings true. Baffled by the king's lack of support, which Montfort felt to be obliged him through the terms of his appointment, he challenged the king by saying: 'Who can believe that you are a Christian? Have you ever confessed?' The king replied with a simple 'Indeed', which led Montfort to ask the rhetorical question: 'What is the use of confession without penance and satisfaction?' As with his criticism of Henry's generalship 10 years earlier, these pointed remarks were deeply hurtful to the king and not easily forgiven or forgotten.

Throughout the hearings, which lasted from early May until early June, it was apparent that Montfort had tremendous sympathy and support among the magnates, including the earls of Cornwall (the king's brother Richard), Gloucester and Hereford, as well as Peter of Savoy and Montfort's good friend Walter de Cantilupe, bishop of Worcester. Indeed, he even seems to have had the support of the queen, who uncharacteristically quarrelled publicly with her husband. The royal council found in Simon's favour, and the king gave his judgment for the earl as well. But all too typically, Henry subsequently reversed this decision and then arranged a largely unsatisfactory compromise. A truce was effected until February 1253, when Henry III and the Lord Edward were to travel to Gascony to address its problems personally. This was, however, a pyrrhic victory: although Simon was 'morally vindicated, he had been politically convicted',[13] and he refused to resign his office under such circumstances.

Henry did not finally set off for Gascony until August, leaving Queen Eleanor behind as regent, with Richard of Cornwall serving as her close adviser. In

September, the king led a highly successful campaign in the Garonne valley. In the course of this campaigning, a reconciliation was effected between the king and earl, who joined Henry at Benauges on 9 November 1253. Montfort did, of course, drive a characteristically hard bargain before relinquishing his office. Nevertheless, he appears still to have felt a genuine sense of obligation and loyalty to Henry. In one of his last letters to Montfort, Bishop Grosseteste (who died on 9 October 1253) had reminded Simon of how greatly the king had honoured and rewarded him throughout his career. Perhaps with this in mind, Montfort made his peace with Henry and also declined an offer to serve as Steward of France in the interim between the death of Blanche of Castile and the return of Louis IX from crusade.

Henry's Gascon expedition was the most successful military undertaking of his reign. Well funded for once, he took a force of 300 knights from England supplemented by another 100 Poitevin knights provided by his Lusignan kinsmen. His mixture of military assertion with conciliation soon brought the duchy under control. Bergerac was taken in July 1254 and the great fortress of La Réole was finally recovered from Gaston de Béarn in August, allowing Henry to return to Bordeaux and settle his affairs. An important aspect of this settlement was to eliminate the threat from Castile. To that end, Henry now arranged a marriage between his son and heir, the future Edward I, and Eleanor of Castile, half-sister of Alphonso X. Queen Eleanor had arrived in Bordeaux on 11 June with her sons Edward and Edmund, along with the archbishop of Canterbury, her uncle Boniface of Savoy. The wedding took place in Burgos in November 1254, and at Alphonso's insistence Aquitaine was conveyed to the prince as a wedding gift. The duchy was henceforth to be considered inseparable from the English crown. Meanwhile, during his prolonged stay in Gascony, Henry initiated another diplomatic scheme involving his second son. He sent proctors to Rome to seek the vacant crown of Sicily for Edmund. Flushed with success in Gascony, the Sicilian Business, as it is usually called, seemed to Henry a means to encircle France with a Mediterranean presence linking Sicily and southern Italy with the Savoyard holdings in the north and then extending across to Gascony. Had the price of this adventure, to which Innocent IV readily agreed, not been prohibitively high, it might have made diplomatic and political sense. In Henry's perpetually straightened conditions, however, it was sheer folly and would lead to the greatest crisis of the reign.

Henry's return journey from Gascony to England was the occasion of a family reunion of sorts and the formation of a real friendship between the kings of

England and France. Henry and Queen Eleanor, with an entourage that included Prince Edmund, Archbishop Boniface and Henry III's half-brother William de Valence, travelled first by way of Fontevrault where Henry visited the tombs of his ancestors. He ordered that his mother's tomb be moved within the church, finding her placement in the cemetery disrespectful. From Fontevrault, the royal party moved on to Orléans, where Henry met for the first time his brother-in-law Louis IX before proceeding on to Paris by way of Pontigny. Henry and Eleanor were also joined by Eleanor's sister, Queen Margaret, her mother Beatrice, Dowager Duchess of Provence, and her youngest sister, another Beatrice, now married to Louis' brother, Charles of Anjou. This remarkable collection of royal brothers and sisters, husbands and wives, made their way to the capital – where Sanchia of Provence would complete the family gathering. Paris would be the site of lavish feasting, as well as generous almsgiving on behalf of both kings. Henry was enthralled with his tour of the city's churches, culminating in the spectacular Sainte-Chapelle, 'the most noble chapel of the king of France with its incomparable relics'. This visit led to the establishment of genuine affective bonds between the two royal families, bonds that would pay substantial dividends to Henry in the years to come.

The Gascon crisis and Henry's direct intervention were costly and had huge unforeseen consequences. During the next 5 years, Henry would struggle to overcome three interrelated sources of friction in the realm. First of all, the king was without funds. The repeated refusal of parliamentary subsidies throughout the 1250s led the king to exploit other sources of income. The sheriffs were squeezed and, in turn, they squeezed their counties, causing hardship more for the middling folk than the magnates. Although the king had frequently turned to the Jews for extraordinary funding in the past, by now their ability to pay had been severely limited. Where a tallage levied in the 1240s had realized some £40,000, in the 1250s it was unlikely to bring in even half that amount. Moreover, as the Jews were pressured to meet royal demands, they were often forced to sell the bonds they held from Christian debtors at discounted prices. The buyers of these bonds, Christians rather than Jews, could force these debtors into court and ultimately gain possession of the lands held in surety for the bonds. This further enflamed anti-government sentiment in the countryside, not least because some of the most prominent players in this game were the king's own Lusignan half-brothers.

The influx of Poitevins had begun in 1247, when Henry welcomed his half-siblings with open arms. Henry saw good, sound political reasons to make common cause with the children of his mother's second marriage. The Lusignans were well placed both to secure the northern frontier of Gascony and to facilitate the recovery of Poitou, a fantasy to which Henry stubbornly clung. Perhaps a hundred Poitevins ultimately made their way to England, roughly two-thirds of them knights (a reverse of the earlier Savoyard profile). They were far less lavishly rewarded than the Savoyards, there being less patronage available at the time of their arrival, but they nonetheless seemed to absorb what little patronage there was. Moreover, they were perceived, probably correctly, as obnoxious, both in their ruthless exploitation of their own lands and the acquisition of other lands in the Jewish bond market. By choice or circumstance, the Lusignans did not assimilate as easily or as fully as the Savoyards had a decade before.

Although the two older brothers, Guy and Geoffrey de Lusignan, soon returned to Poitou, albeit with handsome pensions, two younger brothers and a sister chose to remain in England. A marriage was quickly arranged for William de Valence, who wed the heiress Joan de Munchensy through whom he became Lord of Pembroke and gained lands in Ireland. William's marriage was supplemented by money fees worth more than £800 per annum and possession of Hertford Castle. In the same month that William was wed, Alice married John de Warenne, earl of Surrey. Henry may very well have been aware of the potential problems that his patronage of his Poitevin relations might pose. As already noted, William de Valence was knighted on a very special day, Sunday 13 October 1247, the feast of the translation of the relics of St Edward the Confessor. This was an important day in Henry's personal calendar every year, but particularly so in 1247, for it was on that date that he conveyed the newly received relic of the blood of Jesus Christ in procession from St Paul's to Westminster where the relic was to be housed. Clearly, William was meant to be elevated by his association with this sacred event. Finally, another younger brother, Aymer de Lusignan, sought his advancement through the church rather than the marriage market. Henry had already provided him to the church of Tisbury in Wiltshire prior to his arrival in England, but from 1247 onwards he was lavishly rewarded with benefices and pensions, while he went off to Oxford to study under a certain Master Vincent. Having failed to obtain the see of Durham for his half-brother, in 1250 the king managed to intimidate the monks of St Swithun's into electing Aymer bishop of Winchester, an office to which he seems to have been wholly unsuited by both his youth and temperament.

Despite all this, it must be said that, in these same years, the king also patronized English magnates such as Richard de Clare, earl of Gloucester, and

Roger Bigod, earl of Norfolk. Perhaps it was a naïve hope, but Henry seems to have envisaged an international court that would match his own international outlook and ambitions. Henry's desire for peace and harmony is also seen in his response to the death of his brother-in-law, Alexander II, in 1249. The accession of the 8-year-old Alexander III (1249–1286) presented a potential opportunity for Henry to push forward his notion of English overlordship in Scotland. This had been an intermittent source of tension throughout the reign of Alexander II, nearly leading to open warfare in 1244. Yet Henry did not intervene in Scottish affairs until 1251, and then he acted as an arbitrator with considerable sup-port among the Scottish nobility. Moreover, at York in December 1251, Henry sought to renew the personal link between the two kingdoms when his daughter Margaret married young Alexander. Henry spared no expense on this occasion, perhaps most notably in costuming both himself and his heir in robes adorned with the three leopards of England. Although Henry received Alexander's hom-age for the Scottish king's English lands, when Alexander refused a request to perform homage for Scotland, Henry did not press the issue. He was satisfied merely to register his claim to overlordship. The same was true in September 1255 when Henry entered the Scottish kingdom for the only time in his reign, meeting his daughter and son-in-law at Roxburgh. What he sought during this visit was financial support, already approved by the pope, for his Sicilian venture, but he continued to insist that such a levy of Scottish taxes was not to set a precedent or to prejudice the Scottish king's rights.

The Sicilian Business was not so fully ridiculous as is usually claimed when placed into the context of lordship rather than national kingship, and into the complex diplomatic matrix of the 1250s. On 6 March 1250 in Westminster Abbey, Henry III had taken the cross in an elaborate ceremony presided over by the archbishop of Canterbury. Encouraged by the prospect of a quick success in Gascony under Simon de Montfort, and further energized by the reversals recently suffered in Egypt by his brother-in-law and rival, Louis IX, Henry now proposed to go on crusade himself. His goal was to depart in 1256, toward which end he began the collection of a great war-chest, what has come to be known as his gold treasure. By 1253, the sum stood at nearly 3,000 marks of gold, equivalent to ten times that amount in sterling. A conscious effort had been made to collect a variety of fines and other payments in gold, and Matthew Paris specifically associates this with the king's anticipated crusade 'to the eastern parts where gold is used as money'.[14] Indeed, this is correct, as Henry's will, drawn up in 1253 illustrates, calling for the transport of his gold to the Holy Land along with the king's cross in the event of his death. Unfortunately, however, as we have seen, by 1253 Henry had other needs for this treasure. Henry had vacillated between two different potential responses to Louis's crusade – joining the crusade himself or attacking France in Louis's absence to recover the traditional Plantagenet lands – but in the end he had acted upon neither. His personal intervention in Gascony had required all of his reserve funds. And yet, with papal permission, Henry now sought to translate his Crusading vow from the Holy Land to the Hohenstaufen lands in Italy in support of Edmund's claim to the kingdom of Sicily. Immediately upon his return from Gascony, the king set out to accumulate a second gold treasure to further this cause.

In the summer of 1257, Henry actually minted a gold coinage. William of Gloucester delivered 466 marks worth of the king's new gold coins on 27 August and another 190 marks worth in October. These two mintages, taken together, indicate the production of a minimum of 52,480 gold pennies, of which, remarkably, only six now survive. The coins show the sword in the king's right hand replaced by a sceptre, as had been the case on the gold pennies of Edward the Confessor. The obvious comparison between these coins and Frederick II's magnificent *augustales* can hardly have been lost on contemporaries, but the intended political statement was probably undermined by economic and political reality. These coins were far too valuable to be viable in any monetary sense: in the end, Henry actually lost money on the exchange rate between silver and gold. Symbolically striking, perhaps, Henry's coinage is probably best seen as a golden symbol of his folly. After all, in 1258, Henry's reserves probably stood at about 5,000 marks, a mere pittance compared to his debt to the pope, to whom he had promised 135,000 marks in order to secure Edmund's crown.

The Christmas parliament of 1256 at Westminster had been used as a stage to gather support for the Sicilian Business. Here, it was announced that Richard of Cornwall had been chosen as King of the Romans. His election, we are told, was spontaneous and unanimous. In fact, this was not true. The votes of German nobles and prelates were costly: some 12,000 marks apiece to the count palatine of the Rhineland and the duke of Bavaria; 8,000 marks each for the archbishops of Cologne and Mainz. Nevertheless, Henry III clearly saw this as an enhancement of his overall Mediterranean strategy. Indeed, Richard's success was an implicit riposte to the objections raised against the Sicilian Business: opposition had been easily overcome by the actual, physical presence of the claimant within his realm. That being said, the English magnates were not anxious to see Richard's stabilizing influence removed from his brother's court. Misreading the lack of support for the next stage in his grandiose international schemes, in March 1257 Henry presented Edmund as *puer Apuliae*, dressed in traditional Italian clothing to be invested as king of Sicily by the bishop of Bologna. This was a colossal error. It was to plunge England ultimately into civil war and to bring about the redefining of kingship.

The reform movement of 1258 was not a bolt from the blue. Parliamentary discontent with Henry's government had often been voiced through the reign. The king and his officials were repeatedly criticized for unpopular policy decisions, for failure to enforce the charters, and for the king's refusal to seek nomination or consent for the great offices of state. Parliament's discontent was openly displayed in the repeated refusal to grant extraordinary taxation to the king in 1248, 1252, 1255 and 1257. In 1258, the call for reform was initially focused very specifically on two issues – the Lusignan influence at court, and the king's relationship with the papacy. Interestingly, prior to 1258, Simon de Montfort is nowhere to be found in this opposition. Whatever grievances he held against the king were personal, not constitutional. And yet it was the earl of Leicester who frightened the king. Matthew Paris relates an incident in July 1258 in which Henry was caught in a storm while on the Thames and put to shore at Montfort's temporary residence. Teased about his timidity by his brother-in-law, Henry is reputed to have blurted out: 'I fear thunder and lightning beyond measure, but by God's head I fear you more than all the thunder and lightning in the world.'[15] For the next 7 years, he would have every reason to do so.

The final spark that ignited a revolution was an incidence of violence that took place in Surrey on 1 April 1258. At issue was the seemingly minor matter of the advowson of a church, but in the altercation that broke out between supporters of Aymer de Lusignan and those of John FitzGeoffrey, one of FitzGeoffrey's men was killed. At the ensuing Westminster parliament, FitzGeoffrey demanded justice but received none. Meanwhile, the king was threatened with yet another uprising in Wales, as well as excommunication by a papal envoy unless he made good his debt to the pope for Edmund's Sicilian crown. Henry asked the assembly to grant a tax in support of these challenges, but as had been the case so many times in the past, this was refused. Indeed, on 30 April, a group of magnates – including Simon de Montfort, Peter of Savoy and the earls of Gloucester and Norfolk – marched into Westminster Hall dressed in full armour and forced the king to agree to a general reform of the realm.

A group of 24 reformers was to be named, half chosen by the king and the rest by the barons. Given the split between the Lusignans and the Savoyards, Henry's support was limited, and his dozen appointees included only one earl, John de Warenne, earl of Surrey. It did, however, contain all four of his detested Lusignan half-brothers. This group, in turn, selected a new council of 15 to guide the king, which included Simon de Montfort, as well as the earls of Gloucester and Norfolk. Moreover, the council was to meet along with parliament three times each year and to choose the king's chief ministers. Similarly, the chancellor was to seal no writ without the council's approval. At the Oxford parliament in June 1258, the 'Petition of the Barons' further articulated the grievances against Henry and his administration, indicating that the magnate-driven coup of April had become a broader, national movement in a few short months. The Provisions of Oxford, although never put into law, outlined an overarching programme of reform, placing controls on the central government. Consultation, never Henry's strong suit, had been imposed upon him with a vengeance.

The Lusignans, not surprisingly, refused to swear an oath to uphold the Provisions of Oxford. They fled first to Winchester, and by July to France. Simon de Montfort, now a driving force behind the reform movement with the earl of Gloucester and John FitzGeoffrey, took obvious delight in the discomfiture of William de Valence and his brothers. Matthew Paris reports Montfort telling Valence, 'Either you will give up your castles or you will lose your head'.[16] The papacy also disapproved of the Provisions, and proved even more obdurate than the Lusignans in resisting the call for reform. Alexander IV initially refused to send a legate to England, although in December 1258 he did cancel the grant of Sicily to Edmund.

The Westminster parliament of October 1258 demonstrated conclusively that the reform movement had moved beyond the magnates. It was attended by knights from at least 15 counties and produced the Ordinance of Sheriffs, delineating the duties of that office. This was followed shortly by the appointment of 19 new sheriffs, all of them local knights. Similarities between the recent *Grand Ordonnance* of Louis IX and the Ordinance of Sheriffs is noteworthy. Although it does not mean that the Ordinance was derived explicitly from this or any other source, it does indicate that government reform was in the air on both sides of the Channel, and in Simon de Montfort the barons had a leader who moved regularly between France and England. Montfort was in France again from November 1258 until February 1259, but he returned in time to attend the Candlemas parliament at Westminster. Here, the principles of reform were further extended in the Ordinance of the Magnates and the Provisions of the Barons, which sought to impose similar constraints upon the magnates as had been placed upon the king in the previous year. The earl of Gloucester, in particular, appears to have dragged his feet and slowed the progress of reform at this point. Montfort returned to France immediately after the close of parliament, remaining there until the following October, more concerned perhaps with his own affairs than the movement as a whole.

In the negotiations that would eventually result in the Treaty of Paris, Montfort played an essential, but very likely obstructionist, part. His insistence on the dower settlement owed to his wife Eleanor led him to refuse to relinquish any ancestral claims in France, and this in turn may have prompted Louis IX to delay consenting to the treaty in the summer of 1259. Montfort's involvement with the county of Bigorre was also a continuing source of difficulty. Throughout this period, in the words of his most recent biographer, Montfort acted with 'the same lack of scruple and self-restraint evident at other times in his career, notably in the years in Gascony.'[17] Nevertheless, in November, the king and queen, accompanied by Peter of Savoy and the earl of Gloucester, sailed to France to finalize the peace. The justiciar, Roger Bigod, was left in charge of affairs in England in preference to the Lord Edward, as Henry's relations with his heir were strained at this time. Henry and Eleanor were warmly welcomed by their French counterparts. On 4 December, Henry surrendered all of his lost French holdings and performed homage to Louis, receiving Gascony as a vassal of the king of France and a peer of the realm. The Treaty of Paris was widely decried on both sides of the Channel. With hindsight, it is possible to see the seeds of the Hundred Years War sown in the untenable feudal relationship between two sovereign rulers created in 1259. But the closeness both of family and personality blinded Henry and Louis to the potential problems that their heirs would later face in maintaining this pact.

Henry remained in Paris into the New Year, participating in both solemn and joyous occasions with the French royal family. He served as a pallbearer for Prince Louis on 14 January at Royaumont, following the sudden death of the heir to the French throne. A week later, at St Denis, Henry's daughter Beatrice was married to Jean, son of the duke of Brittany with Louis IX and Queen Margaret in attendance. Despite news of another Welsh rising, Henry spent the remainder of the winter in St Omer – in part because of illness, in part by inclination. While the king was abroad, Simon de Montfort returned to England, where he once again took up the cause of reform with energy. He insisted on adherence to the Provisions of Oxford, most notably in demanding that parliament meet as scheduled in February 1260, despite the king's absence. Montfort now formed a close relationship with the Lord Edward, who made common cause against the earl of

Gloucester and other royalist councilors. When Henry finally did return home in late April, at the urging of King Louis, he was accompanied by 100 mercenaries. The king and his heir, however, were soon reconciled, Richard of Cornwall once again serving as the mediator along with the archbishop of Canterbury, leaving Montfort politically isolated. Indeed, the earl of Leicester was put on trial in Westminster in May, but the proceedings were quickly abandoned – in part, because of Louis IX's support for Montfort and, in part, because of continuing conflict in Wales.

Although the work of reform went on throughout 1260, when Montfort returned to France in December, much of the momentum for reform was lost. Motivated perhaps by the sudden death abroad of his exiled half-brother Aymer de Lusignan on 4 December 1260, Henry used patronage where possible to detach his opponents, while he appealed to Pope Alexander IV to be released from his oath to uphold the provisions. The pope absolved Henry from his oath in June 1261 and, almost overnight, Henry recovered his kingship. He moved with unwonted decisiveness to seize Dover Castle and the Cinque Ports, following which he appointed his own chancellor and justiciar, as well as sheriffs and castellans, and he launched a general eyre to take stock of his circumstances. Henry had overplayed his hand, and there was widespread resistance both to the eyre and the replacement of the sheriffs. Montfort, now back in England, moved to exploit this opposition, but while the country gentry were ready to take up arms in support of reform, the magnates shrank at the prospect of civil war. The result was a negotiated settlement, the treaty of Kingston of November 1261, in which Henry promised to undertake reform. Montfort, frustrated, returned to France.

Restored to regal authority, Henry sought to vindicate himself against Montfort, drawing up a lengthy indictment of the earl. In July 1262, the king crossed the Channel to deliver this indictment to Louis IX in person, but the latter refused to be drawn into this personal confrontation. Meanwhile, Henry – or, more likely, Queen Eleanor, in reaction to her son's earlier support for, first, the Lusignans and then Montfort at the expense of her Savoyard relatives – effected a purge of the retinue of the Lord Edward between May and July 1262. This was a crucial error. These young aristocrats, many of them marcher lords, would soon make common cause with Simon de Montfort, although their natural allegiance was to the crown. In October 1262, Montfort briefly returned to England, appearing before parliament with a papal bull confirming the provisions.

Henry himself returned from France in December 1262 to face yet another

Welsh uprising and renewed calls for adherence to the Provisions of Oxford. On 22 January 1263, he reissued the provisions, but this proved to be a case of too little, too late. The Lord Edward returned to England in February with a new entourage of French supporters, further alienating his own dispossessed retainers and renewing anti-foreign sentiment. Indeed, his former retainers Roger de Leyburn and Roger de Clifford very likely invited Simon de Montfort to return to England and take charge of the opposition to the crown. This Montfort did, arriving back in England late in April. A small but influential group of magnates, including the new earl of Gloucester, Gilbert de Clare, and Richard of Cornwall's son Henry of Almain, met with him in Oxford to plan a course of action.

The summer of 1263 saw a violent series of attacks on the opponents of the provisions, most notably the Savoyards. The lands of Pierre of Aigueblanche, bishop of Hereford, were targeted, and he himself was taken prisoner in his own cathedral on 7 June. It was likely Montfort himself who identified Aigueblanche as the man most closely linked to the Sicilian Business. In July, the lands of Boniface of Savoy, archbishop of Canterbury, were similarly devastated. Central to the baronial policy of 1263 was not only the exclusion of aliens from office as the provisions had sought in 1258, but their deportation with no prospect of return. Montfort's support in 1263 came especially from the bishops and the Londoners. To further legitimize his program of reform, by December 1263, Montfort had begun to use the title Steward of England. After the battle of Lewes in May 1264, this title would appear regularly in government documents, but it was a novel usage in 1263.

Meanwhile, in September 1263, Louis IX failed to support Henry III who once again crossed the channel, as did Montfort, seeking the French king's arbitration. Henry and the Lord Edward returned to England to face the October parliament in Westminster, but Queen Eleanor and Prince Edmund remained behind in France. In mid-October, Edward seized Windsor Castle, where he was soon joined by his father as the kingdom edged towards civil war. A truce was arranged by Richard of Cornwall in which Henry promised to observe the provisions, pending a final adjudication by Louis IX. But the king was hardly as good as his word. From Windsor, he travelled to Oxford, where he dismissed and replaced the chancellor and treasurer. Winchester, too, was taken back into royalist hands, although an attempt to seize Dover failed. Perhaps the most intriguing, and generally overlooked, episode of the period of Montfort's initial ascendancy came on 11 December 1264 when Montfort and his entourage were trapped on the south bank of the Thames at Southwark while two separate royal armies advanced on their position. Montfort and his men apparently feared for their lives, as they confessed, took communion and took the cross in their holy war against the king and anyone who would oppose the provisions. Luckily, a sympathetic group of Londoners broke down the city gates, allowing them to gain the security of the capital. It was during the brief truce that followed this standoff on the Thames that the final arrangements were made, whereby it was decided to submit the dispute to Louis IX.

Henry III made yet another journey to France shortly after Christmas 1263 and made his way to Amiens. The decision by both Henry and Simon to submit to the arbitration of Louis IX has been variously viewed, as either an act of desperation or a sign of overconfidence in each. On 23 January 1264, Louis IX issued his famous 'Mise of Amiens' in Henry's favour, at once dismissing the provisions and confirming Henry's right to appoint his own officials. Louis was careful, however, not to repudiate the Magna Carta or any other aspect of English common law. Whether or not Montfort's absence from Amiens as the result of injuries sustained in a riding accident played any role in the decision is questionable. Hitherto he had been able to persuade his friend Louis IX of many things. Lacking his personal intervention, however, even the rhetorical brilliance of Thomas de Cantilupe was insufficient to carry the day. In England, the general perception seems to have been that Louis had gone beyond the scope of his commission. Indeed, although both sides had agreed to abide by the terms of the arbitration, Montfort immediately rejected the Mise of Amiens on the basis of Louis' detachment of the provisions from the Magna Carta and sent clear signals that he would appeal the decision at Amiens by force of arms.

In the spring of 1264, Henry, or more likely the Lord Edward and Richard of Cornwall, demonstrated considerable military skill in the run-up to the battle of Lewes. Edward managed to blunt the attacks of Montfort's sons in the Welsh marches, while the king summoned an army and made preparations from Oxford. As Montfort held London and Dover, the so-called key to England, and his sons were firmly entrenched in the Midlands, Oxford was well chosen to divide the rebel forces. On 3 April, the king marched out from Oxford to Northampton, which was taken 2 days later. Simon de Montfort the younger and many other prominent supporters of the earl were taken prisoner. Although the elder Simon himself had led a relief force north from London, he only got as far as St Albans before learning of the disastrous defeat. He hurried back to the capital where, on 7 April, he unleashed a savage attack on the Jews, who were rumoured to be conspiring against his faction.

While the royalists secured Leicester, Salisbury and Nottingham, Montfort besieged Rochester on 17 April with the support of Gilbert de Clare. The castle fell on 19 April, but not the keep, and Henry, with uncharacteristic energy, led his army south to Rochester where he successfully raised Montfort's siege, having already taken the submission of Clare's castle at Kingston. The earl of Gloucester's castle at Tonbridge also fell to Henry on 30 April, and the king continued south with the object of securing the south coast and, specifically, the Cinque Ports. On 2 May, as the royal army made its way to the coast, the king's cook Thomas was killed by an arrow as he marched at the head of the king's column. In the aftermath of this failed ambush, Henry ordered the execution of some 315 archers who had surrendered: they were beheaded in his presence at Flimwell in Ticehurst. This uncharacteristically brutal action was said to be taken on the advice of Richard of Cornwall, king of Germany, but perhaps this was also a lesson in terror that Henry had learned from Montfort in Gascony. The next day, the king took a fine of 100 marks from the monks of Battle Abbey for the participation of their peasants at Flimwell. At Winchelsea on 4 May, or shortly thereafter, Henry received the homage and fealty of the men of the Cinque Ports and plans were made to blockade Montfort in London, ending the war once and for all. On 6 May, however, the earl marched out of London.

Having learned of Montfort's movements while at Battle Abbey on 9 May, Henry moved to Lewes with his army on 10/11 May. The king took up residence in Lewes priory, while the castle of John de Warenne, earl of Surrey, provided a strong centrepiece for a defensive position. Montfort made camp at his manor of Fletching, some 8 miles north of Lewes on 11 May. On the morning of 12 May, the royalists dispersed a Montfortian scouting party, and Warenne engaged in a skirmish with a foraging party. In the afternoon, a delegation led by the bishop of Chichester brought an offer of terms to the king. The Provisions of Oxford were to be reaffirmed, with disputed points to be arbitrated by an ecclesiastical panel. A separate delegation, including the bishops of London and Worcester, offered £30,000 in reparations for damages (particularly to Richard of Cornwall). Although Henry is said to have found the offer attractive, he was dissuaded from agreeing by his brother Richard and his son Edward. According to the *Song of Lewes*, Edward declared that: 'peace is forbidden to them, unless they all bind themselves with halters on their necks, and bind themselves over to us for hanging or for drawing'.[18] In response, on 13 May, Montfort sent a letter of defiance 'from the woods of Lewes,' in which he tried, somewhat disingenuously, to separate his attack on the royalists from an attack on the king. Rejected by the king, the Montfortians withdrew their homage and fealty.

On 14 May 1264 at Lewes, Simon de Montfort once again proved his outstanding generalship, while the Lord Edward demonstrated both the skill and energy for which he would later become famous, but without sufficient discretion. Montfort's cavalry force probably stood at no more than 500, one-third the size of that of the king, although each side had several thousand foot-soldiers. Before dawn, Montfort moved his troops up from the west onto the Downs overlooking Lewes. The king held a hastily convened council of war with his brother Richard, their respective sons, the Lord Edward and Henry of Almain, and Roger de Leyburn. The battle most likely took place by the town walls, near the present county prison, Montfort having descended from the heights overlooking the town. The royal army was divided into three divisions, with Edward on the right along with Warenne and William de Valence, Richard in the centre with his son Henry, and the king on the left. Montfort's army also had three divisions opposite the royalists, with the Londoners facing Edward on the left, Gilbert de Clare, John FitzJohn and William de Munchensy in the centre opposite Richard, and Montfort's sons Henry and Guy on the right opposite the king. Montfort himself appears to have been in command of a fourth division held back as a strategic reserve, and he himself will have had the only clear view of all elements of both armies.

Edward smashed through the cavalry and into the Londoners on foot behind them, after which he pursued them off the field for several miles. The centre under Richard and the left wing under the king fared less well. The fighting was heavy, as Montfort presumably threw his reserve in here. The king had two horses killed under him, but despite his personal bravery was forced to withdraw to the priory. Edward, upon his return to the field, engaged the Montfortians, who by then held the town, but much of his contingent fled the battle at this point. Edward made his way to his father in the priory, and the royalists also still held the castle and had taken several valuable prisoners such as John Giffard of Brimpsfield. Although clearly a victory for Montfort, Lewes was not politically decisive. Montfort needed a quick settlement, and this was reached on the following day in what has come to be known as the Mise of Lewes.

The king surrendered his sword to the earl of Gloucester, Gilbert de Clare – not Montfort – and agreed to the enforcement of the Provisions of Oxford. The marchers, including Roger de Leyburn, Roger Mortimer and James Audley, were allowed their freedom, but Edward and Henry of Almain were held as hostages. The disputed points of the Provisions of Oxford were to be arbitrated by Louis IX – although this never happened – and a council would be established to oversee the king's administration. The justification for this new arrangement was articulated and celebrated in the *Song of Lewes*, which trumpeted the end of arbitrary kingship, to be replaced by a new regime, which worked for the good of the entire community of the realm. Nevertheless, this bold new world would prove to be decidedly short-lived. The regime of Simon de Montfort, despite possessing both the king and the heir to the throne, could never be fully secure. Rather than undertake any form of arbitration, Louis IX supported the efforts of Queen Eleanor to raise a force at Damme in Flanders with which to invade. She sought assistance not only from the French king, but also from his brother Alphonse of Poitiers, and she gathered a considerable force not only from the Low Countries and France, but also from Gascony and her own homeland of Savoy. Meanwhile, the papal legate Guy Foulquois awaited in France armed with papal sanctions – both excommunication and interdict – against the new regime. Finally, not all internal resistance had been broken at Lewes, and the freedom of the Lord Edward's supporters among the marcher lords posed a particular danger.

In June 1264, Montfort held a parliament in London, to which he summoned four knights to be elected from each shire. On 28 June, this parliament issued an ordinance for the governance of the kingdom, which completely abrogated the independent authority of the king. The king was to be governed by a council of nine – to be named by a triumvirate composed of Montfort, the earl of Gloucester and the bishop of Chichester – at least three of whom were to be in attendance on him at all times. No appointments to great offices of state, or for that matter even to the offices within the king's own household, could be made without the consent of this council. According to one contemporary chronicle, the king only accepted these constraints upon his prerogative when threatened with deposition and replacement of the Plantagenet line through the election of a new ruler.[19] The mayor and aldermen of London certainly embraced this radical vision of limited monarchy, reportedly renewing their fealty to the king on 17 March 1265 in the most contingent of terms, saying 'Lord, as long as you will be a good king and lord to us, we will be your faithful and devoted men'.[20] Meanwhile, in August 1264, the baronial government sent a draft proposal known as the Peace of Canterbury to Louis IX for his endorsement. Going beyond the terms of the Mise of Lewes, and even the ordinance established by the June parliament, this 'peace' called for the continued restraint of royal power throughout the rest of the lifetime of Henry III and into that of the Lord Edward. Famously, Louis replied 'that he would rather break clods behind a plow than have this sort of princely rule'.[21] Similarly, the papal legate refused to endorse this scheme and continued to threaten excommunication and interdict on the barons.

Some pressure on Montfort was relieved when Urban IV died on 2 October, thereby ending the commission to the legate Guy Foulquois. But, a month later, a failed attempt to rescue the Lord Edward from Wallingford Castle – initiated by Queen Eleanor – demonstrated the continuing resistance to his rule, and was followed by Edward's internment, along with Richard of Cornwall and his son Henry of Almain, in Kenilworth for added security. Montfort was at the height of his power following the defeat of Edward's marcher allies in December 1264 and his effective confiscation of the earldom of Chester from the Lord Edward. In January 1265, summonses were sent out for the Hilary parliament, widely remembered because both burgesses and knights were called to attend; even so, only 5 earls and 18 other magnates were summoned as opposed to 120 ecclesiastics, suggesting the limited nature of Montfort's support. This was a very partisan assembly, not some sort of proto-democratic representative body.

Montfort soon succumbed to the very failing he had long decried in Henry III, the misdirection of patronage. Too much was concentrated too quickly into his own hands and into those of his sons. The Devon and Cornwall estates of Richard of Cornwall – who languished in prison throughout the period from Lewes to Evesham – had been granted to Guy de Montfort. Along with land, Montfort had amassed 11,000 marks in cash prior to his death. He was operating on a kingly scale, travelling with an entourage of upwards of 100 retainers in the spring of 1265, considerably more than Henry III had ever maintained in his own household. On 28 May, Simon de Montfort presented the temporalities to the new abbot of Chester: here was the new 'king', exercising his power in the open. But on that very same day, the Lord Edward escaped from his enforced captivity in a daring and dramatic dash to freedom. A day later, at Ludlow, Edward entered into a pact with Gilbert de Clare, Montfort's former ally and the son of Edward's former opponent. Montfort and Gloucester had begun to quarrel almost at once following the victory at Lewes, disagreeing over the ransoming of the many prisoners taken there, most of whom Montfort had reserved to himself. Now the powerful earl joined the marchers who were already committed to the royalist side.

On 12 June, Montfort sent out letters summoning an ecclesiastical council to meet in Gloucester. He then met with Llywelyn, making an ill-advised pact with him on 19 June. By then, however, Gloucester had fallen to the royalists. Montfort was forced to move south from Hereford to Monmouth and on to Newport by 4 July, where he hoped to ferry his men across the Severn and effect a union with his son. This was prevented, however, by Edward and Gloucester, who forced Montfort to fall back on Abergavenny and Hay-on-Wye before returning to Hereford, where he remained throughout the rest of July. Having failed to bring the elder Simon to battle in July, Edward was now most concerned to prevent the younger Simon from linking up with his father. Simon the younger had moved his forces from London to Winchester, which he sacked on 16 July, and then on to Oxford from where he could threaten Gloucester. By 31 July, he had withdrawn from Oxford to the Montfortian fortress of Kenilworth. On 1 August, Edward took a bold gamble, riding through the night from Worcester to Kenilworth, after a clever diversionary feint toward Shrewsbury, and arriving before Kenilworth near dawn on 2 August. Although the younger Simon de Montfort escaped into the castle, Edward captured the earl of Oxford, William Munchensy, and a number of other valuable prisoners.

Edward returned to Worcester at once, but at the same time the elder Simon crossed to the east side of the Severn at Kempsey. From there, he moved on to Evesham during the night of 3–4 August, with his ultimate goal being to evade Edward's army and move on to Kenilworth and thus combine the Montfortian forces. But Edward was also on the move during the night of 3–4 August, shadowing Montfort's movements and dividing his own forces in order to trap the earl. Edward and Gloucester approached Evesham from the north; Edward from further east at Cleeve Prior and Gloucester from Alcester. Meanwhile, a third royalist force under Roger Mortimer approached from the west from Pershore, following the route taken earlier by Montfort himself. It would appear that Edward displayed the banners captured at Kenilworth a few days earlier and that, initially, Montfort believed his son's forces had come to his rescue. But he was soon disabused of this notion by his barber, Nicholas, who had climbed to the top of the bell tower in Evesham and saw that the city was surrounded by royalist forces: 'We are all dead', he reported from his elevated vantage point, 'for it is not your son as you believed, but the son of the king on one direction, the earl of Gloucester from another, and Roger Mortimer from a third.'[22]

The chronicles are all in agreement that Simon de Montfort refused to flee from Evesham, but the simple reality is that he had no alternative. Edward had skilfully out-manoeuvered him this time, perhaps with the lessons learned at Lewes. Montfort appears to have formed his cavalry into a wedge in order to break through the royalist lines and lead his foot-soldiers out. He marched out to the north, and although he had some initial success in breaking the Edwardian line, this was only temporary. The infantry seems to have failed to march out, let alone to have engaged, leaving Montfort's cavalry on their own. More than 20 Montfortian knights were killed, an astounding number in the context of medieval warfare, with its emphasis on capture and ransoms. The king himself, in a suit of Montfort's armour, was wounded in the neck before being recognized. Following the battle, Montfort was buried alongside his son, Henry, and Hugh Despenser before the high altar in Evesham with the king's permission. The Lord Edward is said to have attended the services for Henry, with whom he had grown up. But these niceties mask the brutal nature of the battle of Evesham. Montfort's corpse had been mutilated on the field of battle – his head, hands and feet were chopped off, as were his genitals, which were repositioned astride his nose. The pent-up rage of the royalist forces could not be contained. Unlike Lewes, the battle of Evesham was decisive: the Provisions of Oxford died with Simon de Montfort.

Henry III summoned parliament to meet at Winchester in September. The king tried to impose some order on the confused state of property rights in the aftermath of civil war, taking the lands of some 254 Montfortian supporters into his own hands. These lands were subsequently redistributed to 71 royalists, particularly members of his own family, suggesting that even now Henry had not learned his lesson in terms of the balanced distribution of patronage. The result was a continuation of resistance and warfare, a situation relished by the Lord Edward, anxious for revenge, if not by the king himself. The last great rebel stronghold, Montfort's castle at Kenilworth, was besieged in June 1266. The king's difficulty in taking it led to a negotiated settlement, the Dictum of Kenilworth, prior to the castle's final capitulation in December. The dictum, revised in the following summer, allowed the former rebels to redeem their lands over a period of years. Henry also brought closure to his longstanding conflict with Llywelyn of Wales, in the Treaty of Montgomery, negotiated by the papal legate Ottobuono in September 1267. The subsequent Statute of Marlborough, issued in parliament in November, once again affirmed the charters, the Dictum of Kenilworth, and in a modified form, the Provisions of Westminster.

When the Lord Edward decided in June 1268 to join the proposed Crusade of Louis IX to Tunis, Henry allocated the revenues of London, along with several counties and royal castles, to his heir in support of this venture. He could ill afford this loss of revenue, but funds were otherwise unavailable. It was only in April 1270, after long negotiation, that parliament finally agreed to a crusading tax of one-twentieth on movables in support of Edward's expedition. Meanwhile, the king presided over a pair of royal weddings, again at considerable expense. Edmund married Avelina de Forz, heiress to the lordships of Holderness and the Isle of Wight, along with the earldom of Devon, on 8 or 9 April 1269. Henry of Almain married Constance de Béarn, the heiress to the lands of titles of the mercurial Gaston VII in an elaborate ceremony at Windsor on 21 May 1269. This union was intended to reinforce Plantagenet power in Gascony and, at the same time, pre-empt any claim by the surviving sons of Simon de Montfort to the county of Bigorre, but Henry of Almains's subsequent assassination in southern Italy by the sons of Simon de Montfort would further confuse the situation. Richard of Cornwall had meanwhile married for the third time, to Beatrix of Falkenburg, a niece of the previously hostile Archbishop Engelbert of Cologne at Kaiserslautern on 16 June 1269. These marriages brought renewed prestige to the royal house, as did the translation of the relics of Edward the Confessor on 13 October 1269. Although the reconstruction of Westminster Abbey was far from complete, Henry III, the Lord Edward, Prince Edmund and Richard of Cornwall bore the relics of the saint-king on their shoulders to the magnificent new shrine. In many ways, this was the culmination of Henry's long reign.

On 4 August 1270, the Lord Edward took his leave of his father in Winchester and set off on his crusading journey. He was never to see his father alive again. Henry seems to have been ill throughout the remaining 2 years of his life. He was unable to travel to France for the commemoration of the death of his brother-in-law Louis IX in the autumn of 1270, and in March 1271 he was so ill that Richard of Cornwall was named protector of the realm. Although the king recovered, he hardly left Westminster after this, and chose not to, or was unable to, attend the funerals of Henry of Almain at Hailes in May, and of his grandson John in Westminster Abbey itself in August. He was ill again at Christmas 1271, and in spring 1272 he excused himself from performing homage to the new king of France, Philip III, on the grounds of his failing health. He died at Westminster on 16 November 1272 at the age of 65, having ruled for 56 years.

Henry III, whose first coronation in 1216 had been such a rushed and imperfect affair, may have sought to make partial amends for this at his passing, for he was buried in coronation *regalia*, possibly that which had been used at his second, more traditional, coronation in 1220. Following his death, the king's heart was quickly removed for eventual transport to Fontevrault, to be interred among the remains of his ancestors. His body, however, was buried on 20 November before the high altar in Westminster Abbey. The king was buried wearing a dalmatic and tunic, and bearing a royal rod. Unlike his father and his Anglo-Norman forebears, Henry III was not buried with a sword. The rod surmounted with a dove was an evocation of his patronage of St Edward, and a symbol unique to the king himself. But one legacy of the Confessor was too precious for Henry to take with him to his grave, 'the diadem of the most saintly king Edward'. This would be left to adorn the head of the next Plantagenet king of England, Edward I.

2

Edward I (1272–1307)

Edward I was born on the night of 17–18 June 1239 at Westminster, the first child of Henry III and his young queen, Eleanor of Provence. He was named after his father's patron saint, Edward the Confessor, and his birth occasioned great joy not only in the royal court and the capital, but throughout the kingdom. Little is known about his childhood, although he was given his own household early on, and raised with other aristocratic children, including his cousin, Henry of Almain. He was placed into the care of Hugh Giffard and his wife Sybil and, following Hugh's death in 1246, into that of Bartholomew Pecche. Every indication is that his education was that typical of his age, with a greater emphasis on military training than academic studies. He may have developed a taste for romance from his mother. His only known act of literary patronage came in the middle of his life when he commissioned Rustichello of Pisa to produce a new work in 1272, the result of which was an Arthurian romance called *Meliadus*. Although frequently sick as a child – in 1246, his mother stayed with him at Beaulieu Abbey for 3 weeks until he had recovered from an unspecified illness – by his teens he had grown to be strong and athletic, becoming an avid tournament knight, participating in his first as early as 1256 at Blyth, while still just 17 years old.

By the time of his tournament debut, the Lord Edward, as he was generally known in his youth, had already married. His marriage to Eleanor of Castile, half-sister of Alphonso X the Wise, had been arranged in response to the threat to Gascony posed by the Spanish kingdom of Castile. In order to arrange the match, Henry III had agreed to endow his son with substantial landed property valued at £10,000 per annum, including the earldom of Chester, the town and castle of Bristol, and substantial lands in Ireland and Wales, as well as Gascony, Oléron and the Channel Islands. Similarly, Eleanor was to be 'dowered as fully as any queen of England ever had been.'[1] Arrangements were made for the prince to be knighted and the wedding to take place in Castile on 13 October 1254, the feast day of Edward the Confessor, which was so significant to Henry III. Unfortunately, there were delays, and in the end Edward appears to have been knighted by King Alphonso on 18 October, with the wedding taking place a fortnight later on 1 November 1254, at the Cistercian monastery of Las Huelgas in Burgos. Edward was 15 years old and his bride was 12 years old.

By the end of November, the royal couple had returned to Gascony and, on 15 December, they made a ceremonial entry into Bordeaux, the city having been lavishly decorated and perfumed at its four corners with incense and spices. As Henry III had already begun his return journey to England, the prince was able to exercise his own authority, probably for the first time. In Bayonne, on his return from the wedding, he had styled himself as 'now ruling Gascony as prince and lord',[2] a clear indication of his intention to assert his own identity. Not only did he engage in military activity, pacifying La Réole and besieging Gramont in July 1255, but he must also have delved into the complex municipal politics of Bordeaux, because following his own return to England, in September 1256, he entered into a treaty with Gaillard de Soler that was designed to give the prince control over the mayoralty of Bordeaux. This was certainly part of a broader policy, as similar arrangements were also made in Bayonne and other towns. Here, we can see some of the administrative acumen that Edward would demonstrate in England, more than a decade prior to his coming to the throne.

Throughout the years to 1258, the Lord Edward can be associated with his mother's relatives, the Savoyards, but in that year he made a dramatic switch in allegiance to his father's Lusignan half-siblings. Edward, always hard-pressed for cash throughout his father's reign, granted Stamford and Grantham to his uncle William de Valence in return for a loan. More significantly, perhaps, Edward planned to install another of these Poitevin uncles, Geoffrey de Lusignan, as seneschal in Gascony, with Geoffrey's brother Guy becoming keeper of Oléron and the Channel Islands. These arrangements certainly suited the Lusignans with their traditional power base in Poitou, but were considered highly suspect and were widely criticized by contemporary English observers.

As we have seen in the previous chapter, the Lord Edward was swept up in the current of baronial reform and revolt in 1258. Perhaps the most noteworthy aspect of his participation in the struggle between his father and Simon de Montfort was his penchant for repeatedly changing sides and the resultant reputation he earned for inconstancy. His pursuit of personal quarrels, and the methods with which he pursued them, further tarnished his image during this period. For instance, in late 1263, Edward revealed an unattractive ruthlessness when – having entered the New Temple by means of a ruse – he proceeded to seize vast quantities of cash that had been placed there for safekeeping, leading to riots in London. Although Edward withdrew to Windsor, which he garrisoned with foreign mercenaries, conditions in the city were so unsettled that the queen was prevented from joining him there when angry Londoners hurled both insults and debris at her barge from atop London Bridge, forcing her to retreat back down the Thames and take refuge at the bishop of London's house.

In the armed conflict that followed the Mise of Amiens, Edward showed himself to be a capable military commander, although, again, his behaviour in the civil war did not always redound to his credit. In early 1264, he forced an entry into Gloucester, but agreed to a truce when confronted by a superior baronial force under the command of the earl of Derby, Robert de Ferrers. Following Derby's own withdrawal, however, Edward returned to extract his revenge – in the form of a heavy ransom – on Gloucester and its citizens. In April, Edward played an important role in the assault on Northampton, but also spent considerable time, energy and resources pursuing his own personal feud with Derby, devastating his lands and seizing Tutbury Castle (Edward and Derby would each pursue the other's undoing until 1269 when the prince finally prevailed and the earl was obliged to recognize a debt of £50,000 to Prince Edmund, effectively thereby surrendering his earldom). At the battle of Lewes on 14 May 1264, Edward led the cavalry on the right wing of the royalist army and would have distinguished himself, had he been able to restrain and reorder his troops after they overran the Londoners who faced them on the baronial side. In the aftermath of the battle, with the king a prisoner, both Edward and his cousin Henry of Almain agreed to become hostages, and Simon de Montfort dictated terms for the governance of England in the so-called 'mise of Lewes'.

Edward was imprisoned for nearly a year until March 1265, when he agreed to accept the reforms, surrendering Bristol as a guarantee of his adherence to his promise. Even then, he was kept under close surveillance until late May when he managed to evade his minders in Hereford and ride to Wigmore Castle, the seat of Roger Mortimer. Edward played a crucial role in the fighting that culminated at Evesham on 4 August 1265, where Simon de Montfort was defeated and killed. Although the battle of Evesham was decisive, it was not final and desperate rebels dug in throughout the country. Edward, rather than Henry III, led the royal forces that inexorably ground down the resistance over the next 2 years. In the campaigning that ensued in the aftermath of Evesham, one incident (in particular) is worth noting. While moving through Hampshire, Edward encountered a force under the rebel leader Adam Gurton in Alton Forest. Although the incident has subsequently been romanticized to make Edward more chivalric than appears to have been the case, the fact of the matter is that the Lord Edward did engage Gurton in single combat and overcame him, demonstrating both his personal valour and martial skills. The end of resistance finally came with the success of the prolonged siege of Kenilworth and the settlement known as the Dictum of Kenilworth on 31 October 1266, by which the former rebels were allowed to buy back their former estates over a specified period of years. The last of the rebels, in the Isle of Ely, surrendered on 11 July 1267.

Shortly after the capitulation of the last of the English rebels, Wales was also stabilized through the Treaty of Montgomery that was sealed with Llywelyn ap Gruffudd on 29 September 1267. Llywelyn was to receive the homages of the other Welsh princes (except for Maredudd ap Rhys) and have a wide general authority, in return for his own homage to the English king and an annual payment of £2,000 to the exchequer. In the end, this treaty left too many disputed issues unsettled, and Edward I would once again face Welsh rebellion early in his reign, but for the moment the area was relatively calm. Meanwhile, in November 1267, the Statute of Marlborough was issued. Drawing extensively upon the Provisions of Westminster, this statute can be seen as a legal lynchpin, connecting the work of the reforming barons of Henry III with the future reforms of Edward I, although it is unclear how much, if any, involvement the prince had in the actual drafting of this legislation.

In the aftermath of the civil war, Edward was at the centre of a group of young English aristocrats who responded to the preaching of the papal legate Ottobuono and took the cross at Northampton on 24 June 1268. Among his fellow *crucesignati* were his brother Edmund and his cousin Henry of Almain, his uncle William de Valence, and the earls of Surrey and Gloucester. Edward seems to have been motivated in taking the cross by his status as heir apparent to the throne, his martial nature, and his respect for Louis IX, under whose leadership the crusade was being organized. There may also have been a penitential element (or at least a spirit of thanksgiving) in his decision. A contemporary poem states that Edward took the cross 'desirous of performing a worthy service to Christ, who had delivered him from this whirlwind of war.'[3] In late August 1269, the prospective crusaders met in Paris, where Louis promised some 70,000 *livres tournois* (£17,500 sterling) to Edward, who in turn promised to arrive at Louis's Mediterranean port of Aigues-Mortes by 15 August 1270. Edward contracted 225 knights in England, presumably at a rate of 200 *l.t.* (£50) apiece, while Gaston de Béarn (to whom Louis had designated 25,000 of Edward's total 70,000) was to raise another 125. Several of the individual contracts survive, including one between Edward and Adam of Jesmond, and another in which Payn de Chaworth and Robert Tiptoft each contracted to serve for 1 year with five knights apiece in return for payment of 600 marks each. Delayed by strained relations with Gilbert de Clare, Edward postponed his embarkation from its scheduled date of 24 June to early August. Even then, he was confronted with unfavourable winds, and despite moving his force from Portsmouth to Dover, was still in England late in August. He finally reached Aigues-Mortes not later than 28 September, but as this was 6 weeks after the agreed-upon date, it must have come as no surprise to him that Louis IX's fleet had sailed without him. Undaunted, Edward sailed on to Tunis, only to discover that Louis had died of dysentery and that Louis's brother Charles of Anjou had entered into negotiations with the Tunisian emir for a settlement.

Remaining committed to his crusading vow, Edward sailed on to Sicily and, in the spring, made for the Holy Land. After obtaining provisions in Cyprus, in May 1271 he landed at Acre, the site of the triumph of his predecessor Richard the Lionheart. Edward faced a critical shortage of horses – he was so desperate that he had to arrange for palfreys to be sent out all the way from England. The campaign that followed was desultory at best, and when Hugh III of Cyprus, titular king of Jerusalem, agreed to a 10-year truce with the Mamluk sultan Baibars, Edward's crusade came to a premature end. He, nonetheless, remained in the east until the following September. He may have been inspired to seek further deeds at arms by an edition of Vegetius's *De Re Militari* that Queen Eleanor commissioned for him at this time, an edition that was updated with reference to Edward's own recent success at the siege of Kenilworth. Meanwhile, on 12 June 1272, Edward was gravely wounded in an attempt on his life by a member of the mysterious Shi'ite sect, the Assassins. He is said to have killed his assailant with the Assassin's own knife, but was seriously wounded in the arm by the same poisoned blade. The wound was only healed after a considerable amount of flesh was cut away. It is unlikely that there is any truth to the romantic tale that Eleanor of Castile sucked the poison from the wound and thereby saved her husband's life, but she did give birth to two daughters while in Acre, only the younger of whom, Joan, survived. Eleanor's pregnancy and Joan's birth may also help to explain Edward's delay in departing the Holy Land. Regardless, Edward remained committed to the ideal of the crusade, and in the 1280s he worked to achieve European peace towards this end. He took the cross for a second time in 1287, but he was never able to embark on another crusade, and with the fall of Acre in 1291, the cause of the crusade in the Holy Land became increasingly chimerical.

As soon as he landed in Sicily, Edward learned not only of the death of Henry III, but also of the passing of his own 5-year-old son John. When Charles of Anjou expressed puzzlement at Edward's lack of remorse at the death of his son, Edward replied in words reminiscent of the callous response of John Marshal, father of William Marshal, at the siege of Newbury in 1152 that it was easy enough to beget more sons.[4] In spite of the news of his father's death, Edward's return to England can only be described as leisurely. In February, he reached Rome and was received by Pope Gregory X in Orvieto. From there, he travelled north by way of Reggio, Parma and Milan, and crossing the Alps through the Mont Cenis Pass he made his way to Savoy, in which his father had put such store. On 25 June 1273, Count Philip of Savoy performed homage to Edward I for the castles he held of the English king, and Edward was treated with lavish hospitality throughout his stay at St Georges d'Esperanche, in the count's newly built castle. It would be the Savoyard architect James of St George who would travel to England later in the decade to become the master designer behind the Edwardian castle-building programme in Wales. It is worth noting that the core of Edward's crusading companions – men such as Roger de Clifford, Otto de Grandson (himself a Savoyard) and John de Vescy – were still with him long after their original contracts had expired. After leaving Savoy, Edward made his way to Châlons-sur-Marne, where he participated in a tournament at the invitation of Count Peter. Indeed, Edward proposed to field his own knights against those of the count and all other comers. Despite urgent entreaties to his own knights in both Gascony and England, Edward took the field outnumbered by two to one. At the outset of the melée, the count is said to have charged together with a company of 50 knights directly at Edward and, when he proved unable to overcome the king with swordplay, he attempted to unhorse Edward by grabbing him round the neck and pulling. This decidedly unchivalric manoeuvre failed miserably when the king turned the tables on the count and, in fact, threw him to the ground. What followed next is referred to by the chronicler Walter of Guisborough as the 'Little Battle of Châlons' rather than a tournament, a battle in which much blood was spilled.[5] Nevertheless, Edward probably enhanced his reputation both as a tournament knight and as a leader of men in this encounter.

From Châlons, Edward travelled on to Paris, where he performed homage for his French lands to Philip III during a 10-day stay from 26 July to 6 August. Although he met with at least one English clerk while in Paris, instead of crossing the channel, he next went south to Gascony to confront a revolt by Gaston de Béarn, 'in the firm belief that his first duty was to Gascony'.[6] While in the duchy, he launched an inquiry into feudal holdings, prior to receiving homage as king-duke. The resultant *Livre des Hommages* may perhaps anticipate the more famous *Quo Warranto* inquests and the generation of the Hundred Rolls in England, once again suggesting Edward's keen interest in administrative efficiency, even if the returns probably added little of material value to the ducal coffers.[7] If nothing else, this process reinforced Edward's personal position as lord in Aquitaine, and strengthened the bonds of loyalty between the king-duke and his Gascon subjects.

Eleanor had parted company with Edward shortly before his arrival in Paris. She was once again pregnant, and travelled ahead to Aquitaine in anticipation of giving birth. Throughout the summer, she encouraged her brother Alphonso to visit her, which he finally did in Bayonne in November when he was present at the baptism of his nephew. The king of Castile stood as godfather for the child, named in his honour as Alphonso. He also took the opportunity presented by this occasion to seek an increase in his sister's dower assignment. During these same months, in the autumn of 1253, Spanish marriages were arranged for two of the four surviving children of Eleanor's marriage to Edward; young Eleanor was affianced to the heir to the throne of Aragon, while Henry was betrothed to the heiress of Navarre.

King Edward I finally returned to England in 1274, landing at Dover on 2 August. The royal family proceeded to London by way of Tonbridge, where they were entertained by the earl of Gloucester, and Reigate, where they were hosted by John de Warenne, earl of Surrey. London, and more specifically Westminster, was a hive of activity in anticipation of the king's arrival. Huge stocks of food were laid in preparation for the coronation, and considerable building activity was likewise put into motion in order to house and feed the throng of both men and beasts expected to descend on the capital.

The coronation of Edward I and Eleanor took place on 19 August 1274, the first such ceremony in nearly half a century. In spite of squabbles over precedence by the king's brother, Edmund of Lancaster (who claimed the right to carry the Curtana sword as hereditary steward of England) and by the archbishop of York, Walter Giffard, which may well have resulted in a boycott of the ceremony by each, on the whole both the coronation and the celebrations that followed seemed to go off without a hitch. Edward did, however, clearly make a point of emphasizing the rights of the crown, which he had seen challenged so forcefully in the reign of his father. During the coronation, he apparently swore to uphold the standard oaths, and one chronicle relates that immediately after Robert

Kilwardby, archbishop of Canterbury, anointed and crowned both Edward and Eleanor, the king removed the crown from his head, refusing to wear it until he had recovered the crown lands relinquished by his father. Nevertheless, the coronation was followed by lavish feasting and merry-making. Indeed, orders for foodstuffs had gone out as early as February, and both staples and delicacies were gathered from across the kingdom and abroad. Prelates were called upon to furnish exotic poultry, including swans, peacocks and cranes, while London fishmongers were hard-pressed to provide enough pikes, eels and lampreys. Temporary lodges, stables and kitchens covered all the open space available in Westminster, and in London the conduit at Cheapside flowed with both red and white wine. The highpoint of the celebration may have come when the king of Scots, accompanied by the earls of Lancaster, Cornwall, Gloucester, Pembroke and Surrey, appeared before the king, each at the head of a force of 100 knights. All dismounted before the king and set these valuable horses free, to be taken and kept by whoever could catch them. Such a grandiose celebration had surely not been seen in living memory and must have inspired great enthusiasm for the new reign.

But what of the man who now, at 35 years of age, had been crowned king? In 1274, Edward was, and must have remained, something of a mystery to his subjects. In many ways, he embodied the very image of kingship. Standing six feet and two inches tall, he was powerfully built, and his experiences on both the tournament field and the field of battle had long since proved his personal courage, a courage he would continue to demonstrate until his dying day. He felt little need to wear rich apparel, confident in the appearance he made, although the impact of his physical presence may have been marred somewhat by a lisp, and by the drooping left eyelid that he had inherited from Henry III. Edward I ascribed to a rather conventional chivalric outlook and was deeply concerned with his own honour and that of the crown, although his behaviour – particularly in his youth, but in some instances right down to the end of his life – may have led some to doubt the sincerity of his conviction to these ideals. Nevertheless, his favourite pastimes – hunting and hawking – fit neatly into this ethos, as did his interest in Arthurian traditions.

Edward's enthusiasm for Arthur and the Round Table has already been mentioned in terms of his literary patronage of Rustichello of Pisa, but it also took a more active form. The king and queen visited Glastonbury in 1278 to witness the translation of the remains of Arthur and Guinevere, and the king organized what were called Round Tables at Nefyn in Wales in 1284 and at Falkirk in Scotland in

1302. Most intriguingly of all, he hosted a little-known tournament in Winchester in 1290, which coincided with the celebration of the impending marriages of his daughters Joan of Acre to Gilbert de Clare, earl of Gloucester, and of Margaret to John, duke of Brabant. Although the tournament was overlooked by contemporary chroniclers, the scraps of evidence that survive in the royal accounts suggest an altogether lavish affair. Considerable sums were expended on building works at Winchester Castle throughout 1289 and 1290 in preparation for the tournament, and during the actual event the king's nephew, John of Brittany, received a grant of 1,000 marks to cover his expenses, while John of Brabant's household consumed 3 tuns (1,088 gallons) of wine during 3 days in Winchester. The most remarkable feature of this tournament is the famous 'Winchester Round Table', which has been displayed on the wall of Great Hall in Winchester since at least 1464, when the chronicler John Hardyng noted that:

> The Rounde Table at Wynchestre beganne
> And ther it ende and ther it hangeth yet.[8]

This massive oak table has a diameter of 18 feet and weighs more than a ton, and although the painted decoration of Arthur and the names of his knights on the rayed surface of the table is a later addition, there can be little doubt of the Arthurian inspiration for this unique artefact that consciously tied the Plantagenet dynasty to the legendary king of an earlier British empire.

On a more mundane level, Edward III was possessed of a thoroughly conventional piety. Like his father, although less extravagantly so, he was generous in the provision of alms, feeding some 200 paupers weekly at the outset of the reign, and more than three times that number towards the end of the reign, with substantial supplements on feast days and other special occasions. On the rare occasions when the king was unable to attend morning chapel, the gifts of alms were supplemented, as they were every year on 25 April, the birthday of his son and heir, Edward of Caernarfon. Edward also demonstrated a devotion to the cult of the Virgin, as well as to that of St Thomas Becket. The king regularly made generous gifts to Canterbury, especially in times of crisis, but these gifts could on occasion take unusual forms. In 1285, the king offered four golden statues, including one of St George, valued at nearly £350. Fifteen years later, the king left four gold florins at the saint's altar 'for the foetus currently in the queen's belly' (Thomas of Brotherton was born to Margaret of France on 1 June 1300). On another occasion in 1297, the king demonstrated both his piety and his interest in hunting when he presented the saint with a wax effigy of one of his falcons in hopes of a cure for the ailing bird. Finally, Edward I may well have been the most devoted of all English kings when it came to the royal touch. Although this practice of healing those suffering from scrofula had begun under his father, documentary evidence suggests that, on average, Edward touched more than a thousand of his subjects for the king's evil each year. This practice, both majestic and humbling at one and the same time – scrofula is a tubercular disease that causes swelling of the lymph nodes in the neck and draining sores – seems to embody the often contradictory nature of Edward I's personality.

His ecclesiastical patronage can not measure up to that of his father. By 1290, for instance, Vale Royal, the Cistercian Abbey which he founded in Cheshire in 1277 in fulfilment of a vow made in the face of shipwreck in the Channel, had foundered. He did, however, patronize painters and sculptors to work on the Painted Chamber in Westminster Palace in the 1290s, and St Stephen's Chapel was begun in 1292. Particularly in the Painted Chamber, some of the differences between the mind of Henry III and that of Edward I become clear. Rather than the depictions of vices and virtues and associations with the Confessor that his father had favoured, Edward sponsored a massive pictorial programme focusing exclusively on the Old Testament, and particularly on the first Book of Maccabees. In Judas Maccabeus, Edward celebrated a warrior king in the mould of both King Arthur and himself. Indeed, in 1323, two visiting Irish friars commented that the Painted Chamber contained all of the warfare of the Old Testament, and observed that Edward himself had been 'the most Maccabean of English kings'. A secondary cycle of paintings depicted the downfall of tyrannical kings and may be combined to articulate Edward's own vision of chivalric kingship.

Edward never let his personal piety stand in the way of political expediency. He was almost constantly at odds with his archbishops of Canterbury, Pecham and later Winchelsey, and according to one chronicler, in 1304, Edward's harsh treatment of the archbishop of York, Thomas of Corbridge, led directly to the prelate's death.[9] Similarly, the king would brook no papal interference in English affairs. Not only did he quarrel with Archbishop Winchelsey over the legitimacy of his appropriation of papal tenths earmarked for crusade in the 1280s, in 1297 when the archbishop attempted to enforce the papal bull *Clericis laicos* to prevent ecclesiastical taxation by laymen, Edward outlawed the clergy and collected fines in the amount of the tax they refused to pay. His relations with Boniface VIII after 1300, when the pope was increasingly consumed in a struggle with Philip IV of France, and with the Gascon pope, Clement V, were more cordial.

There was one kingly virtue, however, that seems to have largely escaped Edward I. *Largesse*, the lavish dispensation of patronage and favours, was a virtue that had posed serious problems for Henry III and would also do so for Edward II. If Edward I had a problem with *largesse*, it was its reverse – parsimoniousness. Perhaps influenced by the events of his youth, Edward I was miserly in the dispensation of patronage. Certainly, he was generous to his family and to a small inner circle of trusted companions and advisors. Men such as Robert Burnell, Walter Langton and Antony Bek were raised to dizzying heights through the king's advocacy. And Edward could make generous, if modest, spontaneous gifts to completely unknown figures when appropriate. But his often-heated relations with the higher nobility has led to a longstanding debate. Although Edward maintained a close relationship with a few of his magnates, notably Henry de Lacy, earl of Lincoln, he found himself unable to get along with many others. His longstanding feud and ultimate destruction of the earl of Derby has already been mentioned, and his dealings with the earl of Gloucester were more often than not troubled. His high-handed acquisition of the earldom of Aumale in 1274, simply to allow it to slip into abeyance, seems to point toward an ongoing policy to diminish the power of the magnates, reinforced by his similar treatment of the earldom of Devon in the 1290s, and his manipulation of the earldom of Norfolk in 1306. Moreover, when comital families were married into the royal family – the earl of Gloucester to Joan of Acre in 1290, and the earl of Hereford to Elizabeth in 1302 – their lands were entailed in such a manner that they would descend through the royal line. Equally telling is the king's failure to elevate new men to fill the ranks of the earls. When Edward came to the throne in 1272, there were fewer than a dozen English earls, whereas when he died in 1307, there were only eight, none of them new creations, and most of them close kinsmen. Although this may have been more of a dynastic than a political policy, which allowed him to concentrate wealth in his family, in the longer term it was one element in the difficult political landscape that would challenge the abilities of his son Edward II following his own death.

Without question, one of Edward I's defining characteristics was a violent temper. His feud with Robert Ferrers, earl of Derby, coloured his youth, and his strained relationship with Roger Bigod, earl of Norfolk and marshal of England, and Humphrey de Bohun, earl of Hereford and constable of England, would similarly colour the later years of his reign. His anger could often boil over into physical action. At the wedding of his daughter Margaret to John of Brabant in July 1290, the king attacked a squire for unknown reasons. That he subsequently felt some remorse is indicated by the payment of 20 marks to the squire. Similarly, in 1297, Edward paid for repairs to a coronet of Princess Elizabeth after having thrown it into a fire in a rage. Even if one doubts the veracity of the well-known account of the chronicler Guisborough set in 1305, in which the king is alleged to have assaulted his son Edward, pulling out his hair and kicking and beating him out of the room over an inappropriate request, the story must have rung true to contemporaries.

And yet, for all the accounts of Edward's explosive temper, he had a gentler side as well. Perhaps the most favourable light that can be cast upon the character of Edward I has to do with his relations with his family. Putting aside the outbursts of temper cited above, and his dismissive reaction to the news of the death of his young son John in 1274, Edward seems to have been genuinely devoted to his family. Although Eleanor of Castile gave birth to perhaps 15 children, only 6 survived childhood. Three boys – John, Henry and Alphonso – died at the ages of 5, 6 and 10 years, respectively, with only her fourth and final son, Edward, surviving. Born in 1284, he grew to adulthood in the last difficult decade of the reign, and his relationship with his father seems never to have been as close as either might have hoped. The situation with Edward's daughters, however, was different. Five of these girls – Eleanor, Joan, Margaret, Mary and Elizabeth – survived into adulthood, and seem to have been closer to their father. Joan did not marry until 1290, when she was 18 years of age, whereas Eleanor was 24 years old at the time of her marriage in 1293. Although Edward was undoubtedly furious at Joan's scandalous second marriage to a mere squire, Ralph de Monthermer, in 1297, he nevertheless forgave her. He was lavish in gifts to the messengers who brought him news of the birth of any of his grandchildren, and he indulged all of his daughters with jewels and clothes, especially Elizabeth and Mary, who were frequent visitors to the royal court.

Finally, we must consider Edward I as a husband. Like his father, Edward appears to have been entirely faithful to his first wife Eleanor of Castile, and later to his young French bride, Margaret. Not only did Eleanor provide the king with numerous children (although only one surviving son), but she was a companion to him, travelling on crusade to the East, as well as to Wales and Gascony. Although she developed a reputation for acquisitiveness in the land market, she did not bring with her the large entourage of aliens that had made Eleanor of Provence so controversial. The king's grief at the death of his consort at Harby in Lincolnshire in 1290 inspired one of the best-known sets of monuments of medieval England, the so-called Eleanor Crosses. The queen's remains were entombed in three different places – her entrails being housed in Lincoln, her heart in Blackfriars, London, and her body in the elegant tomb that survives to this day in Westminster Abbey. More poignant, then and now, than these tombs were the series of 12 crosses constructed on the site of each of the resting places on the route of her funeral cortege. Even if we allow for an element of inspiration coming from the crosses that had commemorated the death of Louis IX in 1270, the three surviving crosses, especially the triangular canopied sculpture at Geddington (Northants), continue to evoke an emotional response that renders Edward more human than perhaps any other relic of his time.

Margaret of France, half-sister of Philip the Fair, was some 40 years younger than Edward I at the time of their marriage in 1299. The wedding was accompanied by 3 days of magnificent feasting, jousting and merry-making (made possible only by loans from the Florentine banking family of the Frescobaldi). She quickly bore the king two sons, Thomas of Brotherton in 1300 and Edmund of Woodstock in 1301, as well as another daughter, Eleanor, in 1306. If she did not accompany the king as Eleanor had done, some of this may be put down to her pregnancies and his absence in Scotland. He seems to have been very solicitous of her well-being, and Margaret played an important role as intercessor at court, particularly in reconciling the king with his eldest son and heir, Edward of Caernarfon, in 1305. She played a very unobtrusive role in the reign of her step-son, although her apparently lavish lifestyle led to considerable debts throughout her lifetime. She died on 14 February 1318, and was buried in Greyfriars' church in London.

Edward I had already indicated his concern with administrative efficiency and order in his activity in Gascony, and his concern with royal rights at his coronation. Now, having appointed his trusted servant Robert Burnell as chancellor, he set out to impose order on the kingdom he had inherited. Commissioners were appointed to discover what rights and lands the crown had lost during his father's troubled reign, an undertaking on a massive scale that was reminiscent of the great Domesday Book of William the Conqueror. By March 1275, their findings had been collected in what are now known as the Hundred Rolls. Very likely, the material generated by this investigation served as a trigger for the creation of the many statutes that radiated out from the king in parliament over the course of the next decade and a half, beginning with the first Statute of Westminster in April 1275. However, along with the elimination of corruption and the insistence on the authority of the crown, Edward's legislation also provided remedies for many of the longstanding grievances of the nobility and people.

Edward I has long been known as the 'English Justinian', and this sobriquet derives from the substantial body of statute law that was produced during the first half of his reign. In some ways, this nickname is misleading, because neither the king nor his councillors set out to create a new body of law. The statutes of Edward I are not analogous to the vast compilation of Justinian, nor, perhaps more germane, to the famous *Siete Partidas* of his brother-in-law Alphonso X of Castile. The statutes, both collectively and even individually, were a series of responses to specific questions of law. The goal was to make the king's courts efficient and equitable. Nevertheless, Edward's reign did have an enormous lasting impact on the direction of English law. The concept that no new writs could be sealed without the consent of the king and his council had been emphatically stated in the Provisions of Oxford. Beginning, albeit tentatively, in the reign of Edward I, changes in the law could only be made by the king in parliament. A shift from 'judge-made' law to enacted law had several consequences. For better or worse, English lawyers hereafter largely ceased to study Roman law until the sixteenth century, leading almost at once to a predominantly lay body of justices. Arguably, but certainly with a good deal of qualification, in avoiding the absolutist tendency embodied in Roman law maxims, and embracing the common law's emphasis, initially established in the Magna Carta, that the king himself must rule by law, late medieval England was guided along a constitutionalist path. However that may be, in the immediate future Edward's outlook and the resultant legislation led to the creation of a powerful legal profession that rapidly grew in prominence as it gained the necessary mastery in case law that now became a central element of the legal system.

Virtually all his major legislation was generated in a 15-year period, beginning in 1275 with the Statute of Westminster, a broad compendium of concerns containing some 51 separate clauses. Land tenure was a central concern of medieval elites, and questions of land tenure recur throughout the statutes. On the one hand, the Statute of Gloucester (1278), also known as *Quo Warranto*, was a natural outgrowth of the inquests that had culminated in the Hundred Rolls. By its terms, all franchises were to be proved, either by writ or assize. Edward's longtime associate John de Warenne, earl of Surrey, famously replied to the challenge of this statute by waving a rusty sword in the air and proclaiming:

'Here my lords, here is my warrant! My ancestors came with William the Bastard and conquered their lands with the sword, and I shall defend them with the sword against anyone who tries to occupy them. The king did not conquer and subject the land by himself, but our forefathers were partners with him and assisted in this.'[10]

On the other hand, the first clause of the second Statute of Westminster, *De Donis Conditionalibus* (1285), enforced the wishes of grantors of lands, while the Statute *Quia Emptores* (1290) forbade sub-infeudation, thereby protecting the interests of the very same feudal lords who were threatened by *Quo Warranto*. Even the Statute of Mortmain (1280), which forbade the alienation of feudal lands to the church without prior royal assent and was viewed by the church as an attack upon its liberties, was not designed to prevent such gifts, but rather to protect the interests of both the nobility and the king in their making. Another concern, more to do with the merchants than the nobility, relates to the enforcement of debts. Both the Statute of Acton Burnell (1283) and the later Statute of Merchants (1285) were designed to provide merchants with security by allowing them access to royal justice. Security, more broadly, was addressed in the Statute of Winchester (1285). Overall, the legislation of Edward I, like his administrative reforms and initiatives, demonstrates a concern with order and process, and the period to 1290 is remarkable for its sustained energy and comprehensive concerns.

Despite Edward's best efforts to create a climate of justice in England, however, his return from an absence of 3 years while in Gascony between 1286 and 1289 exposed corruption among his local officials and within the bench. Over the next 4 years, dozens of royal officers, including the escheator south of Trent, were removed from office or punished with heavy fines. But the greatest purge involved the bench. Four of the five justices of the bench were dismissed, with the chief justice, Thomas Weyland, being forced to abjure the realm and go into exile in France in dramatic fashion. Furthermore, all three judges of the King's Bench were dismissed, as were several of the judges of both the northern and southern eyre circuits. Much of this, however, is misleading. Thomas Weyland, it turns out, was not dismissed for misconduct in his judicial capacity, but rather for harbouring a pair of servants who were guilty of murder. And his fellow justices, such as Ralph Hengham, seem to have been fined more because they were capable of paying than for any particular malfeasance – the king probably netted some £10,000 out of these judicial fines. The conflict between the so-called 'war state' and the 'peace state' has been a subject of considerable interest to historians in recent years, but the purging of the justices proves to be a misleading example of their opposition. Although it is true that Edward's realm seldom knew peace, his consistent interest in the efficient administration of government in all its aspects, meant that to a very great extent the war state and peace state coexisted throughout his reign.

Equally as important to Edward as restoring royal authority over lay society was his concern for relations with the Church. In 1278, Archbishop Kilwardby had been named Cardinal bishop of Porto, and despite Edward's efforts to obtain the see for his chancellor Burnell, Pope Nicholas III appointed the Franciscan John Pecham as the new archbishop of Canterbury. Immediately upon his return to England, Pecham held a provincial council at Reading in June 1279, where he focused on abuses in the church, such as pluralism, and stressed the need for thoroughgoing reform. He also addressed the issue of royal writs of prohibition, which prevented ecclesiastical courts from hearing cases specified therein. He concluded by ordering that the Magna Carta be posted in all cathedrals and collegiate churches, implicitly suggesting that it was not being honoured. In October, he followed up on the Reading council by excommunicating a number of individuals whom he considered to have contravened the council's statutes.

The king's response was both immediate and forceful. Pecham was obliged in parliament in the following month to withdraw his order to publish the Magna Carta, to rescind three orders of excommunication, and to agree that none of the statutes agreed in Reading should be pursued to the detriment of the king or crown. Arguably, the Statute of Mortmain enacted at this same parliament was a warning shot across the bow, cautioning the archbishop against direct confrontation with the king. Nevertheless, Pecham continued his campaign against pluralism with great vigour. Although the continuation of pluralism was crucially important to both the king and his clerks (virtually all of whom held multiple benefices), here the archbishop had papal support and the pronouncements of the recent Second Council of Lyons. At the Lambeth council in 1281, Pecham renewed his excommunications of several royal clerks, and tensions continued to exist between king and archbishop, finally coming to a head in the summer of 1285 when the king ordered the clergy in the diocese of Norwich to desist from hearing cases reserved to royal jurisdiction and ordered the justices in eyre to launch an investigation into clerical conduct there from the beginning of the reign. In the end, however, a compromise was reached, and in the following year Edward issued *Circumspecte agatis*, limiting areas where the writ of prohibition could be applied. This compromise solution was finalized with the Statute of Consultation in 1290.

Archbishop Pecham died in December 1292, and was followed by Robert Winchelsey. Winchelsey was a theologian of note, having been trained at Paris, where he became rector, and Oxford, where he became chancellor; he did not rise to office as a royal clerk. He was, however, elected by the monks of Christ Church, Canterbury, without interference from either the king or the pope. When he returned to England from Rome in 1295, he continued Pecham's opposition to pluralism and other abuses by royal clerks. He was faced by a difficult situation, as in this year the king was seizing papal tenths designated for the crusade in order to fund wars in both Wales and Scotland, and Edward had ordered an unprecedented tax of a half on all ecclesiastical incomes. At the 'Model Parliament' in November 1295, Winchelsey opposed an additional levy of a quarter or third on the clergy. In the following year, emboldened by the papal bull *Clericis laicos*, which prohibited ecclesiastical taxation without papal approval, he refused any further grant to the king. In the crisis that followed in 1297, as Edward I tried to field armies in both France and Scotland, Winchelsey made common cause with the king's noble opponents, led by the earls of Hereford and Norfolk, and his voice can be heard in the Remonstrances of that summer. The *Confirmatio Cartarum* of November 1297 marked a bitter, if temporary, defeat for the king, and a triumph for the archbishop. Winchelsey's relations with Edward I were probably not improved in 1300 when he travelled to meet the king at Sweetheart Abbey in Galloway to deliver the papal bull *Scimus fili*, which pronounced papal overlordship of Scotland. In June 1305, the election of Bertrand de Got, a former royal clerk in Gascony, as Pope Clement V, signalled a reversal of fortune for the archbishop. Still bitter over the failure of the church – and, most particularly, Winchelsey – to respond to the perceived needs of the kingdom in 1297, Edward now charged the archbishop with conspiracy. Winchelsey was summoned to the pope's presence in Bordeaux to answer for his 'perversities' and 'excesses'. He sailed from Dover on 19 May 1306, and would not be recalled until after Edward II had ascended the throne.

The conquest of Wales was by no means inevitable when Edward I came to the throne. Even as earl of Chester, Edward had shown little interest in Wales beyond his ability to extract resources from the region. But this seeming indifference was badly misread by Llywelyn ap Gruffydd of Snowdonia, who had greatly expanded his power during the disturbed conditions that existed in England in the 1260s. First of all, he refused to perform homage to Edward I. Beyond that, he moved to occupy English territory (Caerphilly, for instance, was seized from the earl of Gloucester in 1270) and to consolidate this with the construction of a castle at Dolforwyn in 1273 – despite a prohibition by the English government. Finally, he planned to marry Eleanor, daughter of Simon de Montfort, who was (through her mother, Eleanor) the king's own first cousin: a proxy marriage ceremony was performed in 1275, although both Eleanor and her brother Amaury de Montfort fell into Edward's hands when they were shipwrecked off the Welsh coast. In the end, however, it was the matter of homage that proved non-negotiable and led inexorably to war.

The preparations for the 1277 campaign were extensive and, once again, point to Edward's logistical and administrative awareness. Not only were men and mounts summoned to muster at Worcester on 1 July, but massive quantities of victuals and arms were also ordered – the king ordered some 200,000 crossbow bolts from a single castle in Gloucestershire. Some of the troops who arrived at Worcester were sent south to the king's brother, Edmund of Lancaster, at Carmarthen, but the bulk of the army marched north with the king to Chester, to be joined there by the fleet of the Cinque Ports. The army advanced west along the north coast of Wales, cutting a new road through the forest as they marched, reaching Flint by 25 July. Rhuddlan was reached by late August, and at the end of the month Edward's trusted lieutenants Otto de Grandson and John de Vescy were sent on by sea to Anglesey with a labour force tasked with harvesting the grain there, at once depriving the Welsh and supplementing the stores of the English force.

Llywelyn, wisely, came to terms with Edward in the treaty of Aberconwy in November. The Four Cantrefs were returned to English possession, but Llywelyn was allowed to maintain possession of Anglesey in return for an annual payment of 1,000 marks. He was allowed to continue to receive homage from the Welsh lords of Snowdonia, but not from the rest of the country. Finally, he was saddled with a massive indemnity of £50,000, designed to keep him quiescent rather than there being any expectation of repayment. In fact, the fine was quickly pardoned, the point having been made. He was even allowed to marry Eleanor de Montfort, but on the English king's terms. The wedding took place at Worcester on 13 October 1278, the feast day of Edward the Confessor, with Edward I himself giving away the bride and providing a lavish wedding feast.

Despite the settlement of 1277, tensions remained high between the English and the Welsh. Much of the dissatisfaction of the Welsh arose in response to the increasing imposition of English law, a concern upon which Llywelyn was able to draw. Equally important was the fact that several Welsh princes who had supported the English cause in 1277, and particularly Llywelyn's younger brother Dafydd, felt themselves to have been poorly compensated by Edward I for their efforts. In late April 1282, Dafydd launched a surprise attack on the marcher lord, Roger de Clifford at Hawarden Castle, and other attacks quickly followed on Oswestry, Flint and Rhuddlan, with Llywelyn soon joining his brother's revolt.

In 1282, Edward responded energetically to the Welsh threat, dispatching small contingents under his household knights almost immediately and initially summoning a muster for 17 May. From Rhuddlan, Edward followed a similar strategy to that of 1277, concentrating his own efforts in North Wales, while smaller contingents operated in the marches and South Wales. The English advance was inexorable, and the Welsh were pushed back into the rugged mountains of Snowdonia. Although Welsh morale was boosted by a victory over the royal forces led by Luke de Tany in early November, when the pontoon bridge that the English had built between Anglesey and the mainland collapsed, Edward continued to receive reinforcements, including a sizable contingent from Gascony.

Hoping to take advantage of confusion caused in the Marches by the death (from natural causes) of Roger Mortimer, in November Llywelyn marched out of Snowdonia and made his way toward Builth. Near Irfon Bridge, his force was apparently trapped while attempting to ford the river. Llywelyn, according to the chronicler Guisborough, was not recognized by the English knight Stephen de Frankton, who fatally struck him down with his lance.[11] Dafydd, nevertheless, continued the fight into the following year, but with little realistic hope of success. As another contemporary chronicler puts it, 'After the death of Llywelyn, prince of Wales, his brother David . . . who had lost all his army, wandered aimlessly like a vagabond through little-known regions and at length turned aside to hide in a small cottage, to his own undoing'. Betrayed by Welsh soldiers, he was delivered to the English king at Shrewsbury, where 'he was convicted of treason, lese majeste and sacrilege, and condemned to be drawn, hanged, beheaded, burned and quartered. . . . his bowels were condemned to the flames to punish his crimes of sacrilege, for he had often set fire to churches'.[12] By this time, Edward had secured virtually all of Wales, the last stronghold, Castell-y-Bere, having fallen to William de Valence and Roger Lestrange in April 1283. Wales had been subdued, but at no little expense. The most recent estimate places the cost of the 1282–1283 campaign, including the costs associated with castle building through 1284, at a staggering £120,000.[13]

The settlement that followed the conquest of Wales was not magnanimous. Llywelyn had been decapitated after his death at Irfon Bridge, and Edward I had his head displayed on London Bridge, where it was subsequently joined by that of his brother Dafydd in a grisly declaration of victory. The princes' sons and daughters were sent off to imprisonment in castles and convents: Dafydd's son Owain languished in captivity for more than 30 years. Symbols of Welsh princely power, such as the Neith Cross and the seal matrices of Llywelyn and Dafydd, were taken into Edward's possession to be transformed into symbols of English royal power. Although some Welshmen who had served Edward I loyally were rewarded with marcher lordships, the Welsh aristocracy was virtually eliminated by disinheritance, with powerful new lordships created for some of the English king's closest associates, such as Bromfield and Yale for Earl Warenne, Chirk for the Mortimers, and Denbigh for the earl of Lincoln. Meanwhile, the Statute of Wales of 1284 was designed to extend the scope of English administration, facilitated by the creation of the new counties of Flint, Anglesey, Merioneth and Caernarfon, each with their own sheriff (all of them English) and courts. The statute resounds with the language of conquest, while the Edwardian castles speak of empire.

It was after the first Welsh war that Edward had built the castles at Flint, Rhuddlan, Builth and Aberystwyth under the guidance of the Savoyard Master James of St George and a number of his countrymen. Now, after the second Welsh war, he embarked on an even larger programme, adding Conwy, Caernarfon and Harlech. Along with castles, new towns were also planted, and both towns and castles were designed to have ready access to the sea. These new fortifications were so located as to encircle and isolate Snowdonia, ostensibly making future revolts untenable. Caernarfon, in particular, with its banded masonry that evoked the walls of Constantinople, must be seen as making a symbolic as well as a physical statement of empire. It has been argued, however, that for all their magnificence, the Edwardian castles were ill-suited to the needs at hand. The Welsh had only limited siege technology, so that castles of this scale were unjustified, particularly in light of their enormous cost. And yet, the castles proved their value in both 1287 and especially in 1294.

Yet another Welsh rebellion broke out in 1287, led by Rhys ap Maredudd. The uprising took place while Edward I was absent in Gascony, but it posed little real threat to English rule. Rhys had been loyal to the English king in both 1277 and 1282, but like Dafydd before him, felt poorly rewarded by the English king. Specifically, he was prevented from gaining control of Dinefwr castle. Despairing of justice, despite a direct appeal to the king himself, in June 1287, Rhys seized Llandovery, Dinefwr and Carrag Ceneg castles. Edmund of Lancaster besieged Rhys at Dryslwyn. Although Rhys escaped, the castle soon fell, and he became a fugitive, again like Dafydd before him, constantly on the run until betrayed to the English in 1292. A contemporary chronicler observed that, in the end, 'Rhys, son of Maredudd, the leader of the Welsh, hid himself in the woods. He stirred up sedition against the king of England's peace and devoted himself to robbery and murder. Finally he was captured by some of the king's liege men and led across England to the king at York. He was dragged all through the city and perished by being hanged'.[14]

The final Welsh revolt of 1294 proved more dangerous than its predecessor, and came at a particularly difficult time as Edward was preparing to launch an offensive in France. The combination of an extraordinarily high tax levy, coupled with the mustering of Welsh soldiers to fight in Gascony, proved explosive. Madog ap Llywelyn, son of Llywelyn ap Maredudd, led the revolt in the north. Although Caernarfon Castle, still under construction at the time, was quickly taken, overall the royal castles proved to be worth their cost, for they held out while many baronial estates proved unable to withstand the initial assault. Fortunately, if frustratingly for Edward, the king was able to redeploy troops meant for Gascony to meet this unexpected challenge in Wales. Once again, a royal army was mustered at Chester, this time perhaps twice the size of the initial army of 1277. A second army was mustered at Montgomery under the earl of Warwick, and a third was based in the south at Carmarthen under the command of the earl of Norfolk and William de Valence. In total, the English force exceeded 35,000 men.

In the winter of 1294–1295, Edward found himself besieged in Conwy, which he had reached by Christmas. So desperate was the situation that, on the day after the feast of the Epiphany, the king marched out through Bangor and on to the Llyn peninsula. Unable to force an engagement, however, he soon returned to Conwy, despite the ongoing shortages of provisions there. The turning point came in March when the earl of Warwick defeated Madog at the battle of Maes Madog (near Oswestry). Although the Welsh prince escaped capture for the moment, the revolt was now broken and the various Welsh leaders made peace or were soon captured. Unlike Llywelyn and Dafydd, Madog's life was spared once he fell into English hands, although he appears to have spent the rest of his life in the Tower. Along with taking hostages to ensure the compliance of the Welsh princes in the restoration of English lordship, Edward undertook the construction of one final castle, the most perfect of all the Edwardian castles – Beaumaris in Anglesey. Significantly, it was never completed due to lack of money.

As mentioned earlier, the second Welsh revolt had broken out while Edward I was absent in Gascony. Between August 1286 and June 1289, Edward made an extended visit to Gascony, accompanied by Henry de Lacy, earl of Lincoln. As in 1273, inquisitions were taken into feudal obligations, this time in the Agenais, which had been acquired by the terms of the Treaty of Amiens in 1279. A number of municipal charters were issued as well, many of them to the *bastides*, the new fortified towns that formed an essential part of Edward's programme of consolidation. Finally, in March 1289, a council was held at Condom at which a set of ordinances was drafted for the governance of the duchy. These ordinances are extremely important in that they are the culmination of Edward's vision for Aquitaine in relation to both England and France. Indeed, J-P Trabut-Cussac has argued that the significance of the ordinances is illustrated by Edward's appointment of Maurice de Craon as lieutenant in Aquitaine, prior to the king's own departure in 1289.[15] This appointment, he argues, signals a new orientation in the duchy; by providing more immediate and final justice in Gascony, the lieutenant would serve to render unnecessary appeals to either Westminster or Paris. Moreover, the terms of appointment of Gascon officers after 1289 stated that they held their positions not simply during the king-duke's pleasure, but at that of the lieutenant as well. In theory, the king's lieutenant in Aquitaine was now effectively a viceroy, although in reality the king continued to dictate policy.

While in Gascony in 1286–1289, Edward also arranged for the ransom of his brother-in-law, Charles of Salerno, then captive in Aragon. This is noteworthy, not so much because of the king's concern for Charles, but rather for what it reveals about the loyalty of Edward's Gascon vassals, whom he had been cultivating so assiduously since the 1260s. Among the 76 hostages Edward agreed to deliver to Alphonso III, were not only English household knights such as Hugh Audley, William Latimer and John de St John, but also prominent Gascons, including Gaston de Béarn, nemesis of Henry III and Simon de Montfort, and Arnaud de Gabaston, father of Piers Gaveston, the future favourite of Edward II. The extent of the loyalty of the Gascon nobility to the English king–duke is uncertain, but with few exceptions Edward had the cooperation of these independent-minded lords and was regularly able to draw soldiers from the duchy for his wars in Wales and Scotland. The *Chronicle of Lanercost* relates a story from 1288 that stands as an image of Edward's rule over Gascony. One day as the king and queen sat in their chamber in conversation, a bolt of lightning entered the window of the chamber, passed between them, and killed two domestics who were standing behind them. Those present were said to be amazed, discerning that a miracle had occurred whereby the safety of the royal couple had been ensured.[16] One might add that Edward himself was like a bolt of lightning, highly charged and often dangerous to those around him.

As mentioned earlier, the third Welsh revolt in 1294 had coincided with the initiation of hostilities with France. Throughout the first half of his reign, Edward had enjoyed relatively tranquil relations with his Capetian counterparts. He had visited Paris on three occasions: in 1273 on his return from the Crusade; in 1279 when his wife performed homage for the county of Ponthieu; and in 1286 when he had performed homage to Philip IV. The outbreak of war in 1294 was therefore, in some sense, unexpected. Nevertheless, despite the attention that Edward I paid to Gascony throughout his reign, the duchy remained a frequent source of enmity between England and France, and this remained the case even after the reforms of 1289. In May 1293, the earl of Lincoln was dispatched to Paris along with Edmund, earl of Lancaster, in an attempt to settle Anglo-French tensions centred on piracy and maritime disputes that appeared to radiate outward from the English king's Gascon port of Bayonne. Unfortunately, any hope of a negotiated settlement disappeared with the embarrassment of the French in a naval battle off Cap St-Mathieu on 15 May 1293. The author of *The Chronicle of Bury St. Edmunds* relished this English victory in which he claimed that some 180 Norman ships were captured.[17] Further negotiations were pursued throughout 1293 and early in 1294, primarily by Edmund of Lancaster, and eventually a secret understanding was reached. Edward I agreed publicly to surrender the duchy to Philip the Fair on a 'temporary' basis (an enormous political blunder for which he subsequently apologized to the Gascons). This surrender would not prove temporary. On 15 May 1294 (the anniversary of the battle), Philip the Fair declared Edward a contumacious vassal and moved to confiscate the duchy of Aquitaine, thus triggering war.

Guyenne, as the French called the duchy, had been surrendered to the constable of France, Raoul de Nesle, in March 1294. Some 20 ducal officers were taken as hostages by Nesle, and a large number of Gascon landholders were dispossessed. Edward I planned to fight a holding action in Gascony while he organized a grand coalition of German princes to fight Philip in Flanders. A small force was dispatched to Gascony in October 1294 under John of Brittany, earl of Richmond, and John de St John. This was meant to be followed by a larger force under the leadership of the king's brother, Edmund of Lancaster, but, as we have seen, this force had to be diverted to Wales. The vanguard under St John and the earl of Richmond had some success, sailing up the Gironde and capturing several major fortifications. St John then led a contingent south to Bayonne, whose loyal citizens delivered the city into English hands. These initial successes, however, were compromised in the spring of 1295 when a large French army under Charles de Valois invaded Gascony. By summer, only Bourg and Blaye remained in English hands in the north, Bayonne and St-Sever in the south.

Henry de Lacy, earl of Lincoln, was named king's lieutenant in Aquitaine on 3 December 1295, replacing the king's brother, Edmund of Lancaster. By the time Lincoln landed in Gascony, the military situation was grave. Initially, he followed an ambitious northern policy, including an abortive and unrealistic naval assault on Bordeaux in late March 1296. Falling back on Bayonne, Lincoln then initiated a 'southern' strategy. A failed siege at Dax was followed by a raid into the Toulousain, repeated again in the next year. It has been argued that the French territorial occupation did not extend to subjugation, and the earl of Lincoln's freebooting reflects and reinforces this fact. It is tempting to see, in this raiding, a precursor to the strategic *chevauchée* that would be used by Edward III and the Black Prince with such devastating effect in the Hundred Years War.

The one Battle of Lincoln's lieutenancy took place near Bellegarde, which the English were trying to resupply, in late January or early February 1297. The earl was ambushed by a larger force under the comte d'Artois and heavily defeated. It was this military setback that prompted Edward to propose sending reinforcements to Gascony, ultimately resulting in political crisis in England. Meanwhile, without much support, and despite the defeat at Bellegarde, Lincoln did hold on to what was left of English Gascony. Fortunately, once Edward I landed in Flanders, Philip IV withdrew the comte d'Artois from Aquitaine in order to help lift the siege of Lille.

But getting to Flanders was not easy. Even before the Salisbury parliament met in February 1297, the southern clergy, following the lead of Archbishop Winchelsey, refused to recognize the king's right to levy a tax on them without prior papal consent. Although the northern clergy agreed to pay a tax of one-fifth, the king was forced to extort a similar sum from their southern counterparts by means of fines, further exacerbating relations with the church. At the Salisbury parliament, the earls of Norfolk and Hereford refused to lead troops in Gascony while the king himself campaigned in Flanders, claiming that this would be contrary to the terms of their hereditary positions as marshal and constable of England. The king is said to have threatened Hereford, shouting, 'By God, Sir Earl, either go or hang', only to receive the response, 'O King, I shall neither go nor hang.'[18] Nor did he. Edward I's kingship has been described as 'masterful', but beginning at the Salisbury parliament of 1297 this mastery began to elude him.

In April, the king issued summonses for military service, but in writs that said nothing of the obligation of fealty and homage, nor specified the destination of the troops to be raised. A meeting of magnates at Montgomery demonstrated serious reservations about the proposed muster. In July, the grievances against the king's behaviour were summarized in a document known as the Remonstrances. The king pretended not to have received the document, and set about the collection of a tax of an eighth and a fifth that he claimed had been granted in the July parliament. Critics claimed that it had been granted not by parliament, but 'by people standing around in his chamber'. In August, as the king prepared to sail from Winchelsea, the earls of Norfolk and Hereford (supported by a large number of magnates and knights) appeared at the exchequer and forbade collection of the eighth.

Edward I sailed for Flanders on 23 August 1297, leaving very unsettled political conditions behind for his council and his son Edward to deal with. A parliament was summoned to meet in London at the end of September. The king's opponents made a number of demands for the redress of grievances in this parliament, embodied in a document known as *De Tallagio*, calling for a revised and expanded version of the Magna Carta. The king's council would not – indeed, without the king they could not – go so far, but did agree in October to the *Confirmatio Cartarum*, confirming both the Magna Carta and the Charter of the Forest, and providing assurances (albeit vaguely worded ones) that future levies would only be collected 'with the common assent of the realm'. A tax of a ninth was agreed to (in lieu of the controversial eighth of July) and a negotiated settlement was reached, perhaps in part because the king himself was absent, but even more because of the shocking news that had reached London by the last week of September: John de Warenne, earl of Surrey, had been defeated at Stirling Bridge by a Scottish army led by William Wallace.

As had been the case throughout the reign of Henry III, in the early years of the reign of Edward I, relations with Scotland were cordial. Edward's sister Margaret had been Queen of Scotland from 1251 until her death in 1275. Although the king and queen of Scots had attended the coronation of Edward I in 1274, Alexander did not perform homage to Edward at that time. This issue was settled in 1278, however, with Alexander III performing homage for his English lands, having obtained prior guarantees that this act would set no precedent nor prejudice his position as king of Scotland. Over the next 6 years, both of Alexander's sons and his only daughter predeceased him. His marriage to Yolande de Dreux in October 1285 provided hopes for another son, but these hopes were literally dashed with the unexpected and sudden death of Alexander III on 19 March 1286 in a fall from his horse. Once it was determined that the widowed queen was not, in fact, pregnant, it was clear that the heir to Alexander's kingdom was his 2-year-old granddaughter Margaret, the 'Maid of Norway'. Negotiations were immediately put in train that culminated in the Treaty of Birgham, which elaborated the terms for a marriage between Margaret and Edward I's own son and heir, Edward of Caernarfon. Margaret, however, died in Orkney in late September 1290, throwing the question of the succession to the Scottish throne into turmoil.

Edward I saw the need for judgement rather than arbitration, and opened up the process beyond John Balliol and Robert Bruce to encompass some 14 candidates for the Scottish throne (initially including himself). In June 1291, through a process of negotiations known as the process of Norham, Edward was granted lordship over Scotland in order to settle the Great Cause. Some 104 auditors were assembled at Berwick to hear the cases of the various claimants. The auditors found in favour of John Balliol on 6 November 1292, and this decision was confirmed by Edward I on 17 November. However, King John was made to swear oaths of homage and fealty for Scotland to Edward I, creating an untenable situation from the outset of his reign.

Edward's exploitation of superior lordship in Scotland is one of the most paradoxical elements of his reign, for the very policy he pursued in Scotland was the bane of his lordship in France. As soon as 7 December 1292, he accepted a petition from one Roger Bartholomew, a burgess of Berwick, thereby undermining the judicial independence of the Scottish crown.

In demanding that John Balliol and a number of Scottish aristocrats serve with the English army in France in 1294, Edward eroded the power of the Scottish king beyond recovery. It is not surprising, therefore, that the Scots made common cause with Edward's most formidable enemy, Philip IV of France, entering into the 'Auld Alliance' in February 1296. The Scots launched raids on Wark Castle and the hinterland around Carlisle, thereby justifying Edward's invasion of the northern kingdom.

The army of Edward I, variously estimated at anywhere from 25,000 to 60,000 men, was formidable. Following a minor Scottish attack on Wark and an unsuccessful Scottish assault on Carlisle, soon after Easter, Edward crossed the Tweed, arriving before Berwick on 30 March 1296. Despite the surrender of the castle by Sir William Douglas, Edward ordered the execution of the male population of the burgh for having resisted. The bodies were said to fall 'like autumn leaves' – more than 11,000 of them if we can believe the Hagnaby chronicle.[19] Dunbar soon fell to John de Warenne, earl of Surrey (who happened to be John Balliol's brother-in-law), with the earls of Mar, Ross and Menteith all being taken prisoner along with a number of Scottish barons and knights. Scottish resistance quickly evaporated: Roxburgh, Edinburgh and Stirling castles were all surrendered.

Following negotiations, Balliol too surrendered, unconditionally. Stripped of his kingship, Balliol – or 'Toom Tabard', as he now became known – was sent south to London along with the other symbols of Scottish independence, the Stone of Scone and the Black Rood of St Margaret. In August 1296, Edward I held a parliament in Berwick to establish his administration of Scotland. The conquest was seemingly complete.

The war having been won, the peace proved more difficult. Warenne was appointed king's lieutenant in Scotland, with Henry Percy serving as warden in Galloway and Ayr. English models of administration were imposed, along with English personnel. This was most apparent in the appointment of a treasurer rather than the maintenance of the traditional Scottish office of chamberlain. The traditional three justiciars were retained, but staffed by English officials. If this was an 'alien' regime at the top, it was also so at the bottom, with the sheriffs at the local level. The administration of 1296 is perhaps best seen as a military occupation, and like most such occupations in history, it was resented. Disturbances in the northwest could perhaps be written off to traditional clan rivalries, but unrest soon spread south and found an unlikely champion in William Wallace who triggered a more widespread revolt in early 1297 with the murder of the sheriff of Lanark and raids over into Dumfriesshire. Meanwhile a 'noble' rebellion was led by Robert Wishart, bishop of Glasgow, James the Steward, and Robert Bruce, earl of Carrick, ostensibly over Edward I's demand for military service overseas in Flanders. This noble revolt, however, quickly collapsed, with a capitulation at Irvine.

The Scottish uprising was not over, however, as Wallace, now allied with Sir Andrew Murray, remained in the field. An English army under Warenne and Sir Hugh Cressingham was drawn into battle at Stirling, suffering a disastrous defeat on 11 September 1297. In the aftermath of this defeat, the English hold on Scotland north of the Forth was broken, and the same was also true in the southwest. The silver lining of the defeat at Stirling Bridge was that it shocked the English aristocracy back into allegiance to Edward I at a time of political unrest in England. A new army was raised immediately, and this force included several of the earls who had refused to serve the king in Flanders. By February 1298, Roxburgh and Berwick had been relieved, but Warenne was then ordered to await the arrival of the king in person before proceeding further in the campaign to recover Scotland.

Edward raised an army of perhaps 30,000 men in 1298, including a contingent of some 13,000 Welsh foot-soldiers. To support the war effort, he moved the exchequer and the courts to York, where they would remain for the next 6 years. The English king crossed into Scotland on 3 July 1298. The Scots, led by Wallace, may have been emboldened both by the difficulties of provisioning such a large invasion force, and also by injuries sustained by Edward I when his own horse trod on him. The Scots chose to confront the English at Falkirk. Although the schiltrons – tight formations of spearmen, often likened to a hedgehog – initially held their ground, the Scottish cavalry withdrew without engaging, leading to a devastating defeat. Although it is unlikely that the 100,000 Scots reported killed by the Lanercost Chronicle is an accurate figure, English wage accounts suggest that some 3,000 English foot-soldiers perished on the winning side, indicating how severe the Scottish losses must have been. Immediately after the battle, Stirling Castle was besieged, while the earl of Lincoln led an army northeast to Cupar, St Andrews and Perth. The king marched through Annandale, and by 8 September had retired to Carlisle, having left behind a substantial garrison of 1,000 men in Berwick town, in addition to the garrison in the castle.

Edward returned to Scotland in December 1299, following his marriage to Margaret of France, but troops failed to materialize for his projected winter campaign. In 1300, another campaign was undertaken, aimed at securing southern Scotland, specifically Galloway, Caerlaverock Castle and Selkirk forest. Having paid particular care to the composition of the fleet, which was crucial to the provision of food for the army, Edward arrived at Carlisle on 27 June and reached Caerlaverock on 9 July, which quickly surrendered. But the army achieved little else and never reached Galloway. A truce was arranged through the good offices of Philip IV on 30 October, to run until 21 May 1301. Desultory – and half-hearted – peace negotiations were held at Canterbury in the following spring, but failed to produce an extension to the truce.

Edward arrived at Berwick on 5 July 1301 and mustered his army within a week. He then advanced to Glasgow. A second army, under the Prince of Wales, mustered at Carlisle and then proceeded to Ayr, which was soon taken. Turnberry, chief centre of the Bruce earldom of Carrick, and Bothwell, were also taken in September. The king wintered at Linlithgow in 1301–1302, but his army, poorly paid or provisioned, melted away. Nonetheless, Edward's intentions were made clear by his summons to his master builder, James of St George, to come to Linlithgow in 1302 to strengthen its defences. At Linlithgow, Edward sealed the Treaty of Asnières, establishing a truce with Scotland to run until 1 November 1302. The king may have been induced to seek this truce, in part because of the support of both the king of France and the pope for the Scottish cause, embodied in the fact that John Balliol had been released from papal custody in the summer of 1301 and allowed to return to his ancestral homeland at Ballieul in Picardy. But whatever hopes of French support the Scots derived from the Asnières agreement, those hopes were shattered in July 1302 with the shocking French defeat at Courtrai. The subsequent treaty of Amiens of December 1302 was concluded between England and France without any reference to Scotland. At the same time, the ongoing and escalating conflict between Philip IV and Boniface VIII led the papacy to place increasing constraints upon the Scottish church. Meanwhile, the establishment of Berwick as a free borough in August 1302 points to the increasing consolidation of the English position in the southeast. By late summer 1302, Edward was planning a major campaign for 1303. This, he hoped, would provide the knockout blow.

The Scots enjoyed some modest successes during the winter of 1302–1303, recovering Selkirk Castle and emerging victorious in a skirmish near Roslin. Edward arrived at Roxburgh on 16 May 1303, where he mustered some 7,500 foot-soldiers and 450 men-at-arms, while the Prince of Wales accounted for another 180 men-at-arms. The king issued summonses for military service to Scottish landholders in 1303, and among those who responded was Robert Bruce, earl of Carrick, who was ordered to provide 1,000 foot-soldiers and all the men-at-arms he could find. The English army moved via Linlithgow to Stirling and on to Perth, where it remained throughout June. The Scots meanwhile attacked Cumberland under Sir Simon Fraser and Sir Edmund Comyn, while Sir William Wallace marched through Galloway. Undeterred, in July, King Edward moved north through Arbroath to Montrose before turning inland to besiege Brechin, which fell on 9 July. From there, the king continued on to Aberdeen. He and Prince Edward, who had been operating independently, took several more key fortifications such as Inverness, Urquhart, Cromarty and Lochindorb Castles, before returning south, reaching Dundee on 16 October.

The fact that Edward had been able to penetrate so far north, coupled with his decision to winter in Scotland, left the initiative entirely with the English. Throughout the winter of 1303–1304, raids and *chevauchées* were conducted even as negotiations progressed with Sir John Comyn, guardian of Scotland. Sunday 16 February at Perth was set as the time and place for Scottish submissions to be offered, although those presently residing in France would be given until 12 April to make their way into the English king's presence. The terms were not particularly vindictive, except for those extended to Wallace. Indeed, the terms, somewhat reminiscent of the Dictum of Kenilworth, were generous enough to the Scots that

Edward I was faced with considerable administrative difficulty in restoring the Scots to their former lands without unduly punishing his own supporters.

In March 1304, Edward I held a parliament in St Andrews, at which outlawry was declared on Wallace, Simon Fraser and the entire garrison of Stirling Castle. Some 129 Scottish landholders appeared at this parliament and recognized Edward as their liege lord on 14–15 March. This assembly was followed immediately by the siege of Stirling Castle. Massive quantities of siege equipment were shipped to Stirling from all directions. The king commanded his son to strip the lead from the roofs of all the churches around Perth and Dunblane in order to provide necessary counterweights for his trebuchets; even Greek fire was deployed to overwhelm the garrison commanded by William Oliphant. Indeed, on 20 July, Edward refused to accept the garrison's offer of surrender until after he could test the effectiveness of a device known as 'the Warwolf' against the castle's defences. In the end, however, he spared the lives of the garrison, including Oliphant, when they finally capitulated 4 days later. By then, Sir Simon Fraser had submitted to the king, leaving only William Wallace in open defiance.

Wallace's capture was set as a test of loyalty for Edward's new Scottish liegemen. He was finally rounded up near Glasgow in August 1305 by John of Menteith, who received lands valued at £100 in reward for this service, while his men shared a total of 100 marks in cash. The outcome of Wallace's subsequent trial in Westminster Hall was a foregone conclusion: he must be found guilty of treason and die a traitor's death. His notoriety was such that Wallace was not allowed to speak in his own defence. Wearing a crown of laurel, he was drawn on a hurdle to Smithfield, where he was hanged and disembowelled prior to being beheaded, his entrails burned and his corpse quartered. His head, like that of Llywelyn ap Gruffudd before him, was displayed on London Bridge, while his quartered remains were sent north to Newcastle, Berwick, Stirling and Perth.

In 1304, unlike 1297, Edward chose to rule Scotland with Scots. For instance, the earl of Atholl was made warden and justiciar of Scotland beyond the Forth, whereas prior to this he had been Scottish Sheriff of Aberdeen. Perhaps most prominent of all in this new collaboration was Robert Bruce, earl of Carrick, Sheriff of Ayr and Lanark. In 1305, Wallace's execution was followed by a parliament at Westminster in September in which a Scottish settlement was arranged. A group of ten Scottish representatives had been chosen by a committee comprised of the earl of Carrick, the bishop of Glasgow, and Sir John Moubray. The Ordinance for Scotland of September 1305 specified not only offices, but officeholders for Scotland. All but two of the sheriffs named were Scots, and the justiciars were placed into four pairs with one Scot and one Englishman in each. Although the most powerful official of all, John of Brittany, earl of Richmond and king's lieutenant in Scotland, was English, he was given a Scottish council of 21 members (four bishops, four abbots, five earls and eight barons) in addition to the major officials such as the chancellor and chamberlain. Still, Edward planned to revise 'the laws and customs [of Scotland] which are clearly displeasing to God and to Reason', just as he had 20 years earlier in Wales. The king did not address the paramount concerns of taxation and overseas military service. Nevertheless, in 1305, his settlement appeared to be the culmination of a process going back two decades, which promised at last to provide order and stability to Scotland, even if at the price of English overlordship. The Lanercost Chronicle contains a poem celebrating the benefit of Edward's overlordship for Scotland. It concludes:

> Let Scotia prosper, while, from o'er the border,
> King Edward shields the cause of law and order.[20]

And yet, although it appeared in 1305 that Edward I had conquered Scotland for a second time and would now incorporate the northern kingdom into his own, the dramatic murder of John Comyn, Lord of Badenoch, by Robert Bruce on 10 February 1306, changed everything.

Although the murder at the Franciscan church in Dumfries was reprehensible, it, or at least its consequences, cannot have been unanticipated despite the spontaneous nature of the act. As soon as 25 March, a gathering including four earls and three bishops assembled at Scone for the coronation of Robert I of Scotland. The reaction of Edward I was even more predictable. An army was quickly raised, which under the command of Aymer de Valence defeated Bruce in battle at Methven on 19 June. By summer's end, the would-be king was in flight and his wife and several close kinsmen and associates were prisoners of the English. The earl of Atholl was hanged in London, as was Simon Fraser, and Bruce's brother Neil was put to death at Berwick. Edward I had both Bruce's sister Mary and the Countess of Buchan placed on display in specially constructed cages at Roxburgh and Berwick Castle, respectively, suggesting the depth of the outrage felt by the aged king at Bruce's betrayal.

The following year began encouragingly. In February, both Thomas and Alexander Bruce were captured in Galloway by Dougall MacDouall, their heads being dispatched to the Prince of Wales. On 1 April, John Wallace, brother of

Edward's late nemesis, was also captured. In May, however, Robert Bruce won a minor victory at Loudon Hill against Valence, and 3 days later defeated a separate force under the young earl of Gloucester. The king himself resolved to travel north and lead his army in person and set out from Carlisle. He reached no further than Burgh-by-Sands, where he died on 7 July 1307, the Scottish prize still tantalizingly beyond his grasp.

The war with Scotland dominated the final decade of the reign, but despite the king's apparent success until 1305, the costs of war coupled with continued political controversy had a negative effect on the kingdom as a whole. The crisis of 1297, already discussed above, makes a suitable point of departure for a consideration of the final years of the realm. The grievances articulated in the Remonstrances and *De Tallagio* do not so much challenge the king's right to levy taxes as critique the level and nature of these exactions and the manner of their levying. Although the king spent much of the final decade attempting to undo what he perceived to be the damage done in 1297, his opponents in and out of parliament consistently pressed Edward to hold to the commitments made in his name in 1297, often with mixed results. In March 1299, for instance, the king withdrew from London with considerable haste and a minimum of dignity, rather than confirm the Charter of the Forest in its entirety before parliament. A year later, before a parliament that included representatives from both the shires and the boroughs, the king was confronted by the archbishop of Canterbury and the earl of Norfolk, who advanced the lingering grievances of the clergy and laity. Edward was finally able to obtain the promise of a twentieth only by issuing the *Articuli super Cartas*, although even here he insisted that 'in each and all of the aforesaid things it is the king's will . . . that the right and lordship of his crown be saved', a very broad qualification. In the end, the twentieth having been made conditional upon the king's fulfilment of promises made earlier, this levy was never collected.

In January 1301, parliament met at Lincoln and, interestingly, the king mandated that the same representatives attend as had been at the previous parliament. The king's representative, Chief Justice Roger Brabazon, asked for a grant of a fifteenth. Instead of receiving the grant, Edward was presented with what is now known as Keighley's bill, named for a knight of the shire from Lancashire, but presented to the king on behalf of the whole community. This bill called for the observation of the Magna Carta and the Charter of the Forest, but went beyond this to call for a perambulation of the royal forests and investigation into contraventions against the recent *Articuli super Cartas*, as well as a return to the annual farm for each shire as it had existed in the reign of Henry III. Then, and only then, might a twentieth be considered. The king was clearly offended by this bill, but there was no way round it. Eventually, in 1306, he identified Henry Keighley as the author of this offensive bill and had him imprisoned. But at the Lincoln parliament in 1301, the king was forced to agree to the perambulation of the forests as well as investigation into other abuses. Moreover, it was also argued that the commons should assent to the appointment of the king's chief ministers, a proposal that was probably aimed primarily at the unpopular treasurer, Walter Langton, bishop of Coventry and Lichfield. This proved too much, harking back to the constraints placed upon Henry III by the baronial reformers of Edward's youth. Edward was beside himself with rage and his infamous temper was soon on display. The king personally berated the assembled representatives in a speech dripping with sarcasm, asking why each of them did not request a crown, since they clearly wished to rule the kingdom in his stead.

After 1301, however, the tension between the king and the community of the realm lessened. In part, this reflected the widespread support for the war in Scotland. Equally important, the king sought other, non-parliamentary, sources of revenue to support the war, while allowing the government to run a deficit. For instance, in 1302, the king finally collected a feudal aid for the marriage of his daughter Joan (authorized as long ago as 1290), which netted perhaps £7,000. The first tallage of the reign, in 1303, produced another £5,000, while in 1306 a feudal aid for the knighting of Edward of Caernarfon was negotiated into a more traditional tax of a twentieth and a thirtieth, generating some £26,500. Meanwhile, wool duties accounted for roughly £9,000 per annum, whereas an aggressive programme of re-minting coinage yielded perhaps £7,000 a year from 1300 until the end of the reign.

Another source of financial support, perhaps surprisingly, was clerical taxation. Although Archbishop Winchelsey had held up clerical taxation ever since the promulgation of *Clericis laicos* in 1296, in 1301 Pope Boniface VIII authorized a crusading tenth to be collected for a period of 3 years, with half the proceeds to go to the king. This amounted to £42,000. In 1305, the new Gascon pope, Clement V, authorized a tenth to be collected for 7 years, and by the time of Edward I's death, some £25,000 had been collected. In the end, however, none of this was sufficient to meet the costs of war in Scotland, and Edward turned increasingly to the Frescobaldi. Between 1297 and 1310, the Florentine banking house appears to have lent the English kings some £150,000, and when Edward I died in 1307 the crown was probably in debt to the tune of £200,000 (20 years later at the end of the reign of Edward II, some £60,000 of this debt had still not been cleared from the books). Even the feasts and celebrations that followed the marriage of Edward I to Margaret of France in 1299 had been funded with Frescobaldi money that had been secured by the customs duties on English wool.

Although it probably had little actual monetary impact, faith in the crown and its financial stability must have been shaken, at least symbolically, by the robbery of the royal treasure that took place in 1303. An earlier attempt at gaining access to the royal treasure housed in the crypt beneath the Chapter House at Westminster Abbey in 1296 had led to the imprisonment of a number of monks, including the cellarer, but had been quickly hushed up. So too had been the misappropriation of £100 in silver coins provided to the abbey in support of masses for the soul of Queen Eleanor. In 1303, however, a fairly large and well-organized gang led by an Oxfordshire merchant by the name of Richard Puddlicott succeeded in making off with some £100,000 in plate, jewels and foreign coins. Emboldened by an earlier theft of silver plate from the refectory at Westminster Abbey – clearly with the connivance of some members of the monastic community – in early 1303, Puddlicott and his associates chiselled their way into the crypt, which held the treasure of the royal wardrobe. Over a period of 3 days at the beginning of May, they made off with a massive quantity of treasure. The quantity and the quality of the stolen goods were too great to remain a secret, however, and as these goods made their way onto the London market, suspicions were duly aroused.

The king learned of the robbery by early June while at Linlithgow, and he immediately commissioned an investigation to be conducted by one of his most trusted clerks, John Droxford, keeper of the royal wardrobe and future bishop of Bath and Wells. The commissioners soon uncovered the extent of the conspiracy to rob the treasury. Puddlicott had been aided and abetted by the Sacristan of Westminster, Adam de Warfeld, as well as the sub-prior, Alexander de Pershore, along with a number of monks and their servants. Another key figure in the gang was William Palmer, also known as William of the Palace, who served as deputy keeper of the nearby Westminster Palace, as well as of Fleet Prison. Other accomplices included a mason named John of St Albans, and a goldsmith (significantly, not a London goldsmith) named John of Newmarket. Very likely, one of the sheriffs of London, Hugh Pourte, also had some knowledge of and interest in the robbery, even if he may not have been a direct participant. The audacity of this assault on the royal treasure is shocking, and seems to indicate a disregard for the king that would have been unthinkable earlier in the reign. But with an ageing, and largely absent, ruler, the thieves took their chance. Unfortunately for them, they underestimated the king's continued vigour. Arrests were quickly made, much of the treasure soon recovered, and punishments duly meted out. Five of the malefactors, including William of the Palace, were hanged at the elms at Smithfield in March 1304, while ten Westminster monks languished in the Tower for the better part of a year. Puddlicott, too, was finally executed, once his claim to benefit of clergy had been dismissed, in November 1305. Although the king could not punish the monks of Westminster or the citizens of London as fully as he would have liked, he did have some measure of revenge in 1304 when the former sheriff, Hugh Pourte, was among those appointed to collect the highly unpopular New Customs in London.

The great king's final years were troubled, not only by the theft of his treasure and the recalcitrance of the Scots, but also by other instances of insubordination and disregard for his mandates. In June 1305, the king and the Prince of Wales had a falling out, apparently over a conflict between the young Edward and the treasurer Walter Langton. The king's response was to banish his son from his presence and to cut off his access to provisions of all kinds. It took some 6 weeks and the queen's intercession to achieve a reconciliation. Worse, however, was soon to follow. In the autumn of 1306, the famous royal temper was once again on view when some 26 young knights deserted from Scotland in order to tourney in France. Edward railed against all those 'deserting the king and his son in those parts in contempt of the king and to the retarding of the king's business there', ordering their arrest and imprisonment in the Tower along with confiscation of all their goods. The king planned to deal with them at the parliament scheduled for January 1307 at Carlisle, but this was never held. Instead, in response to the queen's intercession, he issued pardons to the deserters from Lanercost, but the incident left a sour taste in the mouths of both the king and his nobility.

In the meantime, the king's health was failing. Edward had made his way north, arriving at Lanercost Priory on Michaelmas 1306. His stay here was meant to be brief, followed by a move on to Holm Cultram; it soon became apparent, however, that he could not travel. On 4 October, a servant of Master Peter, the king's surgeon, was sent to nearby Carlisle to buy medicinal herbs, while on 1 November the surgeon himself travelled to York in order to obtain needed medicaments. Meanwhile, more, and quite expensive, medicines were obtained from London through the agency of the royal apothecary, Richard of Montpellier, on the orders of the royal physicians. An unguent with aloes was purchased for the legs of the king, as well as balsam and various other aromatic herbs and spices. There is every indication that much of this was purchased in anticipation of embalming the king's corpse, but he survived the winter and continued to prepare for another Scottish campaign.

According to the chronicler Walter of Guisborough, the king and Prince Edward had one final, explosive, confrontation in the spring of 1307. Guisborough recounts that Walter Langton was sent to the king by Prince Edward with the following request:

> "My lord king, I am sent on behalf of my lord the prince your son, though as God lives unwillingly, to seek in his name your licence to promote his knight Piers Gaveston to the rank of count of Ponthieu." The irate king replied, "Who are you who dares to ask such things? As God lives, if not for fear of the Lord and because you said at the outset that you undertook this business unwillingly, you would not escape my grasp. Now, however, I shall see what he who sent you has to say, and you shall not withdraw." Having been called, the king said to the prince, "On what business did you send this man?" He replied, "That with your assent I might be able to give the county of Ponthieu to lord Piers Gaveston." And the king said, "You ill begotten whoreson, do you want to give lands away now, you who have never gained any? As God lives, if not for fear of breaking up the kingdom, you should never enjoy your inheritance." And grabbing the prince's hair in both hands, he tore out as much as he could until finally, exhausted, he threw him out.[21]

These are the circumstances under which the aged king made his way north one final time in the summer of 1307. Unable to ride, he had to be carried in a litter. Finally, he could not go any farther. Edward I died on the morning of 7 July 1307 at Burgh-by-Sands, as his attendants lifted him from his bed. He was 68 years old. Several later traditions developed concerning Edward's final wishes on his deathbed. In one account, he is reputed to have wanted his heart carried to the Holy Land in the company of 80 knights, while another says that the king ordered the flesh to be boiled away from his bones so that these bones could be carried north whenever an English army took the field against the Scots. Finally, the most widely repeated tradition states that Edward called the earls of Lincoln and Warwick to his deathbed and entrusted oversight of Prince Edward to them, specifically enjoining them to prevent the return of Piers Gaveston from exile. There is little reason to believe this account, and considerable evidence to contradict it, yet it has become engrained in historical tradition.

There was considerable delay in publicly announcing the death of the king, at least in part for fear of encouraging the Scots. The king's journal continued on for another 10 days without mention of his passing, and writs continued to be sealed with the great seal of Edward I until as late as mid-August. Meanwhile, the body of the king slowly travelled south to Waltham, where it remained until 18 October. It was then moved to London and the Church of Holy Trinity, on to St Paul's, and finally to Westminster, where his burial took place on 27 October. It was fittingly the bishop of Durham, Antony Bek, who presided at this service, a man whom Edward had favoured greatly and advanced, but with whom he had later fallen out over questions of royal prerogative. Like his father, Edward I was buried in a red silk tunic. His right hand held a sceptre with a cross, the right another sceptre with a dove. He wore an open crown, regal even in death. His tomb, a simple block of Purbeck marble is entirely fitting, as is the inscription later added to the tomb: *Edwardus Primus Scotorum Malleus hic est, 1308, Pactum Serva*: 'Here lies Edward the First, Hammer of the Scots, 1308, Keep Faith.'

3

Edward II (1307–1327)

Edward II is undoubtedly the least well-regarded Plantagenet king. He came to the throne in the shadow of a colossus, and he could not match the expectations aroused by his father. Not all of Edward II's failures were, however, of his own making. He inherited a bankrupt treasury and a complex international situation. The 'Hammer of the Scots' had not, in the end, settled Scotland, and relations with Philip the Fair of France continued to be strained, particularly over the nature of English lordship in the duchy of Aquitaine. Neither in war nor diplomacy was Edward II a match for his adversaries. Yet even nature appeared to conspire against him as England suffered the ravages of the Great Famine in the middle years of the reign, exacerbating the political, military and economic crises that already faced the realm.

The future Edward II was born at Caernarfon on 25 April 1284, the fourth son and the last of 14 children born to Edward I and Eleanor of Castile. There appears to be no truth to the legend that the wily Edward I immediately presented the infant to his Welsh subjects, a native-born prince speaking no word of English. Indeed, Edward of Caernarfon did not become Prince of Wales until he was nearly 17 years old, on 7 February 1301, nor did he set foot in the principality again between 1284 and 1301. Nevertheless, by the summer of his first year, following the death of his 10-year-old brother Alphonso, he was the heir to his father's throne. The infant soon travelled east toward Chester and Bristol, with his first wet nurse, Mary Maunsel, who fell ill at Rhuddlan. Although Mary received a considerable pension of 100 s per annum in 1312, it was Edward's second wet nurse, Alice de Leygrave, with whom he formed a lasting bond of affection. She remained in his service until his marriage in 1308 and thereafter entered the household of the queen: he later referred to Alice with genuine tenderness as 'our mother, who suckled us in our youth'.

It is not surprising that Edward should have developed such feeling for his nurse, as from infancy he was ensconced in his own household, with his sisters, and would have seen little of his parents. In July 1289, for instance, the 5-year-old prince was taken from King's Langley to Dover to greet his parents, who had been out of the country for 3 years. Edward's mother, Eleanor of Castile, died in the following year when he was just 6 years old, while his paternal grandmother, Eleanor of Provence, to whom he might have turned for affection, died 10 months later in September 1291. One by one he also lost the companionship of his five surviving sisters. Mary was sent to become a nun at Amesbury when she was only 5 years old in 1285, while Joan, the most headstrong of the brood, married Gilbert de Clare, earl of Gloucester, on 30 April 1290, and thereafter left the court circle. The eldest of the siblings, Eleanor, married Henry, count of Bar, in 1293; Margaret had earlier married John, son of the duke of Brabant in 1291, although she did not join her husband in the Low Countries until 1297. By then, the youngest sister, Elizabeth, had also married, becoming wife to John I, count of Holland. She returned to England following his death and married the earl of Hereford. Edward's letters as prince in 1304–1305 indicate that he remained close to his sisters – particularly Elizabeth, Mary and Joan – but his direct contact with them would have become less frequent, and his greatest intimacy would have been shared with those who continued to live in his household.

Little is known about Edward's education, which seems to have been entrusted to the elder Guy Ferre, who had served for many years as a knight, and later steward, in the household of the queen mother, Eleanor of Provence. From at least 1295 until his death in 1303, Ferre served as *magister* to the royal heir. What and how much the prince learned from his tutor is difficult to say. By 1300, he was said to be a skilled horseman, although his later lack of martial skill or interest has been often remarked upon and makes one wonder about his aptitude and appetite for chivalric training. He was in possession of a small but varied collection of books, including a primer, a romance that had once belonged to his grandmother Eleanor of Provence, and a book '*de gestis regum Anglie*', which was very likely a version of Geoffrey of Monmouth's history of the kings of Britain. In 1302, he purchased an illustrated account of the life of his grandfather's beloved patron, Edward the Confessor, in French. Although the king was probably more comfortable in French than Latin – a suggestion further reinforced by such well-known instances as the translation in 1317 of a papal bull from Latin into French by Archbishop Reynolds in order to facilitate the king's better understanding of the document – his frequent characterization as *rex illiteratus* seems to have been overstated and to be founded upon no firm evidence.

At an early age, the future king would have accustomed himself to the peripatetic life of a medieval ruler. Throughout much of the year, his household was on the move, as for instance in 1293, when he departed from his winter quarters at King's Langley in mid-April, beginning an odyssey that would see him change residence some 64 times before the end of the regnal year in November. Nevertheless, he did spend long periods at his favourite residences, especially King's Langley in Hertfordshire, and particularly in winter. In 1292, considerable sums were spent on renovations and decorations at Langley, including the painting of four knights on their way to a tournament and 52 shields, perhaps for the prince's edification. In spite of such martial decorations, however, it has been plausibly suggested that it may very well have been at Langley that Edward developed his love of 'rustic arts' – he is said to have been interested in thatching roofs, digging ditches and rowing – as well as his attachment to a small inner circle of trusted companions. This inner circle included clerks such as the future archbishop of Canterbury, Walter Reynolds, and the sons of noble houses, such as Gilbert de Clare. It also perhaps included the young Roger Mortimer of Wigmore, and a few foreigners too, most notably Piers Gaveston. King's Langley continued to hold a place in his affections as both itineraries and building accounts from throughout his life, equally as prince and king, point to his fondness for the place.

From 1295 on, the young Edward became more prominent in the affairs of the kingdom. He was clearly being groomed to rule, and in the last 10 years of his father's life he was given increasing public exposure and responsibility. Unfortunately, these last 10 years also witnessed increasing strain between the king and his magnates, and sometimes between the king and his heir. The young prince played a role in the crisis of 1297 when his father planned a controversial expedition to Flanders. At Westminster on 14 July, the king sought support for his venture, but he also enjoined his people, should he not return, to crown his son as king. The chronicler Guisborough asserts that, following this address, 'all the magnates there present did fealty to the king's son at his father's bidding, and he was acclaimed by all the people, their right hands upraised, as heir, future lord, and successor to the kingdom'.[1] When the king subsequently departed for Flanders, Prince Edward was left behind as titular regent, although he was advised by a council of elders comprised of bishops, earls and barons. The regency council functioned effectively in the highly charged political atmosphere that led the prince to reside in the relative safety of London. With Prince Edward's announcement of the *Confirmatio Cartarum* on 10 October, however, the crisis was defused, and the rest of the regency was taken up with routine administrative business in which the prince probably played only a minor role.

Edward I's Flemish expedition in 1297 proved fruitless, and the king soon returned home to face the Scots who had been victorious under William Wallace at Stirling Bridge. Of greater consequence for the future Edward II than success or failure in Flanders or Scotland was the introduction of a new member into his household in the aftermath of the Flemish campaign. When Edward I returned from Flanders, he brought with him a Gascon squire, Piers Gaveston. Ironically, perhaps, there can be little doubt that Piers Gaveston had been introduced into the household of Edward of Caernarfon by the king himself. The young Gascon, probably a few years older than the prince, had already seen military service in Flanders in the company of his father Arnaud de Gabaston, and appears to have been attached to the king's own household following the 1297 campaign. The senior Gabaston was a minor Béarnaise noble who had served the English crown long and well, having had direct dealings with Edward I as long ago as 1272, even before his coronation.

Piers Gaveston is consistently described in contemporary chronicles as handsome, athletic and well mannered: in short, he appeared to be a suitable companion – indeed, perhaps a role model after whom Prince Edward, lacking elder brothers, might pattern himself. From 1300 until his execution in 1312, his fortunes were inseparably linked to Edward's, and in general his wealth and status rose steadily, if not at first remarkably. According to the *Chronicle of the Civil Wars of Edward II*, looking at Gaveston for the first time, the son of the king immediately felt such love for him that he 'tied himself to him against all mortals with an indissoluble bond of love'.[2] Prior to 1305, there is little evidence that such was the case.

In 1300, the future Edward II entered a new phase in his life. The prince was to accompany his father to war in Scotland. The long progress north was broken at several points, notably at Bury St Edmunds in May, where the prince remained for a week following the king's departure. During this time, a local chronicle relates that 'he had been made in chapter one of our brethren, for the regal dignity of the abbey and the monks' abundance of spiritual comforts pleased him. Every day he asked for a monk's allowance, just as the brethren ate in the refectory, to be given to him'.[3] Passing on by way of York and Durham, the king and his heir reached Carlisle on 25 June. On 4 July, the army moved northward into Scotland, making for Dumfries by way of Lochmaben Castle. Along the way, the army advanced upon Caerlaverock Castle. Prince Edward was in command of the rearguard:

> The fourth squadron, with its train,
>
> Edward the king's son led,
>
> A youth of seventeen years of age
>
> And newly bearing arms.
>
> He was of a well-proportioned and handsome person,
>
> Of a courteous disposition, and well bred,
>
> And desirous of finding an occasion
>
> To make proof of his strength.
>
> He managed his steed wonderfully well.[4]

Edward's squadron contained established knights such as Robert de Tony, Henry le Tyes, William Latimer, William de Leyburn and Roger Mortimer of Chirk. Significantly, it also contained Piers Gaveston, who drew wages as a squire from July until November, when a truce was agreed and the English army returned to the south.

At the subsequent parliament at Lincoln in January 1301, Edward was endowed with the earldom of Chester and all of the crown's lands in Wales except for the castle and town of Montgomery. In May of the same year, he was granted Montgomery too, from which time he was generally referred to as Prince of Wales. During the spring, he toured his new appanage, receiving fealty and homage from his tenants. He also ordered repairs at Chester Castle, where, interestingly, he ordered a painting of Thomas Becket and the knights by whom he was martyred. It is overly romantic to think that he developed a particular attachment to Wales; indeed, a letter from the prince, written to Louis of Evreux in May 1305, leaves little doubt about his sentiments. In this letter, Edward describes his gift to Louis of 'some bandy-legged harriers from Wales, who can well catch a hare if they find it asleep', and goes on to threaten to send 'plenty of the wild men [of Wales] if you like, who will know well how to teach breeding to the young heirs and heiresses of great lords'.[5] On the other hand, he did have one of his minstrels, Richard the Rhymer, travel to Shrewsbury in order to learn how to play the Welsh *crwth* or harp.

Edward received as his own the manor at King's Langley, which had previously belonged to Edmund of Cornwall, and for which the young prince had already shown a great fondness. Over the next few years, considerable sums would be spent on various building projects there. Nevertheless, despite his endowment with Wales and Chester, as well as his mother's county of Ponthieu, Edward was far from independent. The revenues generated from his lands were generally insufficient to support his household (particularly in wartime) and, in many ways, his household continued to be under the supervision of his father. As late as October 1305, for instance, Edward was forced to demur when the earl of Lincoln requested the service of his household steward, Miles Stapleton, as the latter reported directly to the king and it was not within the prince's power to release him.

In 1301, another Scottish campaign was undertaken. This time, Edward was to be given his own command, so that honour in arms might accrue to him. He was to be accompanied by the highly experienced earls of Lincoln and Arundel, and also by a group of younger peers, including the earls of Gloucester (Ralph de Monthermer), Hereford and Lancaster. Edward's household went to war with him. His companions in arms included Sir Reginald Grey, Ralph de Gorges, Guy Ferre the younger, Roderic of Spain, Gilbert de Clare, Robert de Scales, Robert de Clavering, William de Munchensy and Piers Gaveston. Nine of his fourteen clerks, including Walter Reynolds, accompanied his army, which totalled in excess of 300 mounted men and hundreds more of foot-soldiers. Unfortunately, virtually nothing was achieved by either the king or the prince as the Scots refused to offer battle. Perhaps the most interesting insight provided by the movements of the prince's army comes from his unsuccessful attempt to make a pilgrimage to Whithorn Abbey to view the relics of St Ninian, suggesting at the very least a conventional piety not always attributed to him in his later years. The prince wintered at Linlithgow with his father, although Gaveston, ill, was ordered by the king to remain at Knaresborough. A truce being ratified in January, the two Edwards left Scotland in mid-February 1302.

There was no campaign in Scotland in 1302, and the prince appears to have spent much of his time on administrative business of one sort or another. In March, the prince held a parliament in London on behalf of his father, and he was summoned to the subsequent parliaments in July and October at Westminster. In October 1302, the Seneschal of Ponthieu, John de Bakewell, came to England for an audit of the county's accounts for the previous 3 years. The county seems to have generated barely more revenue than expenses, although the prince appears to have received a large quantity of sheet glass from Ponthieu, which presumably was used in renovations at King's Langley. At Christmas 1302, Edward stayed at South Warnborough in Hampshire, where he was entertained on the eve of epiphany by 'three clerks of the town of Windsor', while at the same time he was provided with £5, delivered to him by Gaveston, with which to indulge his passion for gambling at dice.

Although the latter pastime may fit more conveniently into the popular image of Edward II as a dissolute wastrel, records from the same period also indicate something more than just a conventional religiosity. To the evidence of his ease among the monks at Bury St Edmunds and his interest in visiting the relics of St Ninian, can be added a pattern of arranging for or attending requiem masses for those near to him, both great and modest in status. Not only did he attend services in remembrance of his grandmother, Eleanor of Provence, at Amesbury on 16 November, and for his mother Eleanor of Castile on 27 November 1302, but early in the following year he attended masses in February for the king's former squire, Walter de Beauchamp, and for his own yeoman, William Comyn, and another for Guy Ferre in April. In the case of Comyn, his household roll specifically recounts that this mass was held when the prince first heard of William's death.

The summer of 1303 saw the prince accompanying his father's army north on yet another Scottish campaign. This lengthy military adventure lasted from May until early November and was highlighted by a grand, and highly destructive, *chevauchée* north to the Moray Firth. The prince wintered in Perth until March 1304. During this period, he was intimately involved in diplomatic activity, meeting John Comyn, Guardian of Scotland, on 5 February. Spring 1304 saw the siege of Stirling Castle, which surrendered on 24 July. Victory in Scotland was to have been followed by further reconciliation with France. In the autumn of 1304, the prince was to have travelled to France to do homage in his father's stead, but although he made his way to Dover in late October, letters of safe conduct did not arrive from Philip the Fair, and the expedition was ultimately cancelled. Edward spent the winter of 1304–1305 at King's Langley, moving to Kennington in March in order to attend the Westminster parliament. At his temporary residence there, the prince heard petitions from Wales and attended to other business. Now 20 years old, the prince was at the centre of national affairs in both war and peace, and he was clearly in harmony with his father the king: as yet, no inkling of the unfortunate nature of the son's reign could have been foreseen. Leaving Kennington in late April, Edward returned to Langley, where he remained until early June, when he travelled to meet his father at Midhurst in Sussex. Here, on Monday 14 June, father and son had a monumental falling out that brought to the forefront Prince Edward's growing attachment to Piers Gaveston, an attachment that receives no notice in any documentary or chronicle source until this moment.

The initial source of the explosive confrontation was an alleged trespass against

Walter Langton, bishop of Coventry and Lichfield and Treasurer of England. The prince had apparently broken into a wood belonging to the bishop, but more importantly, had verbally abused the bishop following the event. For these 'gross and harsh words', Edward was banished from his father's presence and cut off from financial support. The prince hoped to achieve a speedy reconciliation, and for more than a month he shadowed the movements of the king's household at a reasonably close but respectful distance of 10–12 leagues, a plan he had explained to the earl of Lincoln in a letter written on the very day of his banishment. His sister Joan, Countess of Gloucester, provided him with her own seal in order that he might provide for himself during this difficult period, and by 21 July he was able to return this seal, confident in his ability to support himself once again, as on that same day letters to the sheriffs of England instructed them no longer to prohibit loans or other provision made to the prince.

This was not, however, the end of the prince's punishment, for the king had apparently removed several members of his son's household for an indefinite period. A letter to his sister, Elizabeth, in August noted that two of his companions, John de Haustede and John de Weston, had been allowed to return, and he asked his sister to persuade their young stepmother, Queen Margaret, to intercede with the king in order that Gaveston and Gilbert de Clare might also be restored to his household. In this letter, he says 'if we had those two, along with the others whom we have, we would be greatly relieved of the anguish which we have endured and from which we continue to suffer from one day to the next'. Throughout August and September, the prince resided at Windsor Park at his father's direction, declining offers to visit his sisters, Joan and Mary, for fear of further arousing his anger. Although the worst was over by the end of July, a final reconciliation was not achieved until 13 October, when the prince presided over a banquet at Westminster celebrating the feast of the Translation of St Edward, a particularly important date on the Plantagenet calendar since the reign of Henry III.

During the period of the prince's banishment, the Scottish situation seemed to have been resolved with the execution of William Wallace. All this changed, however, on 10 February 1306, with the notorious murder of John Comyn by Robert Bruce, earl of Carrick, at Dumfries. Edward I immediately issued writs to begin the military preparations for yet another campaign. But there was a noteworthy difference this time: increasingly, the writs spoke of an expedition to be led by the prince, with the king playing a supporting role to his son. In consequence of his growing military leadership, the prince was to be knighted at Pentecost, leaving no doubt about the complete nature of the reconciliation between father and son.

The knighting of Prince Edward was a magnificent affair. The king had issued a summons for all those entitled through succession and having sufficient means to present themselves at Westminster to be knighted. Some 267 young men, including Piers Gaveston, the younger Hugh Despenser and Roger Mortimer of Wigmore, responded. The crowd of aspirant knights was so great that they could not all be accommodated at Westminster Palace. Walls were demolished and fruit trees cut down at the New Temple to make room for the many tents and pavilions required. The prince and a small group of companions passed their vigil on the night of 21–22 May 1306 in Westminster Abbey, while the other aspirants spent the night in the Temple Church. In order to maintain himself 'better and more honourably', the prince at this time was granted, like his father before him, the duchy of Aquitaine along with the island of Oléron and the Agenais.

Edward I knighted his son personally, girding him with the belt of knighthood. The prince then received his spurs from the earls of Lincoln and Hereford. He, in turn, then knighted the other notable aspirants, including the earls of Arundel and Surrey. Gaveston and many others were knighted on the following Thursday, 26 May. The knighting ceremony was followed by the famous 'Feast of Swans', at which some 80 minstrels entertained the throng, and where the king swore an oath to go on crusade, having first avenged himself against the traitorous Robert Bruce, with the prince and others swearing variations on this theme. The prince swore never to sleep two nights in the same place until he reached Scotland.

The prince accompanied his father's army northwards to Scotland again in 1306, and his forces consolidated Aymer de Valence's victory over Robert Bruce at Methven by capturing Lochmaben Castle in June, and Kildrummy in September. But after the king established his winter quarters at Lanercost, an incident occurred that would have far-reaching repercussions into the next reign. A group of some 22 prominent knights – including several who were closely associated with the prince, such as Gilbert de Clare, John Chandos, Robert de Tony and Piers Gaveston – deserted the army to attend tournaments in France, despite specific royal orders to the contrary. The aged Edward I was enraged and ordered the confiscation of all their lands. Eventually, at the urging of his queen, Edward relented, and all of the knights involved appear to have been pardoned except for one: Gaveston.

The young Gascon knight was sent into what was to be the first of his three exiles. That he was singled out for such punishment is significant; but it is equally

significant, and has generally been overlooked, that the decree of exile was temporary – not perpetual – and non-specific with regard to cause. Gaveston could
be recalled and, of course, he would be recalled as soon as Edward I died and
Edward II ascended the throne. Moreover, the terms of his exile were far from
harsh: he was to receive 100 marks sterling annually 'for as long as he shall remain
in parts beyond the sea during the king's pleasure and awaiting his recall'. This
raises the question of the nature of his offence – surely he alone was not singled
out for the desertion of the army – as well as the king's purpose in banishing him
from the realm.

Regarding this episode, the chroniclers are largely silent, except for the highly
colourful, and equally unlikely, account of Walter of Guisborough. According
to Guisborough, when the prince had done everything possible to advance
Gaveston's fortunes, he summoned his old nemesis, Walter Langton, bishop of
Coventry and Lichfield and treasurer to the king. Langton was sent to the king,
to whom he supposedly related the prince's request that the county of Ponthieu
be conferred upon Gaveston. Summoned into his father's presence, the prince
acknowledged his request, only to be verbally and physically assaulted by the
king before being driven from his presence. Immediately after this exchange,
Guisborough continues, the king summoned his council and arranged for
Gaveston's perpetual banishment.[6]

The description of these events in Guisborough's chronicle is suspect for
several reasons. First of all, it is a literary set-piece, with clear resonances of the
biblical account of Saul's confrontation with David over his relationship with
Jonathan, a *topos* that would resurface in the works of other chroniclers writing
about Edward II and Gaveston. Moreover, Gaveston's exile was far from onerous.
Not only did Gaveston receive a generous annuity, he was also allowed to await
his recall in nearby Ponthieu, even though the terms of the original decree of exile
called for Gaveston to return to his native Gascony. This is even more remarkable
when we bear in mind that Prince Edward was scheduled to visit his county later
in 1307 – and that, according to Guisborough, it was the prince's desire to give
Ponthieu to Gaveston that had been at the root of the dispute between the king
and the prince.

What, then, accounts for the king's violent reaction to Gaveston's seemingly
minor transgression? It is possible, even attractive, at this point to agree with the
suggestion that Edward I sought the separation of his son and Gaveston to break
an inappropriate bond of brotherhood between two youths of unequal status, an
inequality that the prince seemed determined to overcome through his elevation

of his companion. Had the union between them been an openly sinful, sexual liaison, as has often been suggested, it is difficult to imagine the king being so lenient in the terms of exile. Having said that, however, and regardless of the exact nature of their relationship, the king had clearly underestimated the depth of the bond between his son and Gaveston. It is worth noting that Edward II was to father at least one illegitimate child, a son named Adam who apparently died while on campaign in Scotland in 1322. Presumably, therefore, this child was born prior to Edward's accession, and this birth might well have reassured Edward I that the relationship with Gaveston, even if sexual, was not exclusive and might prove impermanent. Moreover, the prince was to marry Isabella of France in less than a year, and the king may perhaps be forgiven if he imagined that marriage would turn his son's mind away from any former lover – or lovers – once and for all. Such, of course, was not to be the case.

Edward I died at Burgh-by-Sands on 7 July 1307. By the end of the month, the new king had withdrawn his army from Scotland. Such a military policy was certainly justifiable given the state of the treasury, which was empty, and the limited opportunities for success occasioned by an enemy unlikely to offer battle. Edward attempted to arrange for the security of the north before departing for the south, strengthening garrisons at Stirling, Perth and Dumfries, and calling out the levies of Lancashire, Westmorland and Cumberland. He also installed the experienced commander Aymer de Valence, soon-to-be earl of Pembroke, as Guardian of Scotland. Nevertheless, the economic and military basis for Edward's decision to withdraw from Scotland was quickly overshadowed by other motivations, real or imagined. Most importantly, even before he had crossed the border, Edward had been joined at Dumfries by Gaveston, recalled from exile, and on 6 August elevated to the peerage as earl of Cornwall, a dignity hitherto conferred only on members of the royal family. It had been assumed that the earldom of Cornwall would pass to one of the king's young half-brothers, having previously been held by the brothers of Henry III and Edward I.

The chroniclers express little surprise, if some disappointment, at all of this. Yet it is worth noting that virtually all of the earls appended their seals to the grant to Gaveston and there were no immediate signs of discord between the king and his magnates. The following months were crucial in establishing the tone for the new reign, and these months were not without opportunities for the king to enhance his prestige. Unfortunately, however, he seems quickly to have squandered the initial goodwill shown to him, and to have succeeded in alienating a large section of both the aristocracy and the chroniclers. Edward never really recovered from this initial, failed, exercise in kingship, and his entire reign is best understood in terms of the personal dynamics of distrust and distaste engendered in the first year and crystallized over the next 5 or 6 years. An understanding of these years is central to any explanation of the king's subsequent failures; at the heart of it all lies the intensity of his attachment to Piers Gaveston.

In the meantime, the beginning of the new reign required some sort of formal closure with the reign of Edward I. The body of the late king was conveyed south by stages, stopping at Richmond (Yorks), and then for a long time remaining at Waltham Abbey, before being conveyed into London, where it rested first in Holy Trinity, Aldgate and then St Paul's. The king's remains were thence borne in procession to the family mausoleum, the rebuilt Westminster Abbey, where the king was buried on 27 October. In contrast to the splendour of Henry III's tomb, Edward I was laid to rest in a tomb of Purbeck marble – remarkable as much for its severity as its simplicity. It has recently been convincingly argued that this burial represented Edward I's sense of *gravitas* rather than any lack of respect from his son. The old king – like his adversary Robert Bruce – had apparently wanted his heart to be buried in the Holy Land, but he got no closer than to have the nominal patriarch of Jerusalem, Antony Bek of Durham, preside over his funeral.

This was just as well, perhaps, as within 3 days of the funeral, the Holy Land itself was scandalized, with word reaching England of the shocking suppression of the Knights Templar; this had been undertaken by Philip the Fair of France just 2 weeks earlier, at dawn on 13 October 1307. The detailed charges were stunning: in their rite of initiation, the Templars were said to have denied Christ's divinity and spat on the Cross, worshipped idols and engaged in obscene homosexual acts. After an initial protest against the violation of ecclesiastical jurisdiction entailed in the arrest and trial of the French Templars, the recently elected Gascon pope, Clement V, soon enjoined the other kings of Western Christendom to participate in the suppression of the Order. Remarkably, one of the least enthusiastic of the European kings in his reaction to the charges against the Templars was the young English king, Edward II.

To convince the English court of the justice of the charges, King Philip had sent his trusted clerk, Master Bernard Pelet – who was intimately familiar with the affair, having helped to draft the accusations against the knights – with letters detailing the charges. These letters were duly read before the king and his magnates, eliciting a reply in which Edward said that the charges against the Templars were literally incredible: '*ultra quam credi potest*'. Indeed, on the advice of his council, Edward decided to gather further information, from the seneschal of Agen, William de Dene, in whose region these horrible rumours had apparently originated. Despite the strenuous efforts of Bernard Pelet to convince him, Edward II had, and continued to have, serious doubts about the business. On 4 December 1307, from Reading, he wrote to the kings of Portugal, Castile, Sicily and Aragon, urging them not to give credence to the defamation of the Templars, brought forth 'as we believe, not in zealous righteousness, but excited by cupidity and a spirit of envy'. On 10 December, the king wrote to the pope from Westminster, expressing his continuing disbelief in the rumours, 'terrible to consider, horrible to hear'. Shortly thereafter, however, Edward was constrained to muffle his criticisms, for in December he received the papal bull *Pastoralis praeeminentiae* ordering him to arrest the Templars on the pope's behalf. He issued orders to this effect on the very next day. A little later, he wrote again to the pope from Boulogne, the site of his impending marriage with Isabella of France, assuring him that he would attend to the Templar business in the swiftest and best fashion. Even so, all the evidence clearly indicates that the king's ideas of how 'best' to deal with the Templars were at considerable variance with those of the pope, let alone with those of the king of France.

This early foray into international diplomacy and politics reflects well on Edward II. He had withstood the bullying tactics of his future father-in-law and, while complying with the letter of the law in his dealings with the papacy, he certainly flouted it in spirit. In the end, after going through the motions of various inquisitions, which resulted in none of the spectacular confessions that had been forthcoming in France, the English Templars were largely absorbed into other orders in 1313, and quietly faded from the scene. Nonetheless, Edward has received very little credit for this admirable behaviour. In part, this may be due to the fact that he certainly profited financially from the Templars' fall. For instance, a substantial portion of the resources required to support the 1308 Scottish campaign was derived from Templar revenues. Setting aside the economic benefits, however, Edward ultimately bartered his support for the suppression of the Templars, lukewarm as it was, for papal consent to Gaveston's return from his second exile. This obvious quid pro quo has undoubtedly col- oured interpretations of his defence of the Templars, but is not entirely fair. By the time Edward II exploited the situation for his own benefit, the final suppression of the order had become inevitable. A different king, with a reputation for strong character, might well have been praised for his astute statesmanship in profit- ing both financially and politically from an unfortunate situation. But Edward, whatever his shortcomings, deserves credit for seeing through the farce of the Templars' destruction and for mitigating the severity of this with regard to the English Templars. Perhaps we again see something of his genuine, if simple, faith: he simply could not believe that Christian knights could blaspheme in this way, although in the end he was powerless to stop a process that had the full support of both the king of France and the pope.

If his response to the Templar crisis reflects well on him, his behaviour in other areas during this same period did little to enhance his stature or to strengthen his relationship with his magnates. Less than a week after his father's funeral, he was present at a ceremony of a very different nature. On 1 November 1307, he further dignified Gaveston, as his favourite was married to Margaret de Clare, sister of the young earl of Gloucester and niece of the king himself, in a lavish wedding at Berkhamsted. This union of the upstart favourite with the great house of Clare appears not to have received the same sort of endorsement, however grudging, as Gaveston's elevation to the earldom of Cornwall had done. Among the earls, only Pembroke can be shown to have attended the wedding, although the bride's brother, Gilbert de Clare, earl of Gloucester and Hertford, must also have been present. The king spent in excess of £100 on a variety of gifts, including jewels and horses for the bride and groom, on minstrels to entertain the guests, and on coins to be tossed over the heads of the newly married couple. Edward even paid five shillings in damages to Richard le Kroc, whose adjoining property was apparently damaged in the merry-making that accompanied the wedding.

Gaveston's growing status and unpopularity (and, by extension, the king's) was reinforced by his performance in a tournament held in his honour of Wallingford early in the following month. Although the tournament was attended by the earls of Arundel, Hereford and Warenne, the outcome led to further divisions, rather than reconciliation, between the king and his favourite on the one hand, and the magnates on the other. Opinions about the exact nature of Gaveston's conduct here vary among the chroniclers, the most charitable reporting that all the younger and more athletic knights were arrayed on Gaveston's side, while other writers accuse the favourite of outright fraud, fielding a team of 200 knights when the previously agreed number was 60. The author of the *Vita Edwardi Secundi* dates the onset of the animosity felt by Earl Warenne for Gaveston to this contest, and other magnates would soon join him in turning against the king and his favourite.

The chroniclers, and surely the political community in England, were taken aback, if not outraged, when on 20 December 1307, Gaveston – who was celebrating the Christmas season with the king as guests of the abbot of Battle at his manor of Wye – was named to serve as *custos regni* when the king sailed to France in January for his impending marriage to Isabella, the young daughter of Philip IV of France. It was during the king's brief sojourn to France that the first signs of opposition to his rule began to emerge. The source of discontent was not Gaveston's direct exercise of authority. Unlike Edward's later favourite, the younger Despenser, Gaveston had virtually no interest in politics, *per se*. He seldom witnessed royal charters, and until now had been involved in only one political action, joining with the new treasurer, Walter Reynolds, on 4 October, to issue a proclamation inviting complaints to be brought against the unpopular former treasurer, Walter Langton.

Although he himself was the recipient of considerable royal patronage, what seems to have been most resented was his perceived ability to channel the patronage of the king to others. The *Annals* of St Paul's in London observed that, 'if any of the earls or magnates sought the king's special grace with regard to any business, the king sent him to Piers'.[7] His regency, therefore, although it was both brief and uncontroversial, further reinforced the notion that Gaveston stood as a barrier between the king and his natural councillors and was thereby disrupting the political fabric of the kingdom. It was in many ways reminiscent of the discontent that had been occasioned by Henry III's Savoyard and Poitevin kinsmen half a century earlier.

The wedding of Edward and Isabella did little to dissipate the growing discontent. The wedding had long been planned. Isabella had been born in 1296 – the only, and much loved, daughter of Philip IV and Joan of Navarre. Within 2 years of her birth, she appears in English sources, betrothed to Edward of Caernarfon through the peacemaking efforts of Pope Boniface VIII, the terms of the marriage being further discussed the following year in the Treaty of Montreuil. Shortly after the death of his father, Edward had presented Philip with a series of requests to be considered in light of the pending marriage. These requests apparently included various concessions to be made by the French king regarding such thorny issues as appeals from Gascony to the court of France, as well as the issue of Isabella's marriage portion, which had not yet been specified. Philip's stern response was that Isabella's marriage portion was the return of Aquitaine, which had been forfeited during the reign of Edward I. He also castigated the new king for his temerity in making such impertinent requests.

Nevertheless, the English king made the crossing from Dover to Boulogne on 22 January 1308, and the nuptials took place 3 days later at St Mary's, Boulogne, after some hard dealing between the two kings' representatives, including a substantial increase of the annual value of Isabella's dower. The wedding itself seems to have been a lavish affair, attended by some 32 dukes and counts from the Continent, as well as Edward's own entourage, which included four earls. Edward was showered with gifts of horses, plate and jewels, and he in turn performed homage to his father-in-law for the lands he held of him in France. On 7 February, the king returned home with his young bride; Isabella had in all likelihood just turned 12 years old, while Edward was 23 years old.

While in France, a group of prominent nobles – including the four earls, the bishop of Durham and a number of barons – entered into a compact that has come to be known to historians as the Boulogne Agreement. In this document, the nobles stated that their fealty to the king bound them to safeguard both his honour and his crown. In essence, they separated loyalty owed to the person of the king from loyalty owed to the crown itself. This doctrine of 'capacities' would be more fully articulated and openly stated by the earl of Lincoln and others in parliament in April 1308, but it presents a clear sign of the growing tension between Edward and his nobles at a very early stage of the reign.

As he had done through the extravagant promotion of his favourite in the aftermath of his father's death, on returning from France the king quickly expended whatever political capital he had acquired through the French marriage. Indeed, he must have unintentionally reinforced the convictions of those who had sealed the Boulogne Agreement. When he and his wife landed at Dover, he afforded the young queen and the rest of his audience with a powerful demonstration of her relative position in his affections. According to Trokelowe's chronicle, Edward ran to Gaveston and showered him – and him alone – with hugs and kisses. Moreover, the chroniclers allege that the king conveyed to Piers all of the wedding gifts that he had received from the king of France. There may well be some substance to these rumours, as among the baggage abandoned by Gaveston during his final flight from his enemies in 1312 were several goblets and pieces of plate decorated with the arms of England and France, as well as extraordinary quantities of jewels and precious metals. Unfortunately, this extravagant show of immoderate affection and familiarity was not an isolated incident, and the rapid decline in relations between king and magnates was further exacerbated shortly thereafter at the coronation and subsequent banquet for the royal couple.

The coronation of Edward II took place on 25 February 1308, a week later than originally planned. The reason for the delay seems to have been a last-minute demand from both the English magnates and the French royal family that

Gaveston be sent back into exile. The coronation appears to have gone forward only after the king agreed to submit himself to the guidance of the next parliament to be held. Moreover, a novel fourth clause was inserted into the traditional coronation oath, which was taken in French rather than Latin. This new clause, the significance of which has been much debated, required the king to swear that he would be bound by such laws as the community of the realm would choose in future. The irregularities of the actual ceremony – which seems to have been rushed by the presiding bishop, Henry Woodlock of Winchester – were completely overshadowed by the extravagant prominence afforded to Gaveston. Although the procession was led by William Marshal bearing the king's gilded spurs, followed by five of the earls – including Lincoln, Lancaster and Warwick – the treasurer, the chancellor and various magnates, it was the earl of Cornwall who walked directly in front of the king, carrying the crown of St Edward. It was also he who redeemed the ceremonial sword Curtana, and who fastened the spur onto the king's left foot – the right spur having been fastened by the queen's uncle, Charles of Valois.

If Gaveston's prominence in the coronation ceremony was shocking, contemporaries found his – and the king's – comportment at the subsequent banquet even more outrageous and offensive to the dignity of the crown. As early as the previous October, the king had ordered the production of tapestries bearing the arms of the king and those of the earl of Cornwall, specifically for display at the coronation; but the decoration of the hall could not compare with the decoration of the favourite himself. When Gaveston, 'seeking his own glory rather than the king's', arrived dressed in regal purple trimmed in pearls, one chronicler remarked that he appeared 'more like the god Mars than a mere mortal'.[8] Many present at the feast were outraged that the king spent so little time on the queen's couch, compared with Gaveston's. We are told that the queen's uncles, Louis of Evreux and Charles of Valois, were so deeply offended by this behaviour that they soon departed the kingdom in indignation, while an unnamed earl was said to have been so infuriated by this spectacle that he wished to kill the favourite then and there. Soon, there were reports of Philip the Fair bringing his vast resources and power to bear against the favourite. Isabella is said to have written to her father in the spring of 1308 complaining of her ill treatment, and rumours quickly spread throughout England that the king of France was conspiring against the favourite (if not against the king) with leading figures in the baronial opposition.

Just 3 days after the coronation, parliament met at Westminster on 28 February

1308. The main business of the session was an attack on Gaveston. Led by the earl of Lincoln, the magnates initially sought a written commission from the king authorizing parliament to undertake measures of reform, before addressing the needs of church and state. Interestingly, the demand for this written commission seems to have been balked by an unlikely partnership of the earl of Lancaster and the elder Hugh Despenser. Although later in the reign they would be implacable enemies, in 1308 these two were seen as the strongest royalists among the magnates at this time. Edward, in any case, declined to provide such a written commission and the business of parliament was put off until after Easter. During the next 2 months, the king attempted to strengthen his grip on the kingdom, not least by replacing the custodians of numerous royal castles, in several cases removing men who had sealed the Boulogne Agreement and replacing them with trusted friends such as Gaveston, Despenser and Robert Fitzpain, the steward of the king's household. Meanwhile, considerable sums were allocated for the fortification of the Tower and Windsor Castle, to which the king and favourite retreated. At the same time, the magnates seem to have assembled at the earl of Lincoln's castle at Pontefract.

Parliament reconvened on 28 April, with the earl of Lincoln once again leading the call for Gaveston's immediate exile, along with the confiscation of all his lands. This demand was not casually made, as the earl supported his case with a brief, although legalistic, tract containing three articles in justification of the demands. The first article fully enunciated the doctrine of capacities that had been implicit in the Boulogne Agreement – the king's subjects owed their homage and allegiance to the crown rather than to the person of the king, and therefore must act 'to reinstate the king in the dignity of the crown', should he act unreasonably. The second article pointed to just such a case of unreasonable behaviour, the aggrandizement of Gaveston. The third article said that, since the king and his courts would not act against Gaveston, they, the people, must act on the king's behalf. Clothed in innocuous legal language, this was a revolutionary challenge to the king's authority to rule, as threatening as anything conceived by Simon de Montfort.

Less than a year into his reign, in the spring of 1308, Edward appears to have had little support. Lancaster, it is true, remained at least neutral, but the only other earl to support the king in resisting the call for Gaveston's exile appears to have been Richmond, absent on the Scottish march, and anyway never a powerful political presence. Other than the elder Despenser and a handful of Edward's household knights, the king stood isolated. Moreover, it seems certain that he could look for no assistance from overseas. A letter concerning a disputed election at Westminster Abbey, written in the spring of 1308, affords some insight into the perceived attitude of the queen and her father. The writer bluntly asserts that 'whatever in any way concerns Piers [Gaveston] and his followers, the queen and the earls, the pope . . . the cardinals and the king of France are delighted to hinder'.[9] He goes on to advise his reader to 'let the queen be so informed of all these things, that out of hatred of Piers she may deign to write specially and secretly to the lord king of France her father, to the pope, to the cardinals, and the lord Charles, brother to the said king of France'. Nor was this merely conspiratorial whispering. Philip and his sister Margaret, Edward I's widow, were said to have sent 40,000 *livres* to the earls of Lincoln and Pembroke in order to assist them to proceed against Gaveston; and, if perhaps the sum involved is exaggerated, there seems to have been some substance to this claim. Under pressure from all sides, on 18 May, Edward II capitulated. He agreed to send Gaveston back into exile by 25 June. If the king softened the blow of exile somewhat, both for himself and his favourite, by appointing Gaveston as king's lieutenant in Ireland and sending him to Dublin, the magnates nonetheless had achieved their primary objective of separating king and favourite.

The king immediately bent all of his powers in a single direction, the recall of Gaveston. In the words of the author of the *Vita*, 'he bent one after another to his will, with gifts, promises, and blandishments'. Indeed, even before the favourite had actually departed for Ireland, the king had begun his campaign to reverse the sentence. On 16 June, Edward wrote to both Clement V and Philip IV seeking their support in his cause. A supplementary letter to the pope on the same day specifically sought to have the sentence of excommunication against Gaveston revoked. On the same day, the king also wrote to Otto de Grandson, his personal envoy to the papal curia in Avignon, urging him to act on Gaveston's behalf. Finally, still on 16 June, Edward made a grant of the town and castle of Blanquefort to Bertrand de Got, nephew and namesake of the pope. Valued at 1500 *livres chipotois* (£300 sterling) per annum, this grant innocently declared that it was made solely 'on account of the love we bear towards the most holy father in Christ, the supreme pontiff Clement'. The importance that Edward placed on this business is illustrated by the clerk's notation that all of these letters were drafted, read and sealed in the king's presence, who then took them and placed them on his own bed. The appeasement of the pope continued in January 1309 when several hundred pounds were spent on jewels for Clement and, in May of that year, when the right of justice in Budos was conceded to Raymond-Guillaume de

Budos, another nephew of the pope. During the same period, the king also made political concessions to the pontiff: for instance, he freed the bishop of Coventry and Lichfield, along with the bishops of Glasgow and St Andrews.

Clement V's response to Edward's letters of 16 June was embodied in the papal bull *Faciens misericordiam*, in which the king was enjoined to cooperate, more fully than he had hitherto done, in the suppression of the Templars. Of equal significance, however, were further letters sent the following day exhorting the king and his barons to make peace, and announcing the dispatch of papal negotiators – including Gaveston's kinsman, Betrand de Caillau – to achieve this goal. The timing of these two letters, as well as their import, seems more than coincidentally linked, and Edward's gifts to the pope and his nephews are best seen as part of the same initiative that led him to follow papal directives concerning the Templars more closely. His policy of 'gifts, promises, and blandishments', bore fruit by the spring of 1309, when Clement V lifted the pending sentence of excommunication against Gaveston, clearing the way for the favourite's return.

In England, too, the combination of gifts, promises and blandishments offered to the magnates, frequently including Templar manors, had the desired effect. By the autumn of 1308, many of the most prominent magnates were once again to be found in the king's company, witnessing charters, often in favour of each other. Not only moderates, such as the earl of Gloucester, returned to the royal fold, but even such intransigent opponents of Gaveston as the earls of Lincoln, Hereford and Warwick were frequently found in the king's presence. There was also a solicitous tone in the king's political dealings with the magnates. The St Paul's annalist reports that, at the Northampton parliament, a concord was achieved between the king and his magnates by the agreement to remove six unnamed counsellors from his presence and to be guided by what the earls should ordain at the next parliament. This parliament, held at Westminster in October, was summoned to discuss further matters that had been raised at the parliament held the previous February, whose fuller discussion had been prevented by 'certain obstacles'. By March 1309, Edward was able to send an embassy to the pope, declaring that he had obtained the consent of the English magnates, both lay and ecclesiastical, to Gaveston's return.

Edward's father-in-law, the king of France, presented the last barrier to his goal of recovering his favourite. Here, too, Edward undertook a campaign of blandishment and gifts. Already, in May 1308, he had granted the counties of Montreuil and Ponthieu to Queen Isabella for her personal expenses. On 16 June, Edward wrote to Philip IV seeking his assistance in settling the discord between the English king and his magnates. Philip responded by sending negotiators, his brother Louis and Guy, bishop of Soissons. By mid-September, Louis was in England, and by late November he had negotiated a necessary, but unpopular, truce with Scotland. By the following spring, Edward was ready to proceed with the recall. At the Westminster parliament in April 1309, the king requested a grant of taxation and permission to bring Gaveston back from Ireland. The first was conditionally granted pending the king's addressing a petition of grievances presented on the behalf of the 'community of the realm', but the second was flatly refused. Another parliament was called to meet at Stamford in July. Here, the king received a grant of a twenty-fifth, and consent was given for the favourite's recall. In fact, Gaveston had already returned and was at the king's side in Stamford. A papal bull had arrived in England in June, setting aside Archbishop Winchelsey's excommunication of the favourite, and Edward was able to present his opponents with a *fait accompli*. The king did, however, address the grievances presented in the earlier petition with the Statute of Stamford, largely a recapitulation of the *Articuli super Cartas* of 1300, making it clear that abuses of power by royal officials were at the heart of baronial discontent.

The autumn of 1309 may have provided a brief respite from the tensions that had, up until now, troubled the relations between king and magnates. On the one hand, Gaveston appears to have attempted to effect a reconciliation with at least some of the earls, most notably the venerable earl of Lincoln. He even acted with Lincoln and Gloucester in early December to suspend the collection of the twenty-fifth, as the terms of the Statute of Stamford had not been upheld. Gaveston was here (and in several other minor pieces of business at this time) improbably working as a guardian of the baronial reform. Yet, if the chroniclers are to be believed, at the same time the favourite was once again beginning to control the flow of patronage and to add insult to injury by employing demeaning nicknames to refer to his fellow earls: Joseph the Jew for Pembroke, Black Dog of Arden for Warwick, Burstbelly for Lincoln, and Churl or Fiddler for Lancaster. Over the next few months, tensions once again rose to boiling point. The earls refused to attend a '*secretum parliamentum*' at York in October because of Gaveston's presence. At the subsequent Westminster parliament in February 1310, they refused to come into the king's presence if Gaveston was there, fearing for their safety. It was only after the favourite was sent away that parliament met, and the king's opponents there demanded, and on 16 March 1310 received, a commission to elect a body of prelates, earls and barons to ordain and establish the estate of the king's household and realm.

The work of the Lords Ordainer has been variously interpreted by historians to have had greater or lesser constitutional importance. Although it may be going too far to suggest that the Ordinances of 1311 are nothing more than an expression of personal grievances dressed in constitutional garb, neither is it possible to agree that they represent a clash of diametrically opposed theories of government. By and large, the baronial opposition to Edward II did not so much wish to replace the system of government as to replace the personnel of government. Recent studies of the reign have suggested that there were 'probably as many "baronial policies" as there were barons', and 'probably as many points of view as there were Ordainers'.[10] Consequently, while making due allowance for baronial, and royal, awareness of the political discourse that led from the Magna Carta through the Provisions of Westminster to the Ordinances, in the end it is the personal element of the various recensions of the Ordinances that remains central to their understanding, and which shaped the increasingly violent political climate of the rest of the reign.

Regardless of internal divisions or lack of lofty constitutional principles, the Ordainers moved quickly to set the tone for reform. Even before their formal election, on 19 March 1310, a set of six preliminary ordinances was issued. The emphasis in these preliminary articles, predictably, was on the king's favouritism and his irregular financial policies: the king was prohibited from making gifts without the counsel and assent of the Ordainers; customs were to be paid into the exchequer to Englishmen so that the king would not need to resort to prises; and foreign merchants were to be arrested and their accounts examined. Provision was also made to support the work of the Ordainers, in London, throughout the duration of their commission. These six preliminary ordinances, like the Statute of Stamford, reflect the concerns, and indeed the language, of the barons and reformers since 1297 (but with an additional emphasis on the king's gifts – that is to say, patronage) and they would form the basis for the first eight articles of the final Ordinances in 1311. Meanwhile, Edward did not confirm the preliminary ordinances until 2 August 1310, and even then he did not honour them. The king continued to make grants to Gaveston and others, and generally sought to undermine the magnates' work. This very likely had the undesired effect of hardening the Ordainers' opposition to the king and his close associates even further.

The Lords Ordainers set about their work at once. It is impossible to say with certainty who took the leading role in drafting the Ordinances. The earl of Lincoln and Archbishop Winchelsey were both respected statesmen and were considered to be influential by contemporary chroniclers. Nevertheless, the well-informed author of the *Vita Edwardi Secundi* divided the Ordainers into two groups: genuine reformers led by the earl of Warwick; and another group comprised of the earls of Hereford, Lancaster and Pembroke, who were said to be motivated by their hatred for Piers Gaveston. These four earls were consistently present together in London on occasions when the Ordinances were drafted and seem to have been the core element in framing the document. In August 1310, the earls of Arundel, Hereford, Lancaster and Pembroke refused to leave their business in London to attend the king's council at Northampton. Similarly, none of them served in person with the king in Scotland in 1310–1311. Lincoln, serving as keeper of the realm in London, threatened to resign this position when, on 28 October 1310, the king ordered the removal of the exchequer and the benches to York by the following Easter. The Ordainers, who would thus have been deprived of expert advice, in contravention of the preliminary ordinances, were said to have dispersed to their own districts following the king's order, but in February 1311, Hereford, Lancaster, Pembroke and Warwick were all together again in London – as they still were in July – and it may have been during this period that revisions were made to an earlier draft of the Ordinances.

The king did his best to ignore the implications of the reform commission. He busied himself with a necessary, but ultimately futile, Scottish campaign. In March 1310, Robert Bruce had been able to hold a parliament in St Andrews, at which his right to the Scottish throne was affirmed. Moreover, the Scots were in communication with Edward's disaffected father-in-law, Philip IV, who was attempting to organize a new crusade. Despite the lack of attendance at a parliament at Northampton in August, the king set a muster date for September in Berwick. Among the earls, only Gaveston, Gloucester and Warenne performed their service in person. No significant action took place before the king went into winter quarters, although negotiations with Bruce seem to have been undertaken.

In February, while still in winter quarters at Berwick, Edward received word that the earl of Lincoln had died. This was a serious blow for the king, for although Lincoln was associated with the reform movement, he was also respected and trusted by both Edward and the magnates. Moreover, his death greatly enhanced both the power and prestige of his son-in-law, Thomas of Lancaster, who was now endowed with a total of five earldoms and quickly emerged as the leading figure in opposition to the king. Although Lancaster travelled north to swear fealty to his cousin for his new lands and titles, he is reported to have refused to cross the Tweed in order to do so.

Lancaster's symbolic refusal to endorse Edward's Scottish campaign, and in some sense his kingship, was a sign of greater conflict to come. Although the king finally crossed the Tweed himself, receiving Lancaster's fealty at Haggerston, the earl is said to have refused to acknowledge the presence of Gaveston, thereby causing the king and favourite great offence. Although the latter continued to lead fruitless military operations against the Scots from Perth until May, by the spring of 1311 the king's efforts in Scotland had proved costly and ineffectual. Moreover, his position in London had been weakened both by the death of Lincoln and the dispatch of Gloucester there as *custos*. In the end, he had no real choice but to return south to face his critics.

On 3 August 1311, a draft of the Ordinances was sent to the king and, on 16 August, parliament met, the mayor of London having taken steps to safeguard the Ordainers in the city. The Ordinances were finally published on 27 September 1311, just 2 days before their commission was to expire, in the presence of the earls of Arundel, Hereford, Lancaster, Oxford, Pembroke and Warwick. Two weeks later, sealed with the king's great seal, they were sent to the sheriffs for publication. The primary thrust of the reforms was aimed at the king and his household, but there was also a noteworthy emphasis on the role of parliament, which from now on was to oversee a variety of governmental appointments and functions. There were also articles that called for the abolition of prises and new customs, and for restrictions on royal pardons. Nevertheless, of greatest interest to contemporary chroniclers and presumably the general populace, were the personal clauses, which called for the removal of evil counsellors such as the king's Italian bankers, the Frescobaldi, French courtiers, the Beaumonts and, of course, Gaveston. The *Vita Edwardi Secundi* claims that 'there was one of those Ordinances that more than the rest distressed the king, to wit the expulsion of Piers Gaveston and his exile'. One might argue that it was also most important to the magnates, as in late November 1311 a supplementary set of ordinances, often referred to as the 'Household Ordinances', was issued, which specifically named 27 persons to be excluded from the king's household. Of these, no fewer than 18, two-thirds of those named, had links with the favourite. This supplement is generally thought to have been the work of the earls of Lancaster and Warwick alone, from now on the most stalwart supporters of the Ordinances, and it is eloquent testimony to the limited nature of their reforming vision.

Edward II vigorously resisted the implementation of the Ordinances, although they dominated political thought and activity in the next decade. As early as 12 January 1312, the king issued a proclamation that the Ordinances should be observed only in so far as they were not prejudicial to himself. Later in the year,

Edward sent a delegation to the pope at the Council of Vienne asking for the Ordinances to be annulled should they prove prejudicial to the crown. Similar embassies were also sent to the King of France. In the protracted negotiations between the king and his magnates following Gaveston's death, which stretched through to November 1313, Edward II determinedly avoided confirmation of the Ordinances. This policy, however, proved impracticable after the disaster at Bannockburn (24 June 1314) and, with both his Scottish and domestic policy in disarray, the king was forced to allow the baronial reforms to go forward.

For Edward II, in the autumn of 1312, the most immediate consequence of the Ordinances was that Gaveston was exiled once again, departing the realm from Dover on 4 November. On the strength of their past experience, the magnates had insisted that Gaveston be exiled from all English territories including Ireland, Gascony and Ponthieu. Although the evidence is uncertain, it seems likely that Gaveston, unwelcome and unsafe in France, made his way to Flanders. Despite his absence, tensions between the king and his magnates remained high. Tournaments were banned and, in November, the king felt it necessary to send letters to six of the earls, specifically forbidding them to come to parliament in arms. In order to quell rumours, apparently widely circulated, that the favourite had not actually abjured the realm, the king commissioned two of the Ordainers, Hugh de Courteney and William Martin, to search for Gaveston in the south west. In fact, he was certainly gone, but it was not long before he reappeared in England. Although some of the chronicles date his return to Christmas 1311, Gaveston's actual return took place in January 1312, and the reason for his illicit return was almost certainly the birth of his only legitimate child, a daughter Joan, who was born to Margaret de Clare on 12 January in York.

Regardless of the reasons for Gaveston's return, his presence with the king could hardly do other than provoke another crisis. Edward himself sensed this, issuing letters on 18 January 1312, declaring Piers to be a good and loyal subject whose exile had been decreed in contravention of the laws and customs of the realm. On 20 January, Edward wrote to various sheriffs ordering the restoration of all the favourite's former lands. These letters were followed by a remarkable memorandum entered by the clerk who drafted them and clearly considered them illegal: 'that these writs were made in the king's presence by his order under threat of grievous forfeiture, and that he retained them after they were sealed'. Despite Edward's later order that the Ordinances be observed insofar as they were not prejudicial to the king, his disregard for the Ordinances was clear even to his own servants, let alone to his baronial enemies.

The magnates were not slow to respond to the challenge issued by Gaveston's restoration to favour. While Piers was fortifying himself in Scarborough Castle, an assembly took place at St Paul's in March, at which Archbishop Winchelsey solemnly declared Gaveston's excommunication in accordance with the terms of the Ordinances. According to the chronicler Trokelowe, Thomas of Lancaster was chosen as the leader of the opposition at this time, and the various earls and magnates were assigned specific tasks. Gloucester was given responsibility for securing the south of England, Hereford for the east, Lancaster for Wales and the west, and Robert de Clifford and Henry de Percy for the Scottish marches. Pembroke and Warenne were charged with arresting the favourite. Anyone transgressing the terms of the Ordinances was to be excommunicated. As has been rightly observed, 'the coalition of Earls and clergy, led by Lancaster and Winchelsey, was now stronger than it ever had been before or ever would be again'.[11]

In April, the king and favourite were once again together, moving north to the presumed safety of Newcastle, where they remained for 3 weeks, the length of stay apparently dictated by the fact that Gaveston had fallen ill. The unexpected arrival of an army led by Lancaster, Percy and Clifford in early May forced a hasty retreat, first to Tynemouth, then on to Gaveston's stronghold at Scarborough. In their headlong flight, Edward and Gaveston abandoned vast quantities of jewels, horses and arms (and, according to one account, even the pregnant queen). Although Lancaster certainly seized this royal treasure, the tradition that he consoled the abandoned queen is a fabrication, in which events relating to her later flight from the Despensers in 1321 are conflated with the events of 1312. In reality, the queen also abandoned her own goods at South Shields, and she quickly made her way back to the king, who had left Gaveston at Scarborough and travelled on to York.

Edward's decision to separate himself from the favourite was to prove disastrous. Without the king's presence, the magnates felt no hesitation in besieging Scarborough. Despite royal orders to desist, they would not do so and, on 19 May, Gaveston surrendered himself to the earl of Pembroke. A term of 3 months was set for negotiations to take place between the king and his baronial opponents. Preliminary discussions at York were followed by summonses for a parliament to be held in Lincoln in July. This meeting never took place, however, as in the interim the earl of Warwick intervened, seizing Gaveston from the earl of Pembroke at Deddington in Oxfordshire. Early on the morning of 10 June, Gaveston was awakened to the cry of 'Arise traitor, thou art taken'. He was transported to nearby Warwick Castle and, according to the *Vita*, cast into prison and bound in chains.

A quickly assembled conclave of earls and barons, led by Lancaster, Warwick and Hereford, debated his fate, and in due course sentenced him to death without any semblance of an actual trial. The sentence having been pronounced, Gaveston was taken on the road to Kenilworth as far as Blacklow Hill, within the lands of the earl of Lancaster, and there beheaded by a pair of Welshmen.

Although Gaveston had been the focal point of baronial discontent with Edward II's rule, his death had only a limited effect on resolving tensions in the kingdom. It is true that several of the earls (Pembroke and Warenne, for instance) quickly returned to the king's council, and that the earls of Gloucester and Richmond acted as negotiators between the king and the other earls (notably, Lancaster, Warwick, Hereford and Arundel). With assistance from mediators such as Louis of Evreux, two cardinals, and even a pair of French lawyers dispatched by Philip IV, negotiations proceeded. A tentative settlement was arranged in December 1312, and a final pardon to those involved in Gaveston's execution was issued in October 1313. But, in reality, following Gaveston's death, Edward and his opponents were irreconcilable. Agreements were seemingly made only to be broken and, in particular, the rift between the king and Lancaster, sometimes temporarily healed, was to last until the latter's death in 1322. It is also worth adding here that Gaveston's corpse, which had been taken from Blacklow Hill to Oxford and finally to the Dominican house at Langley, remained unburied. This indicates that although – or perhaps because – he was powerless to extract revenge on his enemies, Edward had not yet come to terms with the loss of his Gascon favourite. He would neither forgive nor forget.

The birth of an heir, the future Edward III, on 13 November 1312 at Windsor, may have helped the king to assuage his bitterness towards his foes, and it certainly occasioned much joy throughout the realm. For instance, the London annals recount the elaborate pageant arranged for the queen by the fishmongers in the following February: they processed to Westminster, dressed in fine robes bearing the arms of England and France worked in gold, and preceded by an ingeniously contrived ship whose raised mast and sail also bore the royal arms displayed in a great variety of ways. Carolling, they then processed on horseback before the queen as she journeyed to the royal residence at Eltham.[12] But, if there was great joy at the birth of an heir, other matters weighed heavily, especially the situation in the north.

Writing under the year 1311, the author of the *Vita Edwardi Secundi* offered the following observation: 'He who hunts two hares together, Will lose now one, or else the other.'

The reference was to the king's difficulty in protecting Gaveston, on the one hand, and establishing control over Scotland, on the other. The first hare was now irretrievably lost, but perhaps it was not too late to snare the other. So it was that Edward II undertook the largest military campaign of his reign.

On the eve of the death of Edward I, the cause of Robert Bruce in Scotland was nearly extinguished, but the passing of the old king revived it. The first years of Edward II's reign proved to be crucial, as late in 1307, in the absence of any English opposition, Bruce was able to march north along the line of the Great Glen successfully confronting his Scottish enemies such as John Comyn, earl of Buchan, and William, earl of Ross. While some of the responsibility for the consequent reversal of Bruce's fortunes can be laid at the feet of Edward II, his prosecution of the war between 1307 and 1314 was not without determination; and if his efforts in Scotland were sporadic and inconsistent, so was the support he received from his magnates. Nevertheless, by 1307, Bruce had evolved a military strategy that proved difficult for the English to counter. One major aspect of this strategy was the 'slighting' of castles. The Edwardian military machine that had reduced Stirling Castle in 1304 made it untenable for the Scots to base a defensive strategy on the possession of castles. Bruce, therefore, had destroyed his own castles at Ayr and Dumfries in 1306; his ally James Douglas of Douglasdale followed suit in 1308. Not only did the destruction of castles deny shelter and forward bases to the English, it also forced Scottish lords to choose sides, unable to sit behind the relative security of their own castle walls. Local communities, beginning in Galloway but spreading throughout Scotland and later northern England, shorn of even the limited security of these castle walls, were viciously harried and forced to pay protection money to Bruce, money used to fund the low-level guerrilla warfare that characterized these years.

An English expedition was not forthcoming in 1308 because of the political upheaval that surrounded the coronation and Gaveston's return into exile. In the absence of meaningful English opposition, Bruce was able to seize the north-eastern port of Aberdeen, while his allies ravaged Galloway and massacred the English garrison of Robert Clifford at Douglas in Lanarkshire. In fact, the English did not mount a Scottish campaign until 1310–1311, and that campaign was itself undermined by the continuing political controversy that had by then resulted in the appointment of the Lords Ordainers. Not only did the Ordainers refuse to serve in person in this Scottish campaign, they viewed it as an oblique – if not direct – attack upon themselves. The threatened removal of the chancery, treasury and both benches to York, for instance, although it had been previously undertaken by Edward I, was now seen as an attempt to deny them the sort of expert assistance they required, not as an effort to shore up the military campaign in Scotland. Short on money, and with little to show for his efforts, in the summer of 1311 Edward abandoned the campaign, returning south in July. His withdrawal was followed almost immediately by savage Scottish raiding into northern England in August and again in September. In the following year, Bruce was able successfully to besiege Dundee and, in the confused situation that surrounded the pursuit, capture and execution of Gaveston, to march into England once more, burning Hexham and Corbridge, and raiding Durham.

Throughout 1313 and into 1314, the northern counties of England bought truces from the Scots at very steep rates. Perth fell in January 1313, followed by Dumfries in the following month. During the summer of 1313, the Isle of Man was taken by the Scots. In the autumn of 1313, Robert Bruce boldly proclaimed that he would disinherit all those who did not come into his peace within 1 year. This fundamental threat to the remaining Scottish supporters of the English cause – dwindling fast as Roxburgh was lost in February 1314 and Edinburgh in March – and not just the specific threat to Stirling Castle, must be what finally provoked Edward II into mounting a new Scottish campaign.

The army that Edward II raised in 1314 compared favourably with those of his father. Although exact numbers are impossible to calculate, a figure of 10,000 infantry supplemented by perhaps 2,000 cavalry is not unreasonable. Even without the personal participation of the earls of Lancaster, Warwick, Arundel and Warenne, who argued that the campaign was invalid, not having been decided upon in parliament as required by the Ordinances, the magnates of England were well represented. The king was accompanied by the earls of Gloucester, Pembroke and Hereford, as well as by numerous prominent knights, especially those from the king's own household. The Scottish army at Bannockburn was composed primarily of infantry, and probably amounted to only about half the size of the English force, but they seem to have been well armed and, in the event, proved to be better disciplined than their English adversaries.

The two armies met in the vicinity of Stirling, although the exact location of the battlefield is still the subject of debate. There is agreement that the field was bordered on one side by the trees of the New Park and on the other side by marsh. More questionable is whether or not Bruce had preselected the site of the battle, and having done so prepared the ground by having his men dig and cover pits in order to confound a cavalry charge. Most modern commentators agree that if Bruce did choose to give battle, in doing so he took an uncharacteristic risk. His decision to fight at Bannockburn certainly surprised the English.

The English army had made good speed from Berwick to the neighbourhood of Stirling – too good according to the author of the *Vita*, who accuses the king of advancing 'not as if he was leading an army to battle but as if he was going [on pilgrimage] to St James's'. Having reached the vicinity of Stirling on the afternoon of Sunday 23 June and come into contact with the Scots, Edward must be faulted for his inability to establish and maintain an effective command structure within his army. Indeed, rather than instilling a united sense of purpose in his army, he sowed dissension among his commanders by naming the earl of Gloucester as constable in preference to the earl of Hereford, who was both hereditary constable of England and a more experienced soldier.

In a series of preliminary encounters on the eve of the battle, the English fared poorly. The English vanguard encountered the Scots and made an undisciplined charge in which Sir Henry de Bohun very nearly ran down Robert Bruce, who instead clove the English knight's head in two with his axe, greatly inspiring his soldiers through this act of personal courage and skill. In the ensuing disorder, the earl of Gloucester was unhorsed, and the English were forced to retreat, not without casualties. Meanwhile, another cavalry detachment, led by Sir Robert Clifford and Sir Henry de Beaumont, was heavily defeated by a Scottish schiltron under the command of the earl of Moray in a separate engagement near St Ninian's kirk.

The English army spent an uncomfortable night. Much of the army had not yet seen, let alone engaged, the Scots; but now they worried about a night attack, and attempted to make the best of the wet conditions in which they had bivouacked. Nevertheless, the English numbers were such that Bruce was reportedly planning a withdrawal until Sir Alexander Seton deserted the English cause, disgusted at the lack of discipline and leadership, and urged the Scottish king to attack the dispirited, and disorganized, English force. In the main battle on Monday morning, Edward II was amazed to see the Scottish schiltrons advance to offer battle. When the earl of Gloucester advised delaying the battle for a day, in order to rest the troops and horses, the king accused him of cowardice and treason. Stung by such criticism, Gloucester led the English vanguard in another impetuous charge against the Scottish spearmen. He was quickly cut off and just as quickly cut down. Joining him in death in this futile charge were the steward of the king's household, Sir Edmund de Mauley, Sir Payn Tibetot, Sir Robert Clifford and Sir John Comyn, son and heir of Bruce's murdered rival.

A Scottish attack on the main English army also had devastating effects. The

English archers, who had been unable to deploy on the Scottish flanks in time to be effective, were quickly dispersed by a cavalry charge. Soon the battle had become a mêlée and a rout. The earl of Pembroke, along with Sir Giles d'Argentein, compelled Edward to leave the field. Whatever else his failings as a commander on this day – and they seem to have been several – none could question his personal courage. Resisting the call to withdraw, he had one horse killed under him before his bodyguard could move him out of danger. Some 500 knights accompanied him to Stirling Castle, but he was denied entrance and was forced to make great haste on his way to Linlithgow and ultimately back to Berwick. Others were not so fortunate. The earl of Hereford, the earl of Angus and his kinsman Sir Ingram de Umfraville, Sir Maurice de Berkeley, Sir John de Segrave and Sir Anthony de Lucy, were all admitted to the castle but then betrayed and imprisoned at Bothwell Castle. They at least escaped with their lives, which was not the case for countless English soldiers, for the king's withdrawal from the field had signalled a general panic and had transformed a defeat into a catastrophe.

The author of the *Vita* compared the disaster at Bannockburn to that which had befallen the French a decade earlier at Courtrai, in the famous battle of the Golden Spurs. In fact, this was far more damaging for, unlike Philip the Fair, who quickly avenged the death of Robert of Artois, Edward II was to prove unable to punish the Scots for his calamitous defeat. Although Edward would refuse to make peace and recognize Bruce's legitimate right to rule in Scotland, the remainder of the reign saw military setbacks such as the loss of Berwick, near-continual Scottish raids in the north of England, and an inability to launch a major campaign north of the border.

Perhaps the true impact of Edward II's defeat at Bannockburn in 1314 can be measured by the subsequent burial of Piers Gaveston. Since 1312, his corpse had remained unburied at Langley. Part of the delay may have been occasioned by the matter of Gaveston's excommunication under the terms of the Ordinances, but by the autumn of 1314 the king seems to have obtained a posthumous papal pardon for his favourite. More likely, the real reason for the delay was Edward's reluctance to acknowledge the implications of Gaveston's execution for his own royal authority. He was apparently biding his time until he could reassert his majesty and compel his enemies to witness the burial of Gaveston with all possible splendour and magnificence. Now such a revenge no longer seemed attainable.

On 3 January 1315, the body of the late earl of Cornwall was finally interred. The service was presided over by the archbishop of Canterbury, Walter Reynolds, and attended by the bishops of Winchester, London, Worcester, and Bath and

Wells. Fourteen abbots were present, as well as the king's half-brother, the young earl of Norfolk, and the man who had inadvertently released Gaveston to his doom, the earl of Pembroke. Also present were the mayor of London, many royal officials and many household knights. Gaveston was dressed in cloth of gold at a cost of £300 and considerable sums were spent on food and wine for those present. But notably absent from the funeral were the men responsible for Gaveston's death, particularly the earls of Lancaster, Warwick and Arundel. For the present, it appeared that the king would not be able to extract his vengeance. After the funeral, he withdrew from prominence, and the years that immediately follow are marked by the ascendancy, and failure, of Thomas of Lancaster.

When Queen Isabella arrived in England in 1308, she was 12 years old and relegated to an inferior position in the king's affections. The chroniclers repeatedly bemoan the king's love for Gaveston in the early years of the reign, describing it with terms such as 'beyond measure and reason', 'immoderate', 'inordinate' and 'excessive'. 'Indeed', wrote the contemporary author of the *Vita*, 'I do not remember to have heard that one man so loved another . . . Our king was . . . incapable of moderate favour.' Although the author goes on to say that Gaveston was thus accounted a sorcerer, Robert of Reading goes even farther in the *Flores Historiarum*, asserting that Edward entered into 'illicit and sinful unions', subsequently rejecting the sweet embraces of his beautiful young wife.[13] Yet, as time went on, and even before the capture and execution of the favourite, the king must have found time for these sweet embraces. For instance, a certain intimacy between the households of the king and queen is suggested by the fact that on Easter Monday 1311, the king was 'drawn forth from his bed' and ransomed for 40 marks by Joan de Villars, his former nurse, Alice de Legrave and other ladies of the queen's chamber. More importantly, on 13 November 1312, Isabella, still barely more than a girl of 16 years old herself, gave birth to the future Edward III. She and Edward went on to produce three more children, another son and two daughters, between 1316 and 1321. Comparisons between the itineraries of Edward and Isabella indicate that, although they did not spend a great deal of time together, they did cohabit at the essential times to suggest the king's paternity of her children.

As the mother of the heir to the throne, Isabella's stature at court must have risen, and indeed she played a significant political role over the following decade, both at home and abroad, several times serving as a diplomatic agent to France. Isabella enjoyed a very favourable image among contemporary writers. While

French sources tend to emphasize her beauty, English writers show tremendous sympathy for her mistreatment by the king, and also point to her role as a mediator between the king and his magnates on a number of occasions. In 1313, she was an important mediator, along with the earl of Gloucester, in resolving the conflict between Edward and his magnates following Gaveston's execution. In that same year, she accompanied her husband to France, attending the Pentecost celebrations in which her brothers were knighted. Both Edward II and Isabella joined the king of France and others present on this occasion in taking a crusading vow, Isabella carefully stating that she would undertake the crusade only in the presence of her husband. During this visit, while at Poissy, considerable concessions relating to Gascony were obtained from Philip IV. While at Poissy, the dwelling in which the English royal couple were residing caught fire. Isabella's hand and arm were injured; she was to require medical attention relating to this injury for the rest of her life. It is unlikely, however, that she suffered a miscarriage, as has sometimes been reported. Nevertheless, in the autumn and early winter of 1313–1314, she was unwell, making it more noteworthy that she was soon dispatched to France once again on diplomatic business.

By late January 1314, a plan was constructed to send Isabella to France, ostensibly as *persona privata*, under guise of a pilgrimage, to negotiate on Gascony. Her entourage included not only intimate courtiers such as Isabella de Vescy and her brother Henry de Beaumont, but also Gilbert de Clare, earl of Gloucester, and most significantly, for the true nature of her business, William Inge, a household knight who had often served Edward on delicate legal and diplomatic business. She crossed the channel in a flotilla of some 26 ships and 13 barges on 28 February and returned to England 2 months later. Although in the interim she visited shrines in Amiens and Chartres, she spent the first half of April, as well as several shorter periods, in Paris. There, she attended a session of the *parlement*. The original petition that she presented to her father, along with his favourable responses, has survived to demonstrate her significant role in this diplomatic exchange. That her husband was pleased with her performance in France is indicated by the grant to her of the reversion of the property held by her aunt, Margaret, widow of Edward I. She was also in Paris at the time of the Tour de Nesle scandal, in which a pair of brothers, Philippe and Gautier d'Auney, confessed that they were the adulterous lovers of Philip the Fair's daughters-in-law, the cousins Marguerite and Blanche of Burgundy, the wives of Louis of Navarre and Charles of La Marche, respectively. Isabella has often been suggested as the informant, triggering the brutal executions of the d'Auney brothers and the imprisonment of her brothers' wives, but there is little evidence, even of a circumstantial nature, to support this claim, which has done much to sustain Isabella's notorious image as the 'She-Wolf of France'.

On 15 August 1316, Isabella gave birth to a second son, John of Eltham. Her role as a peacemaker may be reflected in the fact that she invited the earl of Lancaster to stand as sponsor at the prince's baptism. Two years later, in July 1318, she gave birth to her first daughter, Eleanor of Woodstock. By this time, Isabella had been granted possession of the symbolically important lands of the earldom of Cornwall, and she continued to play an essential role in avoiding open hostilities between the king and the baronial opposition as they negotiated the agreement that would be known as the Treaty of Leake. Demonstrating her diplomatic skills in another area, in the same year of 1318 she managed to arrange the provision of her protégé Louis de Beaumont to the bishopric of Durham through a direct appeal to John XXII, in opposition to her husband, the chapter at Durham and the earls of Hereford and Lancaster.

The importance of the queen is underscored by the 1319 attempt by James Douglas to capture Isabella at York. The author of the *Vita* states that 'Indeed if the queen had at that time been captured, I believe that Scotland would have bought peace for herself.' Sympathy for the queen was once again aroused in 1321 when, pregnant, she was forced to flee from the Scots at Byland. Later that summer, in late June or early July, she gave birth to her fourth and final child, Joan of the Tower, who would soon be married to David Bruce. Also in 1321, she was active along with Aymer de Valence in renewing the peace that resulted in the removal of the Despensers from court. Isabella's growing distrust of the Despensers proved to be well founded, but at this point the consequences of her antipathy were not yet clear.

Rather than by the queen, the middle years of the reign were dominated by a royal cousin, Thomas of Lancaster, who until his death in 1322 played a central role in English politics. Thomas was born in around 1282, the eldest son of Edmund of Lancaster, younger brother of Edward I, and Blanche of Navarre. Very little is known of his early life prior to his marriage to Alice de Lacy, daughter of the earl of Lincoln, sometime between 1292 and 1294. In 1296, he succeeded to the earldoms of Lancaster, Leicester and Derby, and in 1311, with the death of Henry de Lacy, he added the earldoms of Lincoln and Salisbury to consolidate a massive patrimony that generated an annual income in excess of £11,000, making him far and away the wealthiest and most powerful noble in England. Although he supported the king in the first year of the reign, by 1309 he had become a leading figure in the opposition to the king and Gaveston. Given his ancestry, patrimony and massive military retinue, his leadership was almost inevitable. Moreover, as earl of Leicester, Lancaster appears to have seen himself as a political heir to Simon de Montfort. Lancaster had been one of the driving forces behind the Ordinances, and his dogmatic insistence upon their strict enforcement had been his justification for not participating in the Scottish campaign of 1314. Now, in the aftermath of Bannockburn, he finally had his opportunity to implement thoroughgoing reform of the king's government.

Lancaster's programme of reform emerged clearly as early as the York parliament of September 1314 and the subsequent Westminster parliament of January 1315. On the one hand, he committed himself to the vigorous and precise enforcement of the Ordinances, particularly as this related to the king's household and his dispensation of patronage, while on the other, he advocated an aggressive Scottish policy. In 1315, there was an attempt to mount a new campaign against the Scots, with the earl of Pembroke and Bartholomew Badlesmere dispatched north with a force of some 500 men-at-arms. They were unable, however, to achieve much more than to relieve the siege of Carlisle. In August, the earl of Lancaster was appointed king's lieutenant and superior captain of northern forces and given his opportunity to revive the English fortunes of war. But Lancaster could not have taken command at a worse moment in the reign of Edward II. In addition to the danger posed by the Scots themselves, the earl was confronted by several other problems. The Scottish incursions of recent years, greatly intensified after Bannockburn, had led to near-anarchy in the north. To make matters worse, England was entering the throes of a great famine, 2 years' of failed harvests and cattle epidemics that added greatly to the already substantial level of human suffering of the day. The contemporary author of the poem 'On the Evil Times of Edward II', paints a bleak picture:

> I am adred that God [us] hath left out of his honed,
> Thorow wetheris that he hath sent, so cold and unkynde . . .
> He sente derthe on erde an made hit for smert.[14]

A case in point of the shortages affecting England comes from Lancaster's attempt in 1315 to raise horses and carts from 36 northern religious houses in support of his war effort. His total receipt was a mere 22 horses and 14 carts.

At the Lincoln parliament of January 1316, Lancaster was named chief of the king's council, although he was careful about the terms by which he accepted this appointment. At this parliament, enforcement of the Ordinances was thorough-going, especially the resumption of royal grants made since 1310. Among those who lost lands were some of the courtiers who were most closely associated with the king – men such as the elder Despenser, Henry de Beaumont, Roger Damory and the younger Hugh de Audley. In the spring, Lancaster was to have led a group of four commissioners, including Pembroke, Badlesmere, and his own retainer Sir Robert Holand, to meet Robert Bruce and a Scottish delegation at Leicester. This meeting never took place, however, and 1316 was a year of crises throughout the kingdom. Not only was the famine at its height, further reducing royal rev-enues already stretched to the breaking point; in addition, widespread disorder pointed out the ineffectual nature of royal government. In Wales, the king faced the revolt of Llewelyn Bren, while in Bristol discontent with Badlesmere led to riots that ultimately necessitated a full siege of the city. Elsewhere on the Welsh march, the dispute over the lordship of Powys between John de Charlton and John Giffard was renewed with great violence. Against this background, it is no wonder that there was no Scottish campaign in 1316; yet in November, the king's replacement of Lancaster with Arundel as captain of royal forces in the north clearly signalled a vote of no confidence, and a renewed break between Edward and his cousin Thomas.

In February 1317, Lancaster chose not to attend a *colloquium* at Clarendon. The earls of Surrey and Hereford did attend, as did the elder Despenser and William Montagu, and perhaps also the younger Despenser, Damory and Audley. Lancaster again failed to answer a summons to a subsequent meeting at Westminster in April and was therefore declared an enemy of the king and kingdom. Lancaster excused himself from yet another meeting in July, arguing that it was not a legitimate parliament as required by the Ordinances, although he did promise to appear at the muster in Newcastle in August. Meanwhile, on 11 April 1317, John de Warenne, earl of Surrey, had kidnapped Lancaster's wife, Alice de Lacy, from Canford in Dorset. But this was no romantic rivalry. Warenne was said to have done this merely 'in contempt of Lancaster'. The opposition to Lancaster further coalesced on 1 June when, in the king's presence, the leading courtiers – Damory, Audley, Montague and both Despensers – entered into bonds of loyalty to each other for the extraordinary amount of £6,000. During the same period, Edward also entered into indentures with a number of magnates, including the earl of Hereford, Badlesmere, John Giffard and John de Cromwell, while in November 1317 the earl of Pembroke entered into a mutual bond with Badlesmere and Damory.

To a very large degree, the struggle was now between Lancaster and the barons, not the king and his barons. Moreover, Lancaster had made his isolated position even less tenable in September when he was almost certainly involved in the attack on Louis de Beaumont, bishop-elect of Durham. Louis was the brother of Henry de Beaumont, who had been a target for removal from court in the Ordinances. The election of Louis de Beaumont, with the queen's support, over the claims of Lancaster's own candidate seems to have been too great an affront for the earl to bear. So, Gilbert Middleton, a notorious northern knight, in collusion with the Scots, kidnapped the party in which the bishop-elect was travelling, and held them to ransom. But there was a serious miscalculation, even beyond collusion with the Scots, and that was the fact that Beaumont was accompanied by two cardinals who were to attend his consecration and were also attempting to reconcile Lancaster with the king. The pettiness and lack of calculation evident in Lancaster's actions in 1317 was further illustrated not only by his occupation of various estates belonging to Earl Warenne, but even more so by the seizure of the royal castle at Knaresborough from Damory by Lancaster's retainer, Sir John Lilburn, in October. This led to a siege by a coalition of northern magnates, not just courtiers, and, although the situation was finally resolved by negotiation rather than force, it was the rumour that the Scottish earl of Moray was coming to relieve the siege that led to these negotiations, further tarnishing Lancaster's reputation.

Attempts at reconciliation between the king and Lancaster were undertaken by various prelates in late 1317 and early 1318, leading to a meeting at Leicester in April 1318. Here, it became clear, once again, that enforcement of the Ordinances remained a precondition for any settlement with Lancaster, along with the removal of evil counsellors and the resumption of royal grants. By June, the king had largely agreed to these terms in principle, and his inner circle of favourites – the elder Despenser, Damory, Audley, Montague and John de Charlton – had undertaken not to impede or threaten Lancaster or his men in any way. A further meeting between the representatives of the king and those of Lancaster took place at Tutbury shortly thereafter. The king and earl finally met face-to-face on 7 August, exchanging the kiss of peace, and their reconciliation was soon thereafter embodied in the so-called Treaty of Leake. This was further elaborated in the parliament held at York in October, by which a standing council of prelates, earls and barons was formed to provide or deny assent to all actions taken outside parliament; and the York parliament once again reaffirmed the Ordinances.

This standing council has been seen as a revolutionary constitutional innovation, and it does appear to have functioned for the first year or two after its establishment, but in actual fact it seems to have strengthened the king rather than Lancaster, who was hardly represented by those who sat on this council. Furthermore, royal grants since 1310, while reviewed and in some cases modified, were generally approved by the council, and this cannot have suited Lancaster. The York parliament did, however, see the removal of some of the favourites from court. Montagu stepped down as steward of the king's household, while Damory and Audley seem to have left court of their own accord. The great irony, of course, is that in their place a new favourite was to emerge, the younger Hugh Despenser, who was confirmed as chamberlain of the king's household in this same parliament.

In 1319, Lancaster joined the king on campaign in Scotland for the first time in a decade, but this only undermined their relations rather than improving them. The crucial border fortress of Berwick had fallen to the Scots in April 1318, while the king and Lancaster squabbled over their differences through intermediaries. Its recovery was an urgent necessity, and Edward mounted the first serious offensive since Bannockburn, ultimately raising some 14,000 troops, including contingents from all the leading magnates. But the siege of Berwick, which began on 7 September, proved difficult. Meanwhile, the Scots ravaged the north of England, with Sir James Douglas threatening York and nearly capturing Queen Isabella. When Edward decided to maintain the siege of Berwick regardless, Lancaster, for reasons that may have had as much to do with his continuing antipathy to courtiers such as the younger Despenser and Roger Damory as with his concern for his own northern lands, unilaterally withdrew his own troops, forcing the king to follow suit and abandon the siege after just 10 days.

Although Edward certainly deserves his share of the blame, once again demonstrating the indecisiveness and the lack of an effective command structure that had been the case at Bannockburn, Lancaster was widely blamed for this failure. There were even rumours that he had been involved in treasonous communications with the Scots throughout the campaign, rumours made more credible by his almost certain collusion with the Scots in 1317. Lancaster once again withdrew from public life following Berwick, failing to attend parliaments in York and Westminster in 1320, while becoming increasingly critical of the king's favourites, particularly the Despensers.

At the York parliament of January 1320, it was decided that Edward should travel to France in order to perform homage to Philip V for Aquitaine. This trip did not actually take place until 19 June when the king was accompanied to

Amiens by Queen Isabella and a considerable number of prelates and magnates, as well as favourites, such as the younger Despenser and Damory. In the meantime, another delegation, led by the elder Despenser, Badlesmere, and the king's half brother, the earl of Norfolk, was sent to the pope at Avignon. They succeeded in convincing him to release Edward from his oath to uphold the Ordinances, marking a victory over Thomas of Lancaster. Although the Westminster parliament of October 1320 was notable for its moderation – the king even called for the continued enforcement of the Ordinances – it was a short-lived episode. Tensions in the kingdom would soon run high again, this time as a result of the inordinate advancement of the Despensers.

If the early years of Edward II's reign were dominated by the influence of Piers Gaveston, then the final years were shaped by the two Hugh Despensers, father and son. Hugh Despenser the elder was the son of Hugh le Despenser who had died fighting on the side of Simon de Montfort at Evesham, but he himself proved to be a dedicated royal servant throughout his long and successful life. In the reign of Edward I, he served as a soldier in the king's many wars both in Britain and on the Continent, and also served on a variety of diplomatic missions. By 1297, he had been appointed a royal councillor. It is clear from Prince Edward's letters of 1304–1305 that Despenser had already become a trusted adviser to the prince; nor was Edward II's faith in him misplaced. During the crisis of 1308, he was entrusted with several strategic castles. In the subsequent attacks on Piers Gaveston, he stood virtually alone in defending the favourite. Consequently, he was one of the courtiers singled out at the Northampton parliament for dismissal from the council. During Lancaster's ascendancy following Bannockburn, Despenser, who had been present at the disastrous battle, was seldom (if ever) found at court. In the spring of 1316, however, he again became prominent at court and in the royal council, this time alongside his eldest son, the younger Hugh.

The younger Despenser had been knighted by the prince in 1306. In the same year, Edward I had arranged for him to wed Eleanor de Clare, eldest daughter of the earl of Gloucester, and the king's own granddaughter. His prospects were greatly enhanced by the death of his brother-in-law at Bannockburn, although a settlement of the Clare estate was not reached until November 1317, at which time Eleanor Despenser received her share of the Gloucester estates along with her sisters Margaret, Piers Gaveston's widow now remarried to Hugh Audley the younger, and Elizabeth, wife of Roger Damory. Surprisingly, perhaps, the younger Despenser figures little in the royal records until February 1319, at which point he and the king become virtually inseparable until July 1321. Despenser's increased proximity to the king can be attributed to his appointment as chamberlain of the king's household in October 1318, but proximity alone does not account for the violent response to his growing ascendancy. His acquisitiveness, more pronounced than Gaveston's had been, soon led to war. His greed became increasingly apparent after the partitioning of the Gloucester inheritance, as he sought to absorb large portions of the lands assigned to his coheirs. Through his ambition, he created an unusually broad opposition comprised not only of the king's most vocal detractor, the earl of Lancaster, but also the marcher lords led by the earl of Hereford, who resented Despenser's intrusion into the west midlands, and even the other courtiers of Edward II who saw themselves being undermined and isolated.

The younger Despenser's interference in the disputed inheritance of William de Braose's lordship of Gower late in 1320 proved to be the spark that ignited this latest conflagration. Negotiations to end the impasse had failed when Edward, cynically, refused to remove Despenser from his presence on the grounds that he had been appointed chamberlain in parliament, and that to do so would therefore be a violation not only of the Ordinances but of the Magna Carta and the common law as a whole. Left with no alternative, on 4 May 1321, the marchers launched a devastating attack on the Despenser lands, initially in Wales but later in the south and the midlands as well. In the months that followed, the earl of Lancaster set about building a coalition of northerners and marchers with which to oppose the king and his newest favourites, largely on the same lines as he had articulated for the past decade. At parliament in August, the king was faced by a sizeable opposition, and was counselled by the trusted earls of Pembroke and Richmond, by the queen, and by the prelates to send the Despensers away. He may even have been threatened with deposition in the event of his refusal to hear the charges against the Despensers. On 14 August, reluctantly, Edward II agreed in parliament to the exile of his favourites.

Although the king had acquiesced to baronial demands, his insincerity was soon apparent. While the elder Despenser spent his exile in Bordeaux, the younger Hugh took to piracy in the Channel off Sandwich. But if his piratical career was scandalous, it seems not to have bothered the king, who met with his favourite at Harwich before the end of September. An opportunity for revenge, and with it the recall of the Despensers, soon presented itself on 13 October when Queen Isabella was denied entry into Leeds Castle in Kent by the wife of its lord, Bartholomew Badlesmere. Formerly steward of the king's household and an associate of the younger Despenser, by 1321 Badlesmere had gone over to the marchers' side, although his position was complicated by his personal antipathy towards the earl of Lancaster. In any case, with the support of the earls of Pembroke, Richmond and Norfolk, the king quickly launched a siege of Leeds, which in the absence of relief from either the marchers or Lancaster, succeeded by 31 October. The garrison, including its commander Sir Walter Culpeper, was executed on the spot. Based on the consent of convocation rather than parliament, on 8 December the king recalled the Despensers from exile.

Refusing to negotiate or hold parliament, in late 1321 and early 1322, Edward II launched the most effective military campaign of his reign. By swift movement and the use of Welsh allies, he quickly routed the marchers, receiving the surrender of the Mortimers in late January and that of the Berkeleys in early February. He then turned his attention to the north and the greatest enemy of all, Thomas of Lancaster. Although the king was concerned about the small size of his army, and attempted to raise troops from Gascony and even from his brother-in-law, the king of France, in the end he had sufficient means to end the war. He was aided by the desertion of one of Lancaster's most trusted retainers, Sir Robert Holand. As Lancaster's army retreated north toward his great fortress at Dunstanburgh, it was trapped and defeated on 16 March at Boroughbridge by a Cumberland levy led by Andrew de Harcla. The earl of Hereford was killed in the battle and Lancaster himself taken prisoner. Six days later, Lancaster, the most powerful magnate in England, was condemned on the king's record for having 'in his land ridden with banner displayed against his peace as a traitor'. He was not allowed to speak in his own defence, and as a traitor he was sentenced to be drawn, hanged and beheaded. Out of respect for his royal blood, he was spared all but the beheading.

In the years to come, his shrine at Pontefract was to become a site of popular pilgrimage and a cult developed to 'St Thomas' of Lancaster, although he was never canonized by the Church. With him died all meaningful resistance to the Despenser regime that now directed the affairs of the king. Edward II quickly followed up his greatest victory by having the Ordinances repealed in parliament by the Statute of York in 1322. Indeed, not only were they repealed, it was decreed that never again was the royal power to be so constrained. The Statute of York has been the subject of much debate, particularly with regard to its language concerning the role of parliament. In the context of the Ordinances of 1311, however, the Statute of York was clearly an effort to reset the political clock to reflect the *status quo ante* 1310.

Whether or not England had lost a saint at Boroughbridge, the queen in particular had lost a counterweight to the influence of the Despensers in the king's council. The return of the Despensers to power threatened her position as it had not been since Gaveston's ascendancy. On 10 May 1322, the elder Despenser was elevated to the peerage as earl of Winchester, and the following few years saw an orgy of revenge against those who had opposed the favourites, coupled with unprecedented aggrandizement of the Despenser family. The period between 1322 and 1326 saw the Despensers' wealth, power and influence reach their zenith. The younger Despenser, in particular, used a combination of royal favour, legal manipulation and outright force to consolidate his holdings in Wales and the marches, so that by the time of his death his lands were valued at no less than £7,000. The enduring monuments to his lavish expenditures at Caerphilly Castle and Tewkesbury Abbey attest to his exalted stature during these years. Queen Isabella was treated poorly. In 1324, she was humiliated by the confiscation of her lands and the exile of 27 French members of her household, while at the same time Eleanor de Clare, the younger Despenser's wife, was placed into her household as a minder. There were even rumours that Despenser was attempting to have the king's marriage annulled in Avignon.

In 1323, a war broke out between the English and the French over the building of a bastide at Saint-Sardos in the disputed region of the Agenais. The War of Saint-Sardos in 1323–1325 was only a minor military affair, but for Edward II and the Despensers it proved to have major consequences. The king's inability or unwillingness to leave the country prevented a negotiated settlement to this conflict, so in March 1325 he sent his wife Isabella, sister of Charles IV, as his mediator. The settlement arranged by the queen called for Edward II to fulfil his obligation to perform homage to Charles IV for his English lands in France, but Edward was subsequently allowed to send his heir in his place. However, neither the queen nor the prince returned to England following Edward's performance of homage *in absentia*.

In France, Isabella had found considerable support for her opposition to the Despensers from a number of political exiles, including Roger Mortimer of Wigmore. After the defeat of the marchers and Lancaster in 1322, Mortimer had been among the many opponents of the Despenser regime, the so-called Contrariants, imprisoned in the Tower of London. Apparently with the assistance of his custodian, Gerard de Alspaye, he had escaped in dramatic fashion on 1 August 1323 by drugging the Constable of the Tower, Stephen de Seagrave. Once he had reached the safety of Paris, he quickly became the focal point of discontent, and before the year was out he was rumoured to be behind a plot to murder the king and his favourites. By the autumn of 1325, Queen Isabella had certainly become associated with Mortimer and his party, although whether or not she had yet become his lover is unclear. In any case, in November 1325, Walter Stapeldon, bishop of Exeter and one of the prince's guardians, returned to England in haste and secrecy, allegedly in fear for his life at the hands of Mortimer and the queen. It can have come as no surprise to the king in January 1326 when Isabella wrote that she would not return until the Despensers had been removed from the court.

By the summer of the following year, it was clear that the queen would lead an invasion of England. In order to buy support, she had arranged the marriage of her son Edward to Philippa, the daughter of count William of Hainault. With support from the count and also from her cousin Philip of Valois, himself the heir to the childless Charles IV of France, she raised a small fleet of ships in the Dutch port of Dordrecht, sailing on 23 September 1326. Despite elaborate preparations for the defence of the realm on the king's behalf, the queen's landing at Orwell in Suffolk on the following day was virtually unopposed. Within 10 days, the king and the younger Despenser had abandoned London and headed west, towards Despenser's lands and the Welsh allies who had served Edward so well in 1321-1322. The queen pursued them, and Bristol fell to Isabella on 26 October, when king and favourite were at Cardiff, and the elder Despenser was forced to surrender. He was tried in a court of chivalry before William Trussell on the following day, and denounced and sentenced to death under martial law. He was condemned to be drawn for treason, hanged for robbery and decapitated for his crimes against the church, his head to be taken to Winchester, where he had been earl 'against law and reason'.

Meanwhile, the king and the younger Despenser had attempted to sail from Bristol to safety, perhaps in Ireland, but were blown ashore at Cardiff by contrary winds. They then travelled to the favourite's stronghold at Caerphilly, which was afterwards left in charge of Despenser's eldest son, another Hugh. The king and Despenser continued on their westward flight, perhaps still hoping to raise troops in Wales or to take refuge in Ireland and there to regroup. Whatever their plans, on 16 November they were taken prisoner near Neath. Separated from the king, Despenser was transported to Hereford. Outside the city, he was degraded and humiliated by being stripped and redressed with his coat of arms reversed and being crowned with nettles. Having been condemned as a traitor, he was drawn and then hanged from a scaffold raised to a height of 50 feet. Still alive, he was cut down and eviscerated before finally being beheaded. His head was displayed on London Bridge, while his quartered remains were sent to Bristol, Dover, York and Newcastle. The king, meanwhile, was taken to Monmouth by his captor, Henry of Leicester, brother of the late earl of Lancaster. On 20 November, he was made to surrender the great seal. From Leicester's castle of Monmouth, Edward was moved to the royal castle of Kenilworth for greater security; from there, he would observe the final unravelling of his reign.

Until recently, there has been disagreement and indeed confusion with regard to the question of Edward II's removal from the throne. It is now clear, however, that Edward II was in fact deposed, although he was subsequently induced to abdicate in his son's favour. It is also clear that the regime of Mortimer and Isabella subsequently revised historical accounts of these events in order to promote the belief that Edward II had abdicated willingly, making deposition unnecessary. In early January 1327, the king refused to attend the parliament that had been summoned to Westminster in his name, thereby rendering it invalid, in theory, if not in practice. On 12 January, a consensus seems to have been reached to depose the king; these plans were put into motion on the following day. An oath of loyalty to the young king was taken at the Guildhall in the morning, and the deposition was agreed to in parliament in the afternoon. A series of addresses, beginning with a speech by Roger Mortimer and concluding with a sermon on the text 'the voice of the people is the voice of God' by Walter Reynolds, archbishop of Canterbury, culminated in the election and acclamation of Edward III as king. A deputation was subsequently sent to Edward II at Kenilworth, probably on 20 or 21 January, to inform him of his deposition and formally to withdraw fealty from him. The king was presented with a stark choice between acquiescence in his deposition and the continuation of the family line through the elevation of his son, or a forced deposition after which the community of the realm would seek its own successor to wear the crown. Edward therefore assented to his own deposition, following which William Trussell withdrew his own homage and that of those whom he represented by proxy. Thomas Blunt, steward of the king's household, is reputed thereupon to have broken his staff of office, releasing all of the king's servants from their offices. Ten days later, on 1 February 1327, Edward III was crowned.

A deposed king posed certain fundamental problems for any subsequent regime, so it comes as no surprise that Edward II should soon have disappeared from sight. By the autumn of 1327, he was almost certainly dead. His death, on 21 September 1327, was announced as a fact at the Lincoln parliament, which was meeting at that time. There is, however, a highly romantic account of Edward II's death, in which the beleaguered king escaped from his captors in Berkeley Castle, and thereafter embarked on a long and circuitous flight. The fugitive king makes his way from Corfe Castle to Cologne, by way of Avignon – where he gained an audience with the pope – and Paris, and ultimately to northern Italy, where he died, years later, in a hermitage in the diocese of Pavia. This account is supported by a fourteenth-century transcript of a letter written to Edward III by the papal notary Manuel de Fieschi. But while the letter itself may be authentic, historians from William Stubbs to the present, have found it difficult to give much credence to the fantastic claims it makes.

Against this, there is also an incredibly gruesome, and much better known, account of Edward II's death, recounted a generation later by the chronicler Geoffrey le Baker. In this version of events, the king was murdered in Berkeley Castle on the night of 21 September 1327 by having a red-hot plumber's iron inserted into his rectum, thus to mask the foul play inherent in murder, and just possibly to symbolize the late king's homosexual proclivities. Whatever may have happened, the unfortunate, and now superfluous king, disappeared from sight sometime in 1327. He is commemorated – whether or not his remains actually reside within – in the magnificent tomb in Gloucester Cathedral, where his purported remains were interred on 20 December 1327. He is the only Plantagenet king of the thirteenth and fourteenth centuries not buried in Westminster Abbey and, in some sense, this physical absence may symbolize the reign of Edward II as the nadir of the dynasty.

4

Edward III (1327–1377)

The birth of the future Edward III at Windsor on 12 November 1312 was greeted with great joy not only by the royal family, but also by the citizens of London and the kingdom as a whole. Edward II apparently took consolation in the birth of his first son in the aftermath of the recent violent death of his favourite, Piers Gaveston. He awarded the queen's yeoman John Launge an extravagant annuity of £80 for bringing him the news of the birth. Isabella, attended by her father's own surgeon, Henri de Mondeville, expressed her own joy in a letter to the citizens of London. She hoped, with her French relatives, that the child might be named Philip after her father, but the king insisted that his son and heir be named Edward after his own father. The infant Edward was baptized just 4 days later, at Windsor, with the queen's uncle Louis of Evreux standing as godfather, along with John of Brittany, earl of Richmond, and several other bishops and nobles.

A week later, Edward was granted the counties of Chester and Flint, although he was not named prince of Wales or earl of Cornwall, the latter contentious title being so closely associated with Edward II and Gaveston. In any case, he was soon established in his own household, more often than not separated from both his parents. The tradition that he was tutored by the great bibliophile Richard Bury has been challenged, but Bury was certainly a member of his household and later one of his closest advisors. Another figure associated with the prince's education was John Paynel, a parson from Cheshire who may have instructed Edward in reading and writing; he is the first English king known to have been able to write. Edward was comfortable in English and French, had some knowledge of Latin, and probably picked up Flemish and German during his expeditions on the continent. Based on his later interests, however, despite his linguistic facility, the prince probably received more training in the knightly than the scholarly arts. There is no evidence that he ever read either of the two handbooks on kingship written for him: William of Pagula's *Mirror of Edward III* and Walter of Milemete's *On the Nobility, Wisdom, and Prudence of Kings*. Edward appears much more likely to have developed his views on kingship from his own experience.

Between 1318 and 1320, the prince shared his household with his younger siblings, John of Eltham (born in August 1316) and Eleanor of Woodstock (born in July 1318). His steward at this time was Richard Damory, brother of the king's favourite, Roger Damory. In October 1320, Edward made his first appearance at parliament, at which time his household was established at the Savoy Palace in close proximity to the king. Although he may have understood little of the political upheaval surrounding the Despensers over the next few years, he must have been aware of the fact that friends such as Damory ended up in opposition to the king, and that the lives of many nobles, including his uncle Thomas of Lancaster, were lost in this conflict. A few years later, at 12 years of age, Edward was thrown into the maelstrom of politics swirling about England and France and, as it turned out, between his father and mother. In 1325, he was given the titles of duke of Aquitaine and count of Ponthieu so that he could perform homage to his uncle Charles IV in his father's stead. He was duly dispatched to France to join his mother, who had negotiated this settlement with her brother Charles while settling the dispute over the territory of the Agenais that had led to the recent War of Saint-Sardos. Edward performed the required homage at Vincennes on 24 September 1325, but neither the prince nor his mother returned home following this ceremony as expected. Instead, Isabella denounced the younger Hugh Despenser before the French royal court and refused to return to England until this 'Pharisee' had been removed from her husband's side. At the same time, she began a scandalous liaison with Roger Mortimer, a convicted traitor who had escaped from the Tower in dramatic fashion and fled to France in August 1323.

Edward II wrote to his son on three occasions between December 1325 and June 1326, insisting with increasing severity each time that the prince return to England. By March 1326, the king was genuinely alarmed at the prospect that he might marry without his consent. His final letter in June allowed no room for any further excuses on the prince's part for his failure to return, and can only be described as an ultimatum. It concludes:

> Understand certainly, that if you act now contrary to our counsel, and continue in willful disobedience, you will feel it all the days of your life, and you will be made an example to all other sons who are disobedient to their lords and fathers.[1]

Yet Prince Edward had no real freedom and was in no position to act of his own accord in this matter. He soon found himself accompanying his mother and

Mortimer to Hainault, where he was duly betrothed to Count William's second daughter, Philippa. On 22 September, Edward finally began the journey home, setting sail from Dordrecht, not for a joyful reunion with his aggrieved father, but rather as a member of an armed force consisting primarily of Hainaulter mercenaries purchased with his troth.

The little fleet of Isabella and Mortimer landed on the Norfolk coast and quickly gathered nearly universal support. The king's own brother Edmund, earl of Kent, had aligned himself with Isabella and Mortimer in Paris, and now Edward II's other brother, Thomas, earl of Norfolk, likewise joined the rebels. The king and the Despensers fled westward in the hope of regrouping and making a stand, but all to no avail. The elder Despenser was executed on 26 October, while the king and the younger Despenser were finally apprehended near Neath on 16 November. Contrary winds had conspired to return them as they attempted to sail on to safety in Ireland from Chepstow. The younger Despenser was brutally executed at Hereford, while Edward II was taken off to captivity at Kenilworth Castle.

With the Great Seal of England now in their possession, Isabella and Mortimer were able to rule the kingdom through young Edward, who was cast in the role of regent. Political opinion, particularly in London, was manipulated in favour of the deposition of Edward II, through sermons such as that delivered by Bishop Orleton of Hereford on the text, 'Where there is no ruler the people falls'. Nevertheless, on 13 January 1327, Prince Edward, along with the archbishop of York, William Melton, and several other prelates, refused to acquiesce in this, insisting that Edward II must abdicate before Edward III could ascend the throne. This was achieved a week later at Kenilworth Castle, where the captive king tearfully renounced his throne in favour of his son before a large delegation, including the bishops of Winchester and Hereford, as well as the earls of Lancaster and Surrey.

The coronation of Edward III took place on 1 February and, despite the seeming haste with which the ceremony was arranged, it followed the traditional order. Having been knighted by Henry, earl of Lancaster, Edward was crowned by Archbishop Reynolds, swearing the same four oaths as his father had done in 1308. It is interesting that, at the coronation, the tomb of Edward I alone was decorated with cloth of gold, suggesting the lifelong affinity that Edward III would feel for his grandfather. The parliament that followed the coronation 2 days later was dominated by the earl of Lancaster, while the other great power, Roger Mortimer, chose to work behind the scenes. The rebels were pardoned for any offence committed in effecting the recent regime change; Henry's late brother, Thomas of Lancaster, was posthumously pardoned and his estates settled on Henry; and a regency council was established to advise the king during his minority. This council, to be presided over by Lancaster, included Mortimer, as well as four bishops, three other earls and five other barons.

Despite the performance of homage by Edward III in 1325, relations between England and France remained strained in the aftermath of the War of Saint-Sardos. As a consequence, the young king's government sealed an agreement with Charles IV in March 1327 that allowed the French king to maintain control over lands seized in 1324 and also required the English to pay substantial reparations for damage done in previous years. Even more troubling was the situation in Scotland. The French had renewed their alliance with Scotland in the Treaty of Corbeil in 1326 and, perhaps emboldened thereby, on the very day of Edward III's coronation the Scots had launched a raid on Norham Castle. The ageing and ailing Robert Bruce sought formal recognition of his crown once and for all, and he continued to rachet up the pressure. In June 1327, a large Scottish army crossed into northern England, burning and pillaging at will. The young Edward III was eager to meet this challenge and demonstrate his martial qualities, while the regime of Isabella and Mortimer were pressurized by popular sentiment to stand up to the Scots.

Edward led a substantial force north as nominal commander, although Mortimer certainly retained the real authority for the expedition. The campaign got off to a very poor start indeed when Hainaulter mercenaries and English archers from Leicestershire brawled in the streets of York, resulting in the death of some 300 Englishmen if the chronicler Jean Le Bel is to be believed. The young king was able to settle the factions and lead them north, but the actual encounter with the Scots' forces proved equally as unhappy as this inauspicious beginning.

Edward's forces moved north from York towards Durham, with the goal of trapping the Scottish raiders south of the border and bringing them to battle. Having spent ten rain-soaked days huddled on the north bank of the Tyne without adequate food or shelter, on 30 July word of the Scots' position, well to the south near Stanhope Park on the Wear, finally reached the king. The English took up a position directly across the river from the Scots, but were unable to challenge their well-established defensive position. After several days of stalemate, during the night of 4 August 1327, Sir James Douglas led a daring raid into the English camp, inflicting heavy casualties while causing chaos and panic. He actually reached the king's own tent before being driven back. This raid forced the English to maintain their guard both day and night, yet on the morning of the 6 August they awoke to find that the Scots had once again vanished. They had stolen away silently during the night and raced back to the safety of Scotland before the English could respond. The young king, overwhelmed with frustration, wept at the humiliating conclusion to his first military campaign.

In the aftermath of the costly and ineffective Weardale campaign, the government of Isabella and Mortimer sought to make terms with the Bruce regime. Peace negotiations conducted in Edinburgh led to an agreement by March, which was ratified in the Northampton parliament in early May 1328. The Treaty of Northampton renounced all English claims to feudal overlordship in Scotland and recognized the legitimacy of the title of King Robert I. Furthermore, the legitimacy and priority of the Franco–Scottish alliance established by the Treaty of Corbeil was also affirmed. In return for renouncing his claim to Scotland, Edward's government was to receive £20,000 by way of war reparations. Finally, the treaty was to be sealed symbolically by the marriage of the infant David Bruce, son and heir of Robert I, to Joan, sister of Edward III. Although he could not prevent the treaty from being ratified, Edward could and did display his disdain for its terms by refusing to attend this wedding when it took place in July at Berwick. Inept as Edward II may have been as a military leader, even he had never made such a 'Shameful Peace', as the earl of Lancaster and many other contemporaries called it. Necessary as the treaty may have seemed to Isabella and Mortimer, confidence in their regime was irreparably damaged by this humiliating capitulation.

On 31 January 1328, the last Capetian king of France, Charles IV, died. His queen, Jeanne d'Evreux, was pregnant at the time, but subsequently gave birth to a daughter, Blanche, rather than the hoped-for son, bringing an end to more than 300 years of direct male succession. Charles' cousin Philip of Valois immediately claimed the throne, while Edward, who was himself the grandson of Philip IV, had little opportunity to prosecute his own claim to the French throne, concerned as his government was with problems closer to home. Beyond that, the Lanercost chronicle suggests that Edward III was actually prevented from acting by the 'pestilential advice of his mother and Sir Roger de Mortimer'.[2] It is possible that Isabella had entered into an understanding with her cousin Philip during her recent stay in France. It may not be inconsequential that Philip de Valois was the brother-in-law of Count William of Hainault, and this relationship may have influenced the course of events in 1326. In any case, for the time being, Edward did what little he could. The bishops of Worcester and of Coventry and Lichfield were sent to Paris to register Edward's claim to the throne. Philip of Valois was nonetheless crowned at Rheims on 29 May, and immediately demanded that Edward renew his homage for his French lands. After a year of delaying the inevitable, on 26 May 1329, Edward crossed from Dover and met Philip in Amiens, where he performed simple homage for Aquitaine and Ponthieu, implicitly recognizing Philip as king of France.

Edward married Philippa of Hainault in York Minster on 24 January 1328. Their marriage contract had been drawn up as early as August 1326, but as they were related in the third degree (Philippa was the granddaughter of Philip III of France, while Edward was his great-grandson), a papal dispensation was required. This was obtained in August 1327, and a proxy marriage ceremony to confirm the terms of Philippa's dowry was conducted in October. In December, she crossed to England, accompanied by Bartholomew Burgersh and William de Clinton on behalf of King Edward, along with Hainaulters such as Walter Mauny and Jean Bernier, reaching London on 22 December. Interestingly, Philippa was not crowned as queen at the time of her wedding, very likely because the dowager queen, Isabella, was reluctant to share the stage with her son's consort. In the end, her coronation in February 1330 was most likely occasioned by the fact that Philippa was pregnant with her first child (Edward, the Black Prince), who would be born in June of that year, and it was important that she be recognized as queen prior to the birth.

Edward and Philippa appear to have had a genuinely happy relationship. Although it is not clear that there is any foundation to the tradition found in Froissart that Edward himself selected Philippa in preference to her elder sister Margaret (by now married to Ludwig of Bavaria, in any case), the king and queen were probably within a year of each other in age and seem to have been well suited. Not only did the queen produce the requisite son and heir (she ultimately gave birth to seven sons and five daughters, nine of whom survived childhood), she created a warm atmosphere at the royal court that embraced not only her many children, but also the Hainaulters in and about her household as well as members of the English aristocracy. The factional disputes of earlier reigns were almost entirely absent, a tribute to both the king and queen.

Beyond motherhood, Philippa also effectively played the other traditional queenly role of intercessor. As early as 1328 in York, she obtained a pardon for a young girl convicted of theft, and women would often be the objects of her intercession. She is most famous, however, for two more public occasions in which she placated the king's wrath. In 1331, the stands from which Philippa was viewing a tournament in Cheapside collapsed, and the king was determined to extract a heavy penalty from the carpenters who were responsible for risking his queen's life and limbs. She convinced him to pardon them. Even more famously, in 1347, it was Philippa, heavily pregnant at the time, who convinced Edward to spare the burgesses of Calais, whom Edward was determined to execute in recompense for the length and difficulty of his siege of the town.

The fact that Philippa was present in Calais in 1347 is itself noteworthy, in part because it was not unusual for her. Throughout the reign, Edward and Philippa spent far more time together than was typical of royal couples in this period. She repeatedly accompanied her husband on expeditions to both Scotland and the Low Countries. Indeed, she gave birth to their son Lionel in Antwerp in 1338, and 2 years later to John of Gaunt in Ghent. She shared Edward's enthusiasm for tournaments and feasts, and also his passion for fine clothing and expensive jewels, both of which the king lavished upon her. Initially, though, Philippa may have played her most important role of all as the trusted confidante of her teenaged husband as he chafed against the constraints imposed upon him by his mother and Roger Mortimer.

Serious opposition to the Mortimer regime soon emerged. Claiming to fear for his own safety, Henry of Lancaster led a group of magnates in refusing to attend the Salisbury parliament in October 1328 at which Mortimer was elevated to the peerage as earl of March; Lancaster remained at a distance in Winchester. Terms for a safe-conduct could not be agreed, and the earl, supposedly the king's chief councillor, stayed away along with his supporters. Following the parliament, Lancaster's forces actually skirmished with those of the king – or perhaps, more accurately, Mortimer – outside Winchester, leading to anti-Lancastrian rhetoric from the court. Meanwhile, the king's uncles, the earls of Kent and Norfolk, along with several northern lords who had lost lands in Scotland by the terms of the Treaty of Northampton, joined Lancaster's revolt, but the king refused to hear Lancaster's grievances. In early 1329, Mortimer led raids against Lancaster's lands, compelling the earl to submit. In order to be restored to the king's grace, he was forced to agree to a crippling recognizance of £30,000 to ensure his future compliance, much as Llywelyn had been burdened by Edward I in 1277.

Another challenge to the Mortimer regime arose in the following year. The earl of Kent had returned to the royal fold after his flirtation with Lancaster, but dur-ing the course of 1329–1330, he became convinced that Edward II was still alive and began orchestrating efforts to free him. It is likely that Mortimer himself, no longer trusting his former ally, orchestrated the rumours that led Kent down this path, and it was certainly Mortimer who had Kent arrested, tried and convicted of treason before the Winchester parliament on 19 March 1330. Following the conviction, the earl was sentenced to death, but as no one could be found willing to carry out the sentence, Kent waited outside the walls of the castle throughout the day until, finally, a common criminal agreed to carry out the beheading in return for his own pardon. That Edward was powerless to stop this perversion of justice must surely have rankled. More than that, however, this was an assault on the royal blood, and must have given the king further pause to consider his own precarious position.

In the end, it fell to the king himself to launch the coup that would overthrow the earl of March in October 1330. Edward may have been prompted by a number of factors. Mortimer's lavish accumulation of lands and titles, coupled with his haughty behaviour, including his impertinent habit of walking before the king in public, must have been galling. His disregard for the royal family had been demonstrated repeatedly – in his openly adulterous affair with Isabella, his role in the deposition and death of Edward II, and in the execution of the earl of Kent. Another motivation must have been the birth of the king's son and heir, Edward, in June 1330. It is also possible that another pregnancy influenced his thinking as well. Circumstantial evidence exists to suggest that Isabella herself, still only in her mid-30s, may have been pregnant at some point in 1329–1330, perhaps miscarrying Mortimer's child. All of these factors pointed in the same direction: Roger Mortimer posed a mortal threat to Edward III and the Plantagenet dynasty.

Even before the execution of his uncle in March 1330, Edward's growing concerns were revealed in a remarkable letter to Pope John XXII in which Edward directed the pontiff to give credence only to future correspondence bearing the words 'pater sancte' (holy father) in the king's own hand as written on this letter. Only Richard Bury and William Montagu were privy to this secret arrangement, which points to the growing desperation of the king. It was Montagu who is reputed to have challenged Edward with the blunt advice that: 'It is better to eat dog than be eaten by the dog'.[3] Caution was needed, as Mortimer had planted his own spies in the king's council, including a certain John Wyard. Moreover, Mortimer seems to have sensed the king's increasing disaffection. In advance of a council meeting called for 15 October 1330, Mortimer and Isabella had taken up residence in the castle at Nottingham, and the queen mother took personal possession of the keys to the castle. Mortimer took council with his own inner circle, including Henry Burgersh, Hugh Turplington and Simon Bereford, while he also ordered the interrogation of Edward's closest associates – William Montagu, Edward Bohun, Ralph Stafford, Robert de Ufford, William de Clinton and John Neville de Hornby. Having proclaimed their innocence, the conspirators were allowed to leave the castle and return to their lodgings in the town. On the night of 19 October, however, William Eland, described in Geoffrey le Baker's chronicle as 'speculator of the castle', opened a subterranean passage that led under the castle walls and into the keep itself. Led by Montagu, who had apparently suborned Eland, the conspirators made their way to the queen's chamber, where a brief but sharp struggle ensued. Hugh de Turplington was killed by John Neville, along with an usher and squire. Roger Mortimer was taken alive and unharmed, along with his crony Oliver de Ingham, seneschal of Aquitaine. Burghersh, too, was captured, having failed to execute a dramatic flight, attempting to make his way out of the castle through the privy, in which he became lodged. Isabella is famously recorded as begging Edward, 'good son, have pity on gentle Mortimer', but of pity there was none.

The six conspirators who had been interrogated by Mortimer were assisted by several others, including John Molyns, William Latimer, Maurice de Berkeley, Robert Wyville, later bishop of Salisbury (and a favourite clerk of Isabella) and, most interestingly of all, Pancio da Controne, the royal physician. It has been suggested that da Controne provided Edward with a potion that made him appear ill and thereby allowed him to slip away from his mother and her lover at the crucial time. It may also be the case that Henry of Lancaster was aware of the plot, although he cannot have been directly involved. He was, by now, almost completely blind, and he had been forced by Mortimer to take lodgings in the town rather than the castle. Still, he would have taken pleasure in Mortimer's fall. Edward was to show great generosity to his fellow conspirators, many of whom would continue to play major roles throughout the reign. It is significant, however, that no great nobles (with the possible, limited, exception of Lancaster) played a role in the coup to overthrow Mortimer. Edward was wise enough not to exchange one minder for another, and he had taken power by himself in such a way that he was not beholden to any individual or faction. He would set to work at once to bind the aristocracy to him through the creation of a court that exemplified the chivalric virtues of the age.

Rather than hanging Mortimer immediately, as he apparently wished to do, Edward followed the advice of the earl of Lancaster and summoned a parliament to assemble at Westminster on 26 November. There, Mortimer was accused of having ignored the council of bishops, earls and prelates; of usurping royal power;

of murdering Edward II and contriving the execution of the earl of Kent; and a variety of lesser charges. On 29 November, he was executed as a traitor after being dragged from the Tower to Tyburn. Along with the condemnation of Mortimer, this parliament is also noteworthy for the rehabilitation of the victims of the minority regime and even those of the reign of Edward II. Henry of Lancaster was pardoned for having taken up arms against the king in 1328, while Edmund, son of the late earl of Kent, was restored to his father's earldom. Richard Fitzalan, son of the late earl of Arundel, who had been executed as a supporter of the Despensers in 1326, was likewise restored. Even Hugh Despenser, son of the younger Despenser, was pardoned and allowed to collect the quartered remains of his father for interment in the family mausoleum at Tewkesbury Abbey. Although 'gentle Mortimer' suffered a traitor's death, Isabella was quietly removed from prominence, but well provided for. She continued to receive visits from her son, and even as late as the year of her death in 1358, she appears to have been playing an unofficial, but perhaps significant, role in Anglo–French diplomacy.

Edward had already been hard at work to win the hearts of the aristocracy in the spring and summer of 1330, when he had participated in tournaments with them at Dartford, Stepney and Cheapside. A further expression of their sense of solidarity with him came at the parliament of September 1331, where they promised not to protect criminals from prosecution, but rather to aid the sheriffs and other royal agents in seeing that justice was done. Likewise, they would not infringe upon the king's right to purveyance by themselves seizing the crops of their peasants.

Still, even out from under the shadow of Roger Mortimer, Edward III faced enormous challenges. Philip VI had consolidated his position on the French throne, and he was dissatisfied with the simple homage performed in 1329. He demanded that Edward return to France and perform liege homage for Aquitaine and his other holdings. Ultimately, in April 1331, travelling in the garb of a merchant, Edward had made a secret trip to France and acknowledged, at Pont-Sainte-Maxence, that the 1329 homage should be taken as liege. Nevertheless, in September 1331, the chancellor, John Stratford, asked the same Westminster parliament that had agreed to support the king in restoring justice throughout the land whether the continuing dispute over the Agenais should be settled by recourse to war or to diplomacy. The king almost certainly favoured war, but parliament, despite their expressions of good will towards the king on other matters, counselled a course of negotiation.

Scotland, too, posed problems for Edward III. Among other things, the treaty of

Northampton had called for the restoration of Scottish lands to several northern English lords, including Henry Percy, Henry de Beaumont, David de Strathbogie, Gilbert de Umfraville and Thomas Wake. No progress had been made in restoring these estates by the time of Mortimer's overthrow, and 'the disinherited' decided to take matters into their own hands. Henry de Beaumont arranged for the return of Edward Balliol, son and heir of John Balliol, from his ancestral estates in France, seeking to challenge the right of David II to the Scottish throne. Circumstances favoured the English cause in 1332. Robert Bruce had died in June 1329, but his son and heir, David II, was still a mere boy of 8 years old. Moreover, that great soldier Sir James Douglas had died in Spain in 1330, while in July 1332, Thomas Randolph, earl of Moray, also died, robbing the Scots of their most experienced commanders. The presence of Edward Balliol – who almost certainly performed homage to Edward III for Scotland prior to the expedition – added legitimacy to the undertaking. Edward III was subtle in his support for the disinherited. Whatever negotiations were undertaken with Balliol were kept secret, and the English king was careful not to condone this venture publicly, which would have violated his oath to uphold the treaty of Northampton. He forbade the invasion being launched from England, but may have been complicit in providing shipping to transport Balliol's army from Ravenser to Kinghorn; certainly, he did make a substantial gift of £500 to Beaumont as compensation for unspecified past losses. Walter Mauny's participation in the expedition is a further indication of Edward's tacit approval.

After landing at Kinghorn, the small English force (perhaps 1,500 men in total) moved west to Dunfermline and then north towards Perth, but they were soon surrounded by two powerful Scottish armies. The Scottish chronicler Wyntoun reports that the Scots were so sure of victory that they sent to Perth for ale and wine, and passed the night of 10 August in song and dance. After fording the River Earn under cover of darkness, the English routed a small camp of Scots sleeping on Dupplin Moor. However, this merely raised the alarm, and they soon faced an army under the earl of Mar that likely outnumbered them by ten to one. The English formed into a very thin defensive line flanked by archers and backed by a cavalry reserve of only 40 horses. A dispute between the earl of Mar and Lord Robert Bruce (illegitimate son of the late king) over priority, reminiscent of the English quarrels prior to Bannockburn, led to a hastily launched and poorly organized attack. The English archers proved decisive in stopping the charge of the earl of Mar's schiltron, and the second unit under Bruce merely crushed their own compatriots under foot. Both the earl of Mar and Robert Bruce were killed in the mêlée, as were also the earls of Moray and Menteith, along with numerous knights and squires. The earl of Fife survived, only to be captured in fleeing the field. The total Scottish casualties ran as high as perhaps 3,000 dead. The English lost 2 knights, 33 esquires, and not a single archer or foot soldier (or at least none was recorded by the chroniclers). In the aftermath of the battle of Dupplin Moor, Perth surrendered without further resistance.

The earl of Dunbar appeared before Perth with a second Scottish army a week later, but he could not realistically besiege the city, especially when the English fleet prevented a Scottish naval force from completing the encirclement of the city. Soon, Scottish leaders, both lay and ecclesiastical, came to Perth to offer their homage and fealty to Balliol (the bishop of St Andrews being a notable exception). On 24 September 1332, the bishop of Dunkeld crowned Balliol as Edward, king of Scots, at Scone, in a well-attended ceremony. The disinherited were restored: Beaumont become earl of Buchan, Strathbogie earl of Atholl, and Umfraville earl of Angus, while other English lords received grants of land both old and new.

Edward III was anxious to capitalize on Balliol's success. At the York parliament in December 1332, he sought advice; parliament, however, demurred, citing their small numbers, and the session was prorogued until January. Meanwhile, on 16 December, Balliol was surprised at Annan in Galloway by a lightning raid led by the redoubtable Archibald Douglas. Many of Balliol's followers were killed in their beds, while the titular king himself escaped only by breaking through a wall in his bedchamber and was forced to flee southward to Carlisle in total disarray. Although the January parliament advised Edward III to seek counsel from the pope and the king of France, the English king decided to back Balliol. The level of his commitment is clear from his order of 20 February 1333 to move the various administrative offices north to York. Balliol, meanwhile, renewed his homage and other commitments to Edward III and began to recruit an army from a broader community beyond the disinherited, including nobles such as Henry of Grosmont, son and heir of the earl of Lancaster, Ralph Neville, William Montagu and the earl of Arundel.

In March 1333, Edward Balliol invaded Scotland for a second time, marching north from Carlisle and then east to Berwick, which he placed under siege. The Scots responded by raiding into Cumberland and Northumberland in an effort to draw the besiegers away, but to no avail. The Scottish raids afforded Edward III an opportunity to write to Philip VI, portraying the Scots as guilty of breaking the terms of the treaty of Northampton. The raids also, finally, convinced parliament that Edward should assist Balliol. He wasted little time in raising an army and, by 9 May, he had reached Tweedmouth. As the English siege proceeded, Archibald Douglas grew desperate to relieve the town. Appearing before Berwick on 11 July, the day the town had agreed to surrender if not relieved, he also sent another force to threaten Bamburgh, where Queen Philippa was currently resident, but this failed to draw the English away. The Scots launched an assault on one of the gates and a handful of Scots troopers did gain entry into Berwick, but the English argued that this did not fulfill the previously agreed terms of relief. Therefore, a second date of 20 July was set, with very specific criteria being agreed to by both sides as to what would constitute relief, and the siege continued.

On 19 July, a Scottish force of perhaps 15,000 arrived at Tweedmouth, a force that was certainly larger than the combined strength of Edward III and Edward Balliol, perhaps half again as large. The battle began at noon, when the first Scottish schiltron advanced up the slope towards the English position on Halidon Hill. The combination of English archers and men-at-arms proved too much, however, and the Scottish formations quickly broke. A pursuit was maintained to a distance of 8 miles, producing more casualties that the battle itself. The steward, Archibald Douglas, was killed, as were the earls of Atholl, Carrick, Lenox, Ross and Sutherland. Balliol quickly overran the country, and Edward III returned to England from his second Scottish campaign, flushed with victory. He was hailed as a second Arthur. Bannockburn had, at last, been avenged and the north was finally secure. Or so it appeared.

In February 1334, Balliol transferred the whole of Lothian to the king of England and, in June, he performed liege homage to Edward III at Newcastle for the throne of Scotland. Despite this, or perhaps because of it, Edward Balliol's grip on the Scottish throne remained tenuous and he faced mounting resistance from supporters of the Bruce kings. Although David II was sent to France for the sake of safety, and set up a court in exile at Richard the Lionheart's Chateau Gaillard, his cause was steadfastly maintained by John Randolph, earl of Moray, and Robert Stewart. By September 1334, Balliol had fled south to Berwick, and once again implored the English king to secure his kingdom for him. A projected winter campaign in 1334–1335 got no farther than Roxburgh castle, which Edward III set about rebuilding, but, in July 1335, the king led a massive army of 13,500 men on a two-pronged attack that ranged north into Scotland from Carlisle and Berwick as far as Perth, meeting nothing more than token resistance. By August, virtually all of the Bruce supporters had come to terms with the two Edwards, including the earl of Moray, who had been captured, and Robert Stewart, who had negotiated a surrender. On 22 August, Edward III wrote to Philip VI, telling him that the war in Scotland was at an end and that peace had been restored.

In January 1335, negotiators agreed to a draft settlement, by which Edward Balliol would adopt David Bruce as his heir, and the 12-year-old David would be raised at the court of Edward III. When he succeeded Balliol to the Scottish throne, David would hold the kingdom from Edward III on the same terms as Balliol had. Not surprisingly, perhaps, these terms proved unacceptable to David and his advisors, who rejected them out of hand. At the same time, David's ally, Philip VI, was preparing a fleet to launch an invasion to restore the Bruce king to his rightful throne. When the truce expired in May 1336, therefore, hostilities immediately recommenced, with Henry of Lancaster leading one force in the highlands and Edward Balliol another in the lowlands. Edward III himself marched north to Perth with a very small escort, with the strategic objective of preventing a French invasion. From Perth, he launched a *chevauchée* to lift the siege of Lochindorb Castle and rescue thereby the countess of Atholl, Catherine de Beaumont. This has generally been seen as a piece of romantic chivalry on the king's part, but Edward did manage to project English power into the far north, even if he failed to bring any significant Scottish force to battle. More importantly, by burning Aberdeen and much of the east coast, he made a French invasion, or the raising of a substantial Scottish army, much less likely, and could return to Perth with a sense of accomplishment. The king then initiated a building programme, hoping to emulate his grandfather's success in securing Wales by fortifying his own position in Scotland.

Meanwhile, negotiations between England and France over the situation in Agen, as well as a proposed joint crusading venture between Edward III and Philip VI – negotiations that had been continuing since the start of Edward III's personal rule – foundered. Philip VI would not abandon his Scottish ally, David II, and on 20 August 1336 he broke off negotiations with a startlingly blunt conclusion, telling the English ambassadors that 'It seems that all will not be well between the realms of England and France until the same man is king of both'.[4] This was quickly reported to the English chancellor, Archbishop Stratford, who took it as a virtual declaration of war. The king quickly journeyed south to meet with his Great Council, which granted him a tenth and a fifteenth in support of his wars in Scotland and Gascony. He briefly returned to Scotland to oversee the reconstruction of Bothwell Castle, but by mid-December he had returned to England once again, now focusing all of his energy and resources on France.

In October 1337, Edward III sent a diplomatic mission to Paris, the purpose of which was to announce to 'Philip of Valois who calls himself king of France', the renunciation of Edward's homage. This was, effectively, a declaration of war. Aquitaine had once again been confiscated, along with the northern county of Ponthieu, this time on the grounds that Edward was harbouring Robert of Artois who had been sentenced to death by his brother-in-law, the French king. Traditionally, it is Robert of Artois who is said to have convinced Edward to seek the throne of France, famously serving the king a dish of heron, a notoriously cowardly bird. It is difficult to imagine, however, that Edward genuinely considered the French crown within his grasp in 1337. Although his claim was a legitimate one, it was not necessarily stronger in law than the claim of Philip VI, or for that matter the similar claim of Charles of Navarre. Before his renunciation of homage to Philip VI, Edward had already laid much of the groundwork for war with France. The parliament of March 1337 had given its assent to the war, and the subsequent parliament in September 1337 provided the king with a grant of a tenth and a fifteenth for a period of 3 years. Further financing for the war was to be secured through royal intervention in the wool market, but the king's attempt to set up a monopoly on wool proved far from successful, either financially or politically. Nevertheless, Edward marked his preparations with the promotion of his son Edward to the unprecedented rank of duke of Cornwall, while elevating six new earls. These included several of the trusted friends who had helped him to liberate himself from Roger Mortimer: William Montagu became earl of Salisbury; William de Clinton, earl of Huntingdon; Robert de Ufford, earl of Suffolk; and William de Bohun, earl of Northampton. At the same time, Edward also conferred the earldom of Derby on Henry, son and heir of the earl of Lancaster, while Hugh Audley received the earldom of Gloucester, which had been denied to his family by the Despensers in the previous reign. All of these men had campaigned repeatedly in Scotland, and they provided Edward with a solid core of experienced military commanders. The king was generally successful in associating the aristocracy with him in his cause, although there was general surprise at the suggestion that he might revive his claim to the French crown. Despite this support, however, the early phase of the war did not go well, as the king himself seems to have been inconsistent and indecisive in articulating and pursuing his war aims.

Much as his grandfather had done, Edward III attempted to build a grand coalition in the Low Countries. His connections with Hainault facilitated this, but the policy proved unrealistically expensive, as generous subventions were paid to various local rulers and to the Holy Roman Emperor, Ludwig of Bavaria. Even with loans of more than £100,000 from the Italian bankers, the Bardi and Peruzzi, in 1337, Edward was hard-pressed to meet his financial obligations. The Lanercost Chronicle details the composition of the grand alliance of Edward III, no doubt inflating the numbers of every contingent. Even so, his estimate of the cost of this coalition at 'one thousand marks a day, according to others two thousand pounds',[5] is only slightly exaggerated, and probably reflects the general public perception of this astronomically expensive venture.

Edward finally landed at Antwerp in July 1338, but only desultory fighting ensued. Despite the subventions, all of which were in arrears in any case, his allies balked at attacking the king of France until Edward managed to convince the emperor to name him imperial vicar for all Germany in September. Even then, there continued to be disagreements about how to proceed and, in November, Edward formally agreed to follow the advice given to him by his council, now including not only English councillors such as the bishop of Lincoln and the earls of Derby and Salisbury, but also the count of Guelders and the Marquis of Juliers. It was not until the following summer that Edward III would finally initiate his first French campaign. Meanwhile, as Edward, desperately short of cash, awaited his allies at Antwerp, the French made progress on several fronts. In Gascony, French armies captured the key fortresses of Bourg and Blaye, and advanced all the way to Bordeaux. At the same time, a French fleet burned Hastings, and the French also provided assistance to the Scots, who had broken the truce and were besieging Perth, which fell in August.

Finally, on 20 September 1339, Edward III began his first campaign in France, marching out from Valenciennes to Cambrai. Although the Cambrésis was devastated, the city itself was not taken. Philip VI advanced north but would not cross into imperial territory. Edward, although he failed to convince the count of Hainault, did finally persuade his other allies to cross into the Vermandois, into France. Once in France, he elevated Laurence Hastings to the peerage as earl of Pembroke and knighted more than a dozen esquires. But Philip would not take Edward's bait and offer battle, despite several promises to do so. Edward was reduced to conducting a *chevauchée*, brutal and devastating, but ultimately insignificant. While Philip may have suffered some loss of honour for his unwillingness to face the Anglo–German army on French soil, Edward gained little honour and an ever-increasing burden of debt.

On 26 January 1340, in the marketplace of Ghent, Edward III launched a different sort of assault against his French rival, as he assumed the arms and title of king of France. By this public assertion of his claim to the French throne, Edward hoped to shore up the resolve of his continental allies. More importantly, he added a new ally, Jacques van Arteveldt, a wealthy burgess of Ghent who brought the Flemish wool towns into Edward's camp and opened another front in the conflict with the Valois. In February, Edward returned to England and summoned a parliament to assemble at Westminster in late March. With his debts to his allies far in arrears, and having undertaken new commitments of £140,000 to van Arteveldt and the Flemings, Edward was once again desperately short of money. Unfortunately, the parliamentary commons were far from sympathetic. After some hard bargaining, the king received a grant of a ninth, as well as the continuation of the maletolt, a tax of 40 s on every sack of English wool. In return, Edward conceded that royal tax collectors be accountable to parliament and that abuses in the system of purveyance be checked.

Even before Edward returned to the continent, the English campaign of 1340 had begun badly, with the earls of Salisbury and Suffolk taken prisoner during a skirmish outside Lille. There was, however, some comfort in the fact that a French attack on Valenciennes proved equally unsuccessful. Nonetheless, it was imperative for the king to take personal command as soon as possible. Philip VI and his government had undertaken preparations for an invasion of England to be led by Philip's son, the duke of Normandy, commanding a force of 30,000 men. The accompanying French naval buildup posed a genuine threat to Edward's crossing. Indeed, when he sailed from Orwell on 22 June 1340, there was genuine anxiety about his safety. Not only the ever-cautious chancellor, Archbishop Stratford, but also the king's two most trusted naval officers, Robert Morley and John Crabbe, advised the king against challenging the French fleet. Edward is reported to have answered, 'I will cross despite you, and you who are afraid, when there is nothing to fear, you stay at home!'[6] Both men sailed with the king, who was accompanied by fewer than 150 ships and perhaps 15,000 men altogether. Although word did not reach England until several days later, within 48 hours of his departure Edward III had achieved the first significant victory over the French in generations. The naval battle that was fought at Sluys on 24 June was a stunning victory. The French fleet was trapped in the estuary of the Swijn as its commanders bickered over seniority of command and tactics. The English had the further advantages of wind and tide, allowing their smaller force to overwhelm the enemy. Still, it must be said that Edward III seized his opportunity, perhaps foreshadowing the battle-seeking policy that is associated with the later Crécy campaign.

Without heavy artillery, a medieval naval battle resembled a land battle at sea and, at Sluys, English archers played a crucial role in softening up the French resistance prior to grappling and boarding manoeuvres. In a letter written to the Black Prince and meant for more general circulation, the king claimed to have captured 166 of 190 enemy ships and to have killed 30,000 out of 35,000 French combatants. The numbers of the ships involved is probably accurate, as is also the scale of casualties, although the absolute numbers of the French dead are probably exaggerated by a third to a half. English losses were remarkably low, although a number of ladies making their way to the queen at Ghent were drowned when their ship went down after being hit by a shot from a cannon. The king himself was wounded in the thigh and was forced to remain aboard his flagship, the *Thomas of Winchelsea*, for several weeks while he recuperated.

The campaign that followed was rather less successful. A two-pronged attack on Tournai and St Omer proved unsuccessful. On 26 July, Edward sent a letter to Philip VI offering him a choice of single combat, a fight between the two kings with one hundred vassals each, or an all-out battle on the fields beyond Tournai within 10 days. Philip, of course, demurred, saying only that he would drive Edward out of France 'when it seems good to us'.[7] He also added that Edward's offer was unreasonable as he risked nothing of his own, and invited him to include England in the stakes to be fought for. Edward then turned his focus to the siege of Tournai, in the hope that he could force the French to offer battle to relieve the city, much as the Scots had done at Berwick. But Philip VI was resolute, and Edward's allies, particularly the duke of Brabant, their wages and subsidies far in arrears, refused to prolong the siege past mid-September. The truce that was agreed at Espléchin on 25 September, while providing an honourable end to hostilities throughout France, England and Scotland, can only have been viewed as a failure by Edward III. He had once again failed to provoke the French king into battle, and he was now on the point of bankruptcy owing an unfathomable sum of £400,000. Indeed, before he could return to England and try to raise any further funds, he had to agree to leave the earls of Derby, Northampton and Warwick behind as sureties for his debts.

The king returned unannounced, arriving at the Tower on 30 November and unleashing a vitriolic attack on his chief ministers, most especially Archbishop Stratford. The *Libellus Famosus* decried the misgovernance of the regency council, whom Edward accused of deliberately withholding necessary funds for his war effort. The king ordered an inquest into the performance of royal ministers.

Moreover, he determined to end the practice of placing clerics in positions of authority. Edward is reported to have said that 'in his time no man of the church would be treasurer or chancellor, or in any other great office pertaining to the king, but only such persons who, if they were convicted of wrongdoing, he could draw, hang, and behead'.[8]

Stratford fought back, however, waging a war of words from the security of Canterbury, while refusing to receive the king's representatives. On Becket's feast day, 29 December, he declared his intention to emulate the martyr in opposing an unjust king, and he refused to meet the king unless it was before his peers in parliament. But unlike the conflicts of the previous reign, this one did not result in resort to arms. Rather, it was played out in parliament, and this may be the most significant element of the entire episode. When parliament finally convened at Westminster on 23 April, the king set two of his loyal servants, John Darcy and Ralph Stratford, physically to prevent the archbishop from entering the Painted Chamber. Pressured by the earls of Surrey and Arundel, Edward finally relented after a week of obstruction, during which he was unable to move any business. Both magnates and commons made common cause with Stratford and voiced their grievances, and the crisis of 1340–1341 is in many ways reminiscent of the events in the early years of the reign of Edward II that had culminated in the Ordinances of 1311. Edward was forced to make a number of concessions, embodied in a statute, in return for which he finally got a new levy of 30,000 sacks of wool. Among other points, the statute reiterated the right to a trial before one's peers in parliament, and called for both the appointment and confirmation of royal ministers in parliament. It would be wrong to see the king surrendering any fundamental royal rights to parliament in the crisis of 1340–1341, however, as by 1 October 1341 he had annulled the legislation of the spring, and would hold no further parliament until 1343. Nevertheless, the parliamentary commons had found their voice, and the dialogue that had begun in the April 1341 parliament would continue to shape relations between the king and his subjects for the rest of the reign.

It is interesting to note that parliament and the merchant community were not alone in their lack of enthusiasm for the French war; to a large extent, the aristocracy was unequally unsupportive. Despite the fact that the relationship with Aquitaine stretched all the way back to the reign of Henry II and his marriage to Eleanor of Aquitaine, the truth of the matter was that England had never really colonized Aquitaine, and consequently the English nobility had no vested interest in the duchy. This was very different from the situation that obtained in Scotland,

and even, for that matter, in Ireland. Thus, neither a winter campaign in Scotland in 1341–1342 nor a subsequent tournament at Dunstable fully healed the frayed edges of the king's relations with his magnates or led them to embrace the French war. On each occasion, several of the earls declined participation, and tension continued to be evident. When Edward finally summoned another parliament in April 1343, the commons immediately called for the reenactment of the 1341 statute and a promise that legislation duly approved by the lords and commons not be repealed by the king henceforth. The king stood by his prerogative and replied that the 1341 statute was contrary to the law of the land and damaging to the rights of the crown. The issue remained divisive.

Before we return to the war in France, something needs to be said about the character and personal life of Edward III. It is fair to say that, like 1330, the year in which he established his personal rule, 1340–1341 proved to be a watershed in the reign. The period from 1340 into the 1360s forms a clearly defined whole, and a coherence of purpose and behaviour can be seen in the king's personal, as well as his political, affairs. Edward was, in most ways, a thoroughly conventional figure. This is clearly seen in his practice of religion, where he was not merely conventional, but one might even argue conservative. Like his grandfather Edward I, Edward III was deeply devoted to the cult of the Virgin Mary. This was exemplified in his regular visits and gifts to her shrines at Walsingham, St Pauls's in London, and the Lady Chapel in Christ Church, Canterbury. Beyond these major shrines, the king also visited Marian sites at Scarborough, Darlington and St Mary's, York, during his Scottish campaigns in the 1330s. On the continent, he visited similar shrines at Halle, Vilvoorde (Brabant), and Ghent. When offering thanksgiving for his salvation during a storm at sea in 1340, he founded the Abbey of St Mary Graces, London, reminiscent of his grandfather's foundation of Vale Royal under similar circumstances half a century earlier.

Beyond his devotion to the Virgin, Edward III was also particularly attentive to the cult of several English saints. He typically visited Canterbury at least once each year, not only visiting Becket's tomb and the relic of the swords, but also visiting the Lady Chapel at Christ Church, and finally proceeding to St Augustine's Abbey, where he regularly offered alms on behalf not only of St Augustine himself, but also the less well known St Adrian and St Mildred. Edward made regular gifts to St Edmund of Bury and to Edward the Confessor at Westminster: the king had been baptized on the Confessor's feast day in 1312. Of course, when discussing the personal religion of Edward III, one must also mention St George, who was appropriated by the king as a particularly English saint through his connection with the Order of the Garter. It was his standard that English armies henceforth carried into battle in France and elsewhere, his name that became the English war-cry.

If Edward's devotion to English saints communicated a clear political message, so too could his similar devotion to the Virgin. In 1343, Edward presented five gold ships, each worth more than £50, to five prominent pilgrimage sites: Canterbury (both Becket's tomb and the Lady Chapel), Walsingham, St Paul's and Gloucester. The political message of English mastery of the seas – a theme that was also announced at this time on the king's newly minted gold nobles – was coupled with devotion to the Virgin, clearly suggesting divine approval of the king and his accomplishments. Not surprisingly, perhaps, foreign pilgrimages or even the Crusades held little attraction for Edward III. He did make offerings to the shrine of St Mathieu in Brittany in 1342–1343, and to the English saint Edmund Rich at Pontigny in 1360, but these clearly seem to be political gestures that are best understood in the context of the conflict with France.

Edward also promoted the sacral nature of his kingship. From the late 1330s on, the king regularly administered the royal touch to cure scrofula. Interestingly, he was particularly active in demonstrating his thaumaturgical powers between December 1340 and November 1341 during the political crisis at which his prestige and standing in the kingdom reached its lowest point. But he continued to touch for the king's evil throughout the reign, and he also demonstrated his healing powers by distributing cramp rings to combat epilepsy at Easter each year. These rings were made from pennies placed before the Neith Cross on Good Friday and then melted down and made into rings. The household ordinances of 1323 had specified that 5 s should be allocated to this purpose annually, but in the later years of the reign of Edward III, the king, in fact, devoted 25 s to this purpose. Clearly, there was widespread belief in the rings' efficacy, a reflection of the king's standing in God's favour.

Along similar lines, although details are lacking, the king must have encouraged liturgical displays of considerable complexity, designed to emphasize the transcendent position of the royal family. During the course of the reign, the size of the household chapel expanded from five to ten chaplains, assisted by an almoner and a confessor. Similarly, the size and composition of Edward's collegiate foundations at St Stephen's Chapel, Westminster and St George's Chapel, Windsor, point in this same direction. By 1351, each college had a warden, 12 canons, 13 vicars, 4 clerks and 6 choristers. Given Edward's love of display at tournaments and banquets, the great Garter Feast must also have become a splendid event, and so must have other festivals. The provision of vicars choral and boy singers at both Windsor and Westminster points to the performance of polyphonic music, perhaps for the first time at the English royal court.

Edward III also proved conventional in his dedication to the proper commemoration of the dead. For example, he attended the services for the earl of Salisbury in 1344, the earl of Lancaster in 1345 and Sir Walter Mauny in 1372, but perhaps the best illustration of Edward's sensibilities comes in the case of his brother John of Eltham, who died at Perth in September 1336. The funeral was delayed for some 6 months so that the king could be present for John's entombment in Westminster Abbey. The king ordered 900 masses to commemorate his death and commissioned the magnificent tomb still to be found in the Chapel of St Edmund. His anniversary was observed annually with the distribution of alms. Similar care was taken to commemorate the death of the king's own children, William of Hatfield and William of Windsor. The funeral of Queen Philippa in 1370 was a lavish undertaking – including an order from the king to a group of commissioners who were charged with having the streets of Southwark 'cleansed of all dung and other filth'[9] – and the remembrance of both Philippa and Edward's mother Isabella continued to be generously funded throughout the reign. The anniversary of the death of Edward I was always celebrated both at Westminster and wherever the king happened to be, regardless of whether he was home or abroad. In the end, Edward III declared his intention (in 1359) to be laid to rest in Westminster Abbey alongside 'that most illustrious and courageous soldier, and the most prudent statesman', Edward I.[10]

Another area in which Edward III showed himself to be rather conventional was in his devotion to his family, and to the Plantagenet dynasty more broadly. Edward and Philippa were blessed with a remarkably large family – five sons and four daughters surviving into adulthood. Although Shakespeare and many subsequent historians would trace the problems of the fifteenth century back to this unwieldy brood, neither Edward nor his contemporaries viewed this as other than a sign of divine approbation. Of course, providing for such a large family was a great challenge. Since the loss of their overseas possessions, the Plantagenet kings from Henry III onward had faced the necessity of assigning English earldoms to their sons, a not entirely satisfactory solution, as recently demonstrated in the reign of Edward II. From the 1340s until the final decade of his reign, Edward III took a rather different approach as he worked to balance and merge his own policies and ambitions with the interests and needs of his family.

Edward's concern for his family, in a broad sense, commenced as soon as he asserted himself in Nottingham in 1330. As discussed earlier, at the ensuing parliament, he restored the heir of his uncle Edmund, earl of Kent, and also pardoned all those involved in the recent revolt of Henry of Lancaster. A further sign of his reconciliation with the house of Lancaster was his continuing support for the canonization of Thomas of Lancaster, a popular political martyr since his execution after Boroughbridge in 1322. In his own generation, Edward rewarded Henry of Lancaster's son, Henry of Grosmont, with large annuities 'for the special affection which the king bears him'. In 1337, Grosmont became earl of Derby, linking him with the king's other favourites. Any doubt about the value of creating solidarity in the royal family was removed during the crisis of 1340–1341: that Henry of Derby chose not to play the contrariant role that Thomas of Lancaster had played in 1311 had been crucial to Edward's survival. Had he thrown his weight behind Archbishop Stratford and the parliamentary opposition, events might have turned out very differently. Instead, he remained a trusted lieutenant of his cousin for the rest of his life.

In the aftermath of the crisis of 1340–1341, Edward's political designs for his family became increasingly clear. In 1342, Edward III's second son, the 4-year-old Lionel of Antwerp, was betrothed to Elizabeth de Burgh, heiress to the earldom of Ulster. Soon thereafter, Elizabeth's recently widowed mother Maud (sister of Henry of Grosmont) was married to Ralph de Ufford, who would be appointed Justiciar of Ireland in 1344. At the same time, in 1342, Henry of Grosmont was granted Carmarthen, while in 1343 Prince Edward was appointed Prince of Wales. The inquiries into landholding and the behaviour of local officials that these various lords carried out in 1343–1344 clearly demonstrated Edward III's policy of reimposing effective royal lordship throughout his entire realm.

In 1342, Edward's third son, John of Gaunt, received the title earl of Richmond, a title that had long been connected with the dukes of Brittany, and must be seen as part of Edward's wider ambitions. No further English titles were bestowed on any of Edward's children between 1343 and 1362, while during this same period only Edmund of Langley and Isabella received any English territories. Moreover, by 1358, only one of the king's children had been married, and his only grandchild was the daughter of Lionel of Antwerp and Elizabeth de Burgh, Philippa of Ulster. Some of this was simply a result of chance. Marriage negotiations had been undertaken with Flanders in the 1340s and with Brittany in the 1350s only to have fallen through, and Joan had died of the plague on her way to Spain in 1348. Isabella was betrothed to the heir of the important Gascon lordship of Albret in 1351, but simply refused to consent to the union.

Still, all of these failed marriages were continental rather than English, and illustrate Edward's overall policy to expand the reach of the Plantagenet dynasty.

If we accept that the settlements arranged in the Treaty of Berwick in 1357 and Brétigny in 1360 were not entirely satisfactory – Berwick making no mention of English suzerainty and Brétigny, while recognizing English sovereignty in Aquitaine, requiring the renunciation of the claim to the French crown as well as suzerainty in northern France – both arrangements left considerable room for the next generation to advance the Plantagenet cause. They also prompted the king to return his consideration to the family's position within Britain. In 1358–1359, Princess Margaret was betrothed to John Hastings, earl of Pembroke, while Philippa of Ulster was betrothed to Edmund Mortimer, son and heir of the earl of March. These unions, especially the combination of the de Burgh and Mortimer holdings in Ireland, greatly consolidated the position of the royal family in the Celtic west. It is no coincidence that, in 1361, Lionel of Antwerp finally became king's lieutenant in Ireland and the first member of the royal house to set foot in Ireland since King John. Meanwhile, John of Gaunt was married to Blanche, the youngest daughter and co-heiress of Henry of Grosmont, duke of Lancaster. As it turned out, by 1362, both Henry and his eldest daughter Maud had died, and John succeeded to the entire massive Lancastrian inheritance. He became, almost by default, the natural representative of the English government in the Scottish March.

A similar pattern can be discerned in Edward's continental undertakings after 1360. The creation of the prince of Wales as prince of Aquitaine in July 1362 was a circumvention of the treaty of Brétigny, especially as Edward III immediately took the role of superior lord for the new principality. Meanwhile, he continued to exercise suzerainty in Brittany, where he recognized the claims of his ward John de Montfort, was had recently been married to the king's daughter Mary. Edward also entered into negotiations aimed at arranging a marriage between Margaret, heiress to Flanders and Burgundy, and his fourth son, Edmund of Langley. Arguably, it is this broad family settlement, both in Britain and abroad, that allowed Edward to condone the unlikely marriage of his eldest son Edward to his cousin Joan of Kent in 1361, a love match that brought little political benefit to the crown. All in all, Edward III provided both opportunities and challenges to his children within the framework of English expansion, while limiting internal conflict and rivalry. If the solid foundation upon which this settlement was built had already begun to crumble by the time of the king's death in 1377, the achievement of three decades should not be dismissed out of hand.

Edward returned to France in 1342 with a fresh strategy in mind. Laying aside the grand coalition that had failed both Edward I and himself, he now initiated a strategy of placing several English armies in the field simultaneously. This was first employed in Brittany. Duke John III of Brittany had died on 30 April 1341, leaving no obvious heir, the succession being contested between his niece Jeanne of Penthièvre and her husband Charles of Blois on one side, and his half-brother John de Montfort on the other. Charles of Blois was the 'official' candidate of Philip VI and of the Breton nobility, yet John de Montfort showed more initial energy and was able to establish himself in Nantes, Rennes and Dinan. Soon, however, he was summoned to Paris, where his refusal to renounce his claim led to his arrest and imprisonment in the Louvre. His wife, Jeanne of Flanders, showed great resolve in maintaining the Montfortian position and successfully sought English support for her husband's cause.

Edward III's trusted commander Walter Mauny landed at Brest with a small English force in May 1342, and a larger army under the earl of Northampton and Robert of Artois followed in August. They were able to push back the forces of Charles of Blois, and had some success in battle against him outside Morlaix. On 26 October, the king himself finally landed on his flagship, the *George*. From Brest, the king turned his attention to Vannes. Unfortunately, however, Robert of Artois, commanding the English fleet, reached the city first and attacked before the main army arrived. His initial success was short-lived, and he died of wounds suffered in the attack. More importantly, Edward had lost the element of surprise. While Edward sat down to besiege the city, the earl of Northampton invaded the territory of Rohan, after which, accompanied by the earl of Warwick and Hugh Despenser, he led a raid against Nantes. Meanwhile, the earl of Salisbury burned the suburbs of Dinan. The presence of the English in so many places at once was devastating to French morale. In March 1343, a truce was negotiated at Malestroit, recognizing the status quo on the ground not only in Brittany, but also in Flanders, Gascony and Scotland. All in all, this was positive from Edward III's point of view, and it allowed the English to consolidate their hold over the south and west of Brittany to an extent that Philip VI seems not to have understood. Brittany, despite its peripheral geographic location, was home to French – not just Breton – nobles with extensive holdings elsewhere. Men such as Olivier de Clisson and Godfrey de Harcourt rallied to the cause of Edward III. Clisson was foolish enough to attend a tournament in Paris in the summer of 1343, believing himself to be protected by the truce. He was arrested by Philip VI there, convicted of treasonous dealings with the king of England, and brutally executed. Harcourt, however, would be a different matter.

In June 1345, following 2 years in which the shaky truce held as much from financial limitations as diplomatic progress, Edward III repudiated the truce of Malestroit. He planned a three-pronged offensive, with himself campaigning in Flanders, the earl of Northampton in Brittany, and Henry of Grosmont, earl of Derby, and after September 1345, earl of Lancaster, in Aquitaine. Northampton had already sailed from Portsmouth to Brest in early June, and Derby awaited only a favourable wind. If the royal fleet at Sandwich had indeed been intended for Flanders, plans changed suddenly. On 3 July, the king did sail to Sluys, where he would remain until 22 July. His repudiation of the truce of Malestroit had allowed the count of Flanders, Louis of Nevers, to disrupt the pro-English urban oligarchies of the great wool towns. On 7 July, Edward met with Jacques van Arteveldt, the demagogue of Ghent, but van Arteveldt was now a broken reed. He returned to Ghent only to be beaten to death by a mob led by a rival faction. Nevertheless, Edward was able to seal agreements with each of the major towns undertaking not to allow the count to assume control of government in Flanders. It took 4 days to sail from Sluys back to Dover, as the English fleet was buffeted by storms. The English troops, which had remained on their ships in Sluys, were now disembarked. Indeed, they were released from service. Edward had to arrange for new, smaller, armies to be mustered in late summer in support of the campaigns in Brittany and Gascony. He would see no action in 1345.

In the following year, the king raised a massive army, and if he could not keep the scale or timetable of his preparations secret from the French, he could withhold his destination. Brittany and Aquitaine seemed the logical targets; Brittany had seen early successes by the earl of Northampton evaporate, while in Aquitaine the earl of Lancaster now faced a major French force commanded by the heir to the throne, John, duke of Normandy. But, ultimately, the king of England sailed to neither of these destinations. Instead, he landed unexpectedly in Normandy. Whether this was the original target of Edward's planning remains uncertain. A tradition recorded in Froissart relates that the king was convinced to invade Normandy on the advice of Godfrey de Harcourt, who assured him, 'I promise you, on my life, that once you reach it, it will be easy to land there. There will be no serious resistance, for the inhabitants have no experience of arms and the whole cream of the Norman knights are at the siege of Aiguillon [in Aquitaine] with the Duke'.[11] For whatever reason, Edward did choose Normandy, and much of what Harcourt is reputed to have said was true. The English force of some 7,000–10,000 men sailed from Portsmouth on 28 June. The king was accompanied by his eldest son, Edward, now a young man of 16 years old.

The first child of Edward III and Philippa of Hainault was a son, Edward, later known as the Black Prince, born at Woodstock on 15 June 1330, when the king was still some 3 months short of his eighteenth birthday, and the queen of a similar age. The king was certainly delighted in the birth of his son and namesake, rewarding Thomas Prior, the 'yeoman' who brought him the news at Westminster with a remarkably generous pension of 40 marks per annum.[12] It may well have been the birth of a son and heir that finally emboldened Edward III in launching his coup against his mother and Roger Mortimer at Nottingham 4 months later.

The young prince was endowed with the earldom of Chester in March 1333 and the duchy of Cornwall in 1337 prior to being granted the principality of Wales in 1343. By the time he had been made prince of Wales, his father had claimed another title for himself as king of France, and it was in support of this claim that the younger Edward would earn his reputation as a great captain. Very little can be said about his childhood. Although he may have been tutored by the philosopher Walter Burley, his education was more likely to be entrusted to the masters of his household, Nicholas de la Beche and Bartholomew Burgersh the elder. In any case, his education very clearly leaned toward the practical, and specifically the military, aspects of life, and throughout his life the inventories of his armour and jousting equipment were to be more extensive than the catalogue of his books. One other interesting aspect of his upbringing is deserving of mention. By 1334, he already had a tailor, William Stratton, who would be knighted by the prince in 1355. As early as 1337, we find Prince Edward splendidly garbed for a ceremonial entrance into London with a pair of cardinals, robed in purple and wearing a hat trimmed with scarlet and pearls. His taste for extravagant clothing and jewellery later in life may well have been acquired at an early age. So was his taste for war.

The campaign of 1346 may have seemed to contemporaries a desperate attempt by Edward III to salvage his claims to the French throne. For the prince, it was the beginning of a glorious military career. He was accompanied by a powerful retinue that included 11 bannerets, 102 knights, and well over 1,000 assorted men-at-arms, archers and foot-soldiers. Following the landing at Saint-Vaast-la-Hougue, the king knighted his eldest son, along with other young notables including both Roger Mortimer, son of his former nemesis, and William Montagu, son of the man who had helped him seize his throne. The

prince himself then knighted many other aspirants. The prince's column participated in the devastating advance that not only served to punish the French, but
may very well also have been designed to lead to the pitched battle that finally
resulted at Crécy. In the meantime, its target was Caen, which was reached on
26 July. The prince, like many of the young tiros in the English army, was anxious
for action, and the fighting at Caen began prematurely when some of his men
seized one of the western gates to the city, leading to an all-out struggle led by
the earl of Warwick. The city quickly fell, as more than 100 French knights and
120 esquires surrendered for ransom, including the Constable and Chamberlain
of Normandy. More than 2,500 lesser men lay dead in the streets. Before leaving
Caen 5 days later, Edward III sent out orders for reinforcements, seeking an
additional 1,200 archers from East Anglia with the requisite supply of bows and
arrows to meet the army later at Le Crotoy. Along with these orders, the valuable
prisoners taken at Caen were sent to England, and this, along with the booty
already returning with English sailors, made clear the success of the campaign
so far. The king reinforced this message, writing newsletters to the archbishops
of York and Canterbury, calling for the prayers of the people while celebrating
his own achievements at arms.

The king's next target appears to have been Rouen, or perhaps even Paris itself.
Edward was delayed briefly at Lisieux after entering into unproductive negotiations with a pair of cardinals dispatched by Philip VI offering the same terms as
ever: Aquitaine and Ponthieu held in fee from the king of France. After 2 days,
the English army moved on toward the Seine, but by now Philip had arrived at
Rouen with a substantial army of his own, intent upon keeping Edward's army on
the left bank. To that end, he reinforced or destroyed all of the bridges across the
river. Nevertheless, on 14 August, Edward was able to repair the broken bridge
at Poissy, cross the river, and open the way north toward Picardy and his Flemish
allies. Interestingly, Edward paused for 2 days at Poissy, raiding the countryside
around Paris. Two royal manors, at Montjoie and Saint-Germain-en-Laye, were
burned to the ground, yet Philip did not march out to confront his adversary
despite this clear provocation.

On 16 August, the English army moved off, now covering 15 miles per day
as it hastened north. According to a contemporary journal of the campaign on
18 August, the vanguard of the English army under the command of the Black
Prince lingered before Beauvais while hoping for the king's permission to attack:
this was firmly refused. Two days later, however, a similar scene played itself out
with the rearguard at Poix, where a delay in the advance for such a small prize

might have endangered the entire English army. Meanwhile, the French army also marched north, very nearly catching the English just as they crossed the Somme at Blanquetache at low tide on 24 August, but unable to pursue them across the river. Philip withdrew to Abbeville, while Edward, having gained needed supplies with the capture of Le Crotoy, advanced another 9 miles to Crécy-en-Ponthieu.

The battle of Crécy took place on 26 August 1346. The battlefield had been chosen by the earl of Warwick and other seasoned commanders. Still, the French outnumbered the English by two, perhaps three, to one. At about 5 p.m., as the skies darkened and rain began to fall, the French attacked. The Genoese cross-bowmen led this assault, but they were quickly broken by the English longbows and cannon. Outraged at the apparent cowardice of the Italian mercenaries, the count of Alençon charged forward with the second French battalion and was followed by the rest of the cavalry. They trampled their Genoese allies underfoot, but the French horses were likewise shot down by English arrows and cannon: nonetheless, they continued their charge toward the centre of the English line and the prince of Wales.

The prince led the vanguard in the engagement with a collection of his father's great captains, including the earls of Warwick, Northampton and Kent, as well as Godfrey de Harcourt and John Chandos. Under the weight of the initial French cavalry charge, the prince's standard fell, and the prince himself was struck down, to be rescued by Richard FitzSimon, his standard-bearer. In the midst of repeated French cavalry charges, King Edward was approached about the question of removing his 16-year-old son from harm's way and famously answered, 'let the boy win his spurs, for if God has so ordained it, I wish the day to be his'.[13] And so, of course, it happened.

Late in the day, the blind and aged king of Bohemia ordered his men to lead him into the English line directly at King Edward. Shouting his war-cry of 'Prague', he and his men were quickly cut down in an empty but glorious chivalric gesture. Meanwhile, the English cavalry now remounted and charged the remaining French units. The French infantry fled. Philip VI was largely abandoned, but for his personal bodyguard and some foot-soldiers from Orléans. His standard bearer was cut down and the *oriflamme* fell to the ground. Wounded in the face, the French king had two horses shot from under him but managed to escape the field with the assistance of John of Hainault, Edward III's erstwhile ally and mentor. The defeat was devastatingly complete. At least 2,000 French knights and esquires died at Crécy. As well as King John of Bohemia, the dead included the counts of Alençon, Blois, Flanders and Harcourt, along with the duke of Lorraine.

Despite the scale of the defeat, however, Crécy was strategically insignificant. Although Edward III had earlier proclaimed in Normandy that he 'had come into this land not to lay it waste, but to take possession of it', in fact the reverse was true. With limited financial and human resources at his disposal, Edward had been unable to occupy the territory he had devastated earlier in Normandy or to capitalize now on his victory in Ponthieu. He chose, therefore, to march north to Calais hoping to capture the port and thereby secure a permanent gateway into France.

In 1346, Calais was not a major port in the way that Boulogne, St Omer or Dieppe were; its population was well under 10,000. Its attraction to Edward lay in its proximity to Flanders, whose border stood just a few miles to the north-east. All the same, Calais was well fortified and strongly garrisoned. When the English arrived before the city in early September, it was clear that it would not fall easily to assault, but would only be taken as the result of a prolonged siege. With recently arrived reinforcements, the English dug in just to the south of the city. The command centre, wryly referred to as 'Villeneuve-le-Hardy', served as a distribution point for the badly needed food and clothing brought in by sea or overland from Flanders via Gravelines. By the time the siege ended 11 months later on 4 August 1347, some 32,000 troops had taken part in the single largest English military undertaking of the Middle Ages.

The siege had both a primary and secondary purpose: capture of the port was crucial to the continuation of the English war effort, but the siege may very well have been designed to entice Philip VI into a second battle, with the stakes being raised higher still by the outcome of Crécy. Edward made this clear when parliament was informed in September that 'he did not intend to conclude [the siege of Calais] before he had conquered the town, with the help of God, and . . . after this conquest he would go after his enemy in pursuit of his quarrel, without returning to England before he had brought an end to his war overseas'.[14] Jean le Bel was even more precise, reporting that the king had declared 'neither for winter nor for summer would he depart until he had the town at his mercy, unless King Philip would come to combat him, and defeat him'.[15] Philip attempted to draw Edward away with an attack on Flanders, but a siege at Cassel failed. He also wrote to his Scottish ally David II, urging the opening of a second front, although in the event this proved disastrous.

Although the French did manage to obtain supplies by sea in March and April 1347, thereafter the English were able to close the shipping lanes and further tighten the noose around Calais. On 25 June, a supply fleet was intercepted by the

English, prompting the Commander of Calais, Jean de Vienne, to write a desperate letter to Philip VI stating that, having eaten horses, dogs and cats, 'we can now find no more food in the town unless we eat human flesh . . . Unless some other solution can be found this is the last letter that you will receive from me, for the town will be lost and all of us within it'.[16] In fact, the letter was intercepted by the English, but Edward, having read it and appended his own personal seal to it, sent the letter on to his cousin of France.

After yet another supply convoy was captured by the English in July, the mounting pressure felt by the beleaguered garrison of Calais is vividly illustrated by the decision to expel some 500 townspeople who could not aid in the defence. Given the harsh conditions being endured by the English army, it is difficult to accept the account of the chivalric chronicler Jean le Bel who reports that Edward fed them all and then sent them on their way, each with a gift of 4 s. Knighton's chronicle rings truer: trapped between the walls of their native city and the English lines, they suffered and died of hunger. Finally, on 27 July 1347, the king of France arrived at Sangatte, overlooking Calais, with some 15,000–20,000 troops. Recognizing instantly that he could not challenge the English position, he entered into several days of perfunctory negotiations. During the night of 1 August, however, the French army burned their tents and marched away. Two days later, Jean de Vienne rode out with a rope around his neck, followed by his knights and the leading burgesses similarly encumbered, to surrender. Edward would have executed both the garrison and the burgesses, but Walter Mauny appealed to his chivalric sense to spare the garrison and Queen Philippa convinced him to spare the burgesses as well. Calais was now an English town.

Although the siege of Calais was settling into a prolonged and painful stalemate, the Scots fulfilled their obligation to the French, as embodied in the Treaty of Corbeil. In October, an army led by King David II and Sir William Douglas invaded northern England, besieging the castle of Liddell. Lanercost Abbey and Hexham Priory were pillaged – much to the dismay of the contemporary Lanercost Chronicler, who expressed his utter disdain by referring to the Scottish king as 'not David the warrior, but David the defecator'.[17] On the morning of 17 October 1346, in a thick fog, a Scottish raiding party under Douglas encountered an English force under the command of the archbishop of York, William de la Zouche. Having suffered heavy losses in the ensuing skirmish, Douglas hastened back to the main Scottish army, but could not rouse King David to action. According to the Lanercost Chronicle, David scoffed: 'There are no men in England, but wretched monks, lewd priests, swineherds, cobblers and skinners.

They dare not face me: I am safe enough.'[18] But he was not safe at all. At the battle of Neville's Cross, near Durham, disaster befell the Scottish cause. Not only was the king himself captured, but so were Douglas and the earls of Fife, Menteith and Wigtown.[19] The earl of Moray, John Randolph, was killed in the fighting, along with the earls of Strathearn and Sutherland, as well as the Constable, Marshal, Chancellor and Chamberlain of Scotland. Both the military command and the administrative centre of the Scottish kingdom were destroyed in a single day. Amid the defeat of the French king at Crécy, the capture of the Scottish king at Neville's Cross, and the fall of Calais, Edward III had much to celebrate upon his return to England.

The central element in the celebrations that ensued was the foundation of the Order of the Garter in 1348. This was an event that has more often than not been mischaracterized and devalued. The traditional tales of Edward III picking up and replacing the garter of his alleged mistress, the countess of Salisbury, has no basis in historical fact. In actuality, the king had adopted both the symbol of the garter and the Order's famous motto, *Honi soit qui mal y pense* ('Shame on him who thinks ill of it'), for the Crécy campaign. It appeared on streamers displayed from the ships that had carried his troops to Normandy, as well as robes and other accoutrements (including a bedcover) displayed by the king during the campaign. That the motto was in French (whereas all of Edward's other mottoes were in English), and the streamers and robes were in the blue and gold of French royalty, reflects the audience to whom Edward was issuing this defiant challenge. The vindication of his cause at Crécy and Calais justified the use of both the symbol of the garter and the motto in the creation of a chivalric order to commemorate these victories. Much more than his earlier scheme for a Round Table in 1344, or the pageantry of his many tournaments in the previous decade, the Order of the Garter has a *gravitas* about it that is altogether lacking earlier in the reign. The simplicity of the rules of the Order, and the emphasis on the annual Feast of St George, convey this seriousness of purpose. The Order was limited to 26 members: the king, the prince of Wales, and two teams of 12 knights attached to each. Although this may initially have reflected the origins of the Order in the context of a tournament with two teams of knights attached to the king and prince, respectively, over time the exclusivity of membership in the Order added to its prestige, and the success of these knights as commanders in France reinforced this image. This was soon recognized by those well outside the aristocratic circle who formed its founding membership. As early as 1352, the author of the Middle English poem *Wynner and Wastere* described Edward's tent decorated:

With English bezants full bright, beaten from gold,
And each one gaily encircled with garters of blue . . .

He then goes on to give, in English, the Order's motto suggesting the burgeoning English national identity and pride. The founding members of the Order of the Garter included King Edward and the Black Prince, Duke Henry of Lancaster, and five present and future earls. All had fought at Crécy or the concurrent campaigns in Brittany and Aquitaine. Membership was based on chivalric accomplishments, so that alongside the king and his heir we find simple knights, largely unknown otherwise, such as Sir Otho Holand and Sir Walter Paveley. Not all were English: Sanchet de Abrechicourt was from Ponthieu; Henry Eam from Brabant; and Jean de Grailly, captal de Buch, from Gascony. The Order of the Garter, and its headquarters at Windsor Castle, physically embodied Edward III's vision of kingship, chivalric in nature and international in scope. Unfortunately, the same year that saw the articulation of this vision by Edward III also witnessed an unprecedented vision of disease, despair and death as the bubonic plague made its way across Europe.

The great pestilence, or the Black Death as it is generally known, was a catastrophic event of unprecedented scope. The bubonic plague had not visited the Mediterranean world since the sixth century, and in consequence there was little if any resistance to the virulent bacillus, *yersinia pestis*. Moving from east to west, the disease devastated both the Byzantine and Islamic civilizations before making its way into western Europe. As many as 200,000 were said to have died in Constantinople following the arrival of the plague there in the spring of 1347, while half the population reportedly perished in both Alexandria and Cairo. The disease quickly made its way across the Mediterranean, reaching Sicily and Italy in the autumn, and from there spreading throughout the continent. The pestilence first made landfall in England at Bristol in late June 1348. According to Higden's *Polychronicon*, the pesitilence 'raged so strongly that scarcely a tenth of mankind was left alive'.[20] Although this sort of hyperbole is typical of the contemporary chronicles, recent research has convincingly demonstrated that the traditional estimate that one-third of the population perished in the first outbreak of the plague is too low a figure: in all likelihood, 50–55% of the people in England died in 1348–1349.

From Bristol, the plague moved quickly on to Dorset, Devon and Somerset. Turning inland from the south coast, the pestilence reached London on or about the Feast of All Saints. According to Robert of Avebury, 'between Candlemas

[2 February 1349] and Easter [12 April], more than 200 corpses were buried every day in the new burial ground next to Smithfield, and this was in addition to the bodies buried in other churchyards in the city'. The disease continued its inexorable spread, reaching York in the spring of 1349. Even Scotland was stricken by 1350 as recorded in the *Scotichronicon* of John of Fordun. In Ireland, the Franciscan friar John of Clynn chronicled the spread of the disease from Dublin to his own house in Kilkenny. Clynn appears to have been a victim of the plague himself, and he concluded his entry with this poignant ending: 'I leave parchment for continuing the work, in case anyone should still be alive in the future and any son of Adam can escape this pestilence and continue the work thus begun.'[21]

The first wave of the great pestilence was an indiscriminate killer. Even the royal family was touched, as Edward III's daughter Joan died of the plague in Bordeaux on 2 September 1348 as she travelled to Spain for her marriage to Pedro, heir to the throne of Castile. The king's pain at the loss of his daughter is evident in his subsequent letter to the Castilian court. Nevertheless, he demonstrates an outward courage and dignity that must have impressed all those who suffered a similar grief. The king wrote:

> No fellow human being could be surprised if we were inwardly desolated by the sting of this bitter grief, for we are human too. But we, who have placed our trust in God, and our life between his hands . . . give thanks to him that one of our own family, free of all stain, whom we have loved with pure love, has been sent ahead to heaven to reign among the choirs of virgins, where she can gladly intercede for our offences before himself.[22]

Here, as elsewhere, the king's rather conventional, but altogether genuine, faith provided him with strength in a moment of crisis.

To the medieval mind, the cause of the Black Death was obvious. No agency other than God Almighty was capable of unleashing such a horrible scourge. The initial reaction in England was not unlike that in other lands: Edward III ordered prayers and public penance. But this was the occasion of a social and economic crisis as well as a spiritual one, and here too the king took action. Making common cause with his aristocracy, as early as 18 June 1349 Edward issued the Ordinance of Labourers, which obliged agricultural workers to accept employment at the wage rate that had been established in 1346. Refusal to accept employment under these terms was cause for imprisonment. This ordinance was reissued in statutory form by the first post-plague parliament in February 1351.

Justices were commissioned to hear labour cases in the county quarter sessions, and the records indicate that enforcement of the statute was vigorous, with some £10,000 collected in fines between 1352 and 1354. These fines testify to the fact that the great landowners clearly struggled to find the necessary labour to continue direct demesne farming, but in an ironic case of adding insult to injury, heriots and entry fines imposed upon the survivors of the Black Death boosted manorial incomes throughout England in the short run and may have slowed the transition away from direct demesne farming despite the greatly diminished labour pool. These factors, along with the increasing concentration of land in the hands of the greatest noble houses, help account for the class tensions that would erupt at the very end of the reign.

The great pestilence also interrupted the war with France, as both kingdoms came to terms with reduced tax revenues and manpower. Nevertheless, in the immediate aftermath of the first visitation of the plague, while the royal court celebrated Christmas 1349 at Havering, word reached the king of a plot to betray Calais to the French. In an episode of chivalric derring-do, unequalled except perhaps by his grandfather's struggle with a knife-wielding Assassin while on Crusade, both the king and his son Edward hastened to Calais in secrecy with a small force of household knights. There they fought incognito under the banner of Sir Walter Mauny, overwhelming the French army led by Geoffrey de Charny and saving the English gateway to France. Edward followed this up by defeating the Franco–Castilian fleet off Winchelsea the following summer, and there continued to be sporadic fighting, particularly in Gascony, but neither side was willing or able to launch a major campaign.

The death of Philip VI in August 1350 provided the English king with some breathing space, and over the next few years Edward was able to concentrate his attention more fully on domestic affairs. Ever since the crisis of 1340–1341, Edward had been served by a corps of talented administrators, William Edington most of all. Edington had been sponsored in royal service by his early patron, Bishop Orleton. In November 1341, he became keeper of the wardrobe, and was responsible for guaranteeing the flow of cash to support the king's wars in Scotland and Brittany. He excelled at the task and was made treasurer in April 1344. He was to serve in that capacity for 12 years, until November 1356 when the king made him chancellor, an office he would hold for a further 7 years. Meanwhile, Edward had arranged Edington's provision to the see of Winchester in 1345, reversing his promise of 1341 not to appoint clerics to high administrative posts. Other trusted administrators such as John Thoresby (chancellor,

1349–1356), Sir John Stonor (Chief Justice of the Common Pleas, 1342–1354) and Sir William Shareshull (Chief Justice of the King's Bench, 1350–1361) provided a continuity of tenure that had been lacking in English government since the reign of Edward I.

During this relatively stable period in domestic affairs, one legal enactment stands out and reinforces the king's relationship with his magnates, the Statute of Treason of 1352. This was a landmark in that it defined treason to a number of specific acts, such as: plotting to kill the king, queen or heir to the throne; raping the king's spouse or eldest daughter; waging war against the king in his realm; counterfeiting the great seal or money; and killing officials such as the chancellor, treasurer or royal justices when they are in their places performing their offices. The statute marked an end to the cycle of political violence that had marred the entire reign of Edward II and the early years of Edward III, and it provided the aristocracy with greater assurance about the security of tenure of their estates. As such, it can be seen as the culmination of a process of reconciliation that had begun as early as 1330. In these same years, the crown also addressed the increasingly contentious issue of relations with the papacy. The Statutes of Provisors (1351) and *Praemunire* (1353) responded to the xenophobic atmosphere occasioned by an increasingly French-dominated papacy, restricting the pope's ability to reserve ecclesiastical appointments and provide his own nominees for them. While part of the inspiration for these statutes came from commons petitions, they were very much the product of the king's council, and remind us that although parliament was becoming an increasingly important institution, Edward III maintained his prerogative powers throughout his reign while nonetheless cooperating with the political community. Unfortunately, in the later years of the reign, this cooperation broke down. The king put his trust in William Wykeham (Chancellor, 1367–1371), who (like Edington) became bishop of Winchester, but by then the combination of failure in war with other social and economic crises precluded a continuation of the smooth relations that had characterized the middle years of the reign.

In 1354, a draft peace settlement between Edward III and Philip VI's successor John II was negotiated, the treaty of Guînes, by whose terms the English stood to receive Aquitaine, Poitou, Ponthieu and Calais in full sovereignty in return for Edward's renunciation of his claim to the French crown. These were the terms that Philip VI had never been willing to grant and, as it turned out, neither was John. In the end, neither side ratified the treaty and the war soon recommenced. Edward planned to launch a two-pronged attack in 1355, with one army under the Black Prince going to Aquitaine, while he himself led another, larger, force to Normandy in cooperation with Charles of Navarre. Unfortunately, Charles of Navarre was playing a complicated diplomatic game and he reached an understanding with John II: he withdrew from the English cause altogether, even trying to set a trap for Edward in Normandy. Although the king finally sailed to Calais in late October, the ensuing campaign was brief and unmemorable. Moreover, the king returned to England to discover that the Scots had seized Berwick in a daring dawn raid on 6 November 1355, forcing him to redirect his attention to the north. Meanwhile, the Black Prince sailed on to Bordeaux and down in the south he undertook a *chevauchée* of unprecedented scale.

If the Black Prince 'won his spurs' at Crécy, then he cemented his reputation with the stunning success of his campaigns in 1355 and 1356, which culminated in the victory at Poitiers. His army of 6,000–8,000 men left Bordeaux on 5 October 1355 and marched south and east right to the Mediterranean coast. Along the way, they burned Carcassonne and pillaged Narbonne before retracing their steps, very nearly, to Bordeaux. This was the *grande chevauchée*, perhaps the most destructive military operation of the entire Hundred Years War, and one that might seem difficult to square with the image of the Black Prince as the paragon of chivalry that was indelibly sketched by Froissart and Chandos Herald. More than 500 villages were burned – the lands of the French commander in Gascony, the count of Armagnac, being particularly targeted. Despite this, Armagnac refused to offer battle to the prince's numerically inferior force, instead defending the principal towns and fortifications of the region. Whether or not the prince himself was seeking battle during the *chevauchée* remains a controversial topic. Contemporary letters written to the archbishop of Canterbury by Sir John Wingfield on 23 December, and by the prince himself to the king on Christmas Day, certainly indicate that this had been the prince's intention. When, in late November, Armagnac had finally marched out from Toulouse to oppose the prince, the latter had marched his army toward an engagement only to have the French withdraw before him. Ultimately, with winter coming on and a long march still ahead, the prince was forced to return to Bordeaux, albeit with carts heavily laden with booty.

In early 1356, a second English army under the duke of Lancaster landed in Normandy, while the prince maintained his position in Aquitaine. The king had returned to England and now turned his attention to the Scots. Edward led a brutal winter campaign that recovered Berwick and devastated Lothian so thoroughly that the campaign was long remembered by the Scots as the 'Burnt

Candlemas'. With the north once again secure, the English could resume their French offensive. In early August 1356, the prince left Bergerac with a force estimated at between 6,000 and 7,000 men, planning to link up with the northern army under Lancaster, which had been operating in Normandy. Marching north through Périgord, the Limousin, and Poitou, this march does not seem to have been marked by the same sort of destructive violence as that of the previous year, perhaps suggesting a different intent – conquest and occupation rather than destruction and intimidation. It proved impossible to combine the two English armies as planned, as John II had broken the bridge over the Loire at Angers, leading Lancaster to use his forces to garrison Maine and Anjou rather than continue south.

The Anglo–Gascon army of the Black Prince, which was encamped near Tours by mid-September, had marched some 320 miles in 32 days. Moreover, the French army under the command of John II was certainly numerically superior to that of the Black Prince. When the efforts to arrange a truce undertaken by Cardinal Talleyrand of Périgord proved fruitless, the prince seems to have favoured discretion as the better part of valour. Despite recent arguments suggesting that the prince was deliberately trying to provoke an attack at Poitiers, his own letters suggest ambivalence at best: 'Because we were short of supplies and for other reasons, it was agreed that we should retreat in a flanking movement, so that if they wanted to attack or to approach us in a position which was not in any way greatly to our disadvantage we would give battle.'[23] He ordered the earl of Warwick to lead the baggage train away towards the river Miosson, and it was this withdrawal that triggered the French attack, suggesting that the initiative for the battle did indeed lie with the French.

Once begun, the battle of Poitiers on 19 September 1356 followed a pattern that was remarkably similar to that of Crécy. An initial pair of charges led by Arnaud d'Audrehem (accompanied by Sir William Douglas and some 200 Scottish men-at-arms) and Robert de Clermont, both marshals of France, was repulsed by the English archers. A subsequent attack on foot by the dauphin Charles with the French first division was driven back by the dismounted Anglo–Gascon men-at-arms after 2 hours of hand-to-hand combat. The English, with the exception of the earl of Warwick, held their positions and did not pursue the retreating French, as a large part of the enemy army had yet to engage. The dauphin was now led from the field, perhaps on King John's orders, but the young duke of Orléans followed the dauphin with the entire second division of the French army, leaving the remaining French forces in an untenable position. King John was left alone on the field with a single division: nevertheless, he resolutely ordered an advance on foot. The Black Prince, in turn, ordered a counter-attack. The captal de Buch drove into the left rear of the French army with a small force of men-at-arms and mounted archers, while the English knights and men-at-arms now remounted and were hurled forward under Sir James Audley. Between the impact of this charge and the continuing hail of arrows from English longbows, the French formation was broken. In the ensuing chaos, King John was surrounded and overwhelmed. The *oriflamme* fell to the ground and the French king was taken prisoner and led from the field by the earl of Warwick and Reginald Cobham. The French casualties were horrific: the duke of Bourbon, the Constable, Marshal Clermont, the bishop of Châlons, and Sir Geoffrey de Charny (the king's standard-bearer), were all killed, along with some 2,500 noble men-at arms. Along with the king, the archbishop of Sens, 17 counts and viscounts, 22 bannerets (including d'Audrehem), and the seneschals of Saintonge, Tours and Poitou, along with some 1,900 men-at arms, were taken prisoner. The victory at Poitiers was complete.

In the aftermath of Poitiers, a settlement with the Scots was arrived at fairly quickly. Edward's devastating winter campaign had broken Scottish resolve, while the capture of the French king had deprived them of their main foreign ally. Edward Balliol having surrendered his claim to the Scottish throne to Edward III at Roxburgh on 20 January 1356, a treaty was sealed at Berwick on 3 October recognizing David II and the Bruce dynasty in Scotland in return for a ransom of 100,000 marks to be paid in instalments prior to David's release from captivity. Negotiations with France proved more difficult. The first draft of a proposed treaty of London in 1358 called for Edward III's renunciation of his claims to the French throne in return for sovereignty over Calais, Ponthieu and an enlarged Aquitaine (Edward's traditional demands), along with a massive ransom of 4 million gold écus (£666,666) for the release of John II, which was ten times the sum demanded of the Scots for the release of David II. The refusal of the French regency government to agree to these terms may have reflected their inability to raise even the first instalment of such a staggering sum, rather than any matter of political principle. The ensuing stalemate led Edward, anxious to capitalize on his son's victory at Poitiers, to raise a fresh army while increasing his demands. In 1359, a second draft of the treaty of London added Normandy, Maine, Touraine and Anjou to the sovereign territories of the English king, with Brittany to recognize his suzerainty: Edward was demanding nothing less than the restoration of the Angevin Empire of Henry II and Eleanor of Aquitaine.

On 28 September 1359, the king sailed from Sandwich to Calais with a well-equipped army of 10,000 men. His aim was to capture Rheims, the coronation city of French kings, and Edward had in fact brought a crown with him in his baggage. He invested the city on 4 December 1359, but Gauchier de Châtillon refused to surrender. After just 5 weeks, on 11 January 1360, Edward III withdrew. He was short on supplies, suffering from atrocious weather and ultimately reluctant to storm the city. He did go on to lead a successful raid through Burgundy, forcing the duke of Burgundy to pay a ransom of 700,000 gold écus in return for the withdrawal of the English army. The duke also promised to support Edward's claim to the French throne. The English king then marched past Paris, but was unable to lure the dauphin out of the city and into battle. Moving off west down the Loire, on 13 April the English army was caught in a violent storm outside Chartres, in which large numbers of both men and horses were killed. In an age attuned to signs and prophecy, both the failure before Rheims and the catastrophic storm spoke volumes. Edward was not destined to ascend the throne of his Capetian ancestors.

Negotiations recommenced at Brétigny within weeks, and by 8 May a draft treaty had been completed. The ransom for John II was cut down to 3 million gold écus from the original 4 million, and Edward's traditional territorial demands (Calais, Ponthieu and Aquitaine) were set out as the price of his renunciation of his claim to the French crown. The treaty was ratified at Calais on 24 October 1360, but with one profoundly consequential change. The renunciations (of sovereignty over Aquitaine, Ponthieu and Calais by John II, and of his claim to the French throne by Edward III) were made contingent upon the completion of the transfer of territories between the two sides to take place not later than 12 November 1361. Edward was committed to Brétigny, even if the dauphin/ Charles V was not. He did not use the title or arms of France between 1360 and 1368. But in the end, the details of the settlement were never finalized, and the French successfully chipped away at the edges of the English-controlled territories. Slowly, but surely, the lustre of the magnificent victories of Edward III and the Black Prince began to tarnish and fade from view.

The plague returned to England in 1361–1362, perhaps portending other coming difficulties that would soon face the king and his kingdom. Edward III turned 50 years of age on 12 November 1362, and to commemorate the occasion he issued a general pardon. In the same parliament, he addressed the perennial problem of abuses in the system of royal purveyance. The same year had seen the creation of the principality of Aquitaine for the Black Prince, which was meant to be a central feature of Edward's dynastic legacy. Unfortunately, neither the principality nor the prince himself as its ruler was destined to live up to its promise. By now, the prince was in his 30s, and none of the various diplomatic marriages that had been considered for him had come to fruition. Now, rather unexpectedly, he married his cousin Joan of Kent in a public ceremony performed by the archbishop of Canterbury at Lambeth on 6 October 1361. Four days later, the wedding was celebrated in the presence of the king and queen, John of Gaunt and Edmund of Langley, and a wide array of lords and ladies at Windsor. The marriage would have to be described as a surprise. Joan was, by all accounts, a great beauty, although like the Black Prince himself she also had a reputation for extravagance. Moreover, marriage to a woman satirized as the 'Virgin of Kent', on account of her earlier, scandalous, marital history, was of doubtful utility. After the execution of her father Edmund, earl of Kent, in 1330, Joan had been raised in the royal household by Queen Philippa. At 12 years of age, in 1340, she entered into a clandestine marriage with Sir Thomas Holand. In the following year, while Holand was absent in Prussia, she was pressed by her mother to marry William Montagu, son of the king's trusted friend, the earl of Salisbury. Holand appears to have acquiesced in this, as he served as Montagu's steward upon his return from abroad. But, having made a fortune for himself through the capture of the count of Eu at the battle of Crécy, he began proceedings in the papal court at Avignon in 1347 to recover his wife. He was eventually successful, and a papal bull on 13 November 1349 declared Joan's marriage to Montagu null and void. She and Holand went on to have five children prior to his death in 1360, two of whom, Thomas and John, would play significant roles in the reign of their half-brother Richard II. Her third marriage to the Black Prince produced two sons, both born in Aquitaine. Edward of Angoulême was born in 1365 but died in 1371, just 5 years old, while the future king, Richard II, was born at Bordeaux on 6 January 1367.

The principality of Aquitaine to which Edward and Joan moved in 1363 was an artificial creation at best, extending well beyond the traditional borders of English Gascony. Several times larger than the territory inherited by Edward III in 1327, it included two dozen bishoprics and more than a dozen senechausées. Political divisions aside, this enlarged Aquitaine also lacked linguistic and cultural unity. As such, it was never likely to succeed. Perennial disputes, such as the status of Béarn, were reopened, and new controversies arose as formerly French territories and their leaders disputed the legitimacy of the Brétigny settlement. The counts of Périgord, Armagnac and Comminges all refused to recognize the Black Prince's authority from the outset.

The prince was to establish himself in the castle of the Ombrière in Bordeaux, a city of between 20,000 and 30,000 people. The fact that Aquitaine was located in a frontier zone – facing challenges not only from France, but from Navarre and Castile as well – is reflected in the strong military presence at the prince's court. He sailed to Bordeaux in April 1363 with 3 bannerets, 60 knights, 250 men-at-arms and 320 archers. As Chandos Herald recounts: 'Every day there were more than eighty knights at his table and four times as many squires. They jousted and held revels at Angoulême and Bordeaux.'[24] These revels lead us to another aspect of the prince's court that has often occasioned comment – its lavishness. It has been noted that the prince moved with greater alacrity in making provision for his goldsmith and embroiderers in Bordeaux, than for his administrative officials. A convincing case can be made, however, that such extravagance was necessary. Although the prince has traditionally been seen, following Froissart, as the very embodiment of chivalric virtue, the chivalric ideal to which he subscribed was one rooted in loyalty and duty to one's lord, and indeed one's sovereign. This model was not nearly so universal in southern France, a region with considerable allodial land and fierce independence. The paramount 'chivalric' virtue in the south seems to have been *largesse*, even if the importance of this particular virtue was exaggerated by self-interested troubabours. The Black Prince's nearby rivals, Charles of Navarre and Gaston Fébus of Béarn, patronized musicians such as the renowned master, Guillaume de Machaut, while Gaston Fébus himself wrote the *Livre de Chasse*, a famous treatise on another chivalric interest – hunting. The prince could do no less, and he hosted lavish feasts at which musicians entertained his guests, while he and Joan presided dressed in fashionable clothing and opulent jewels. The problem was not the extravagance of the prince's court, but rather how to pay for it.

Although the court of the Black Prince at Bordeaux was a centre of courtly culture and suggests a comfortable transition to English rule over the new enlarged Aquitaine, such was not the case. There was resentment against the imposition of English, or for that matter Gascon, taxes and legal restrictions that were considered to be 'foreign' in previously French-ruled areas. Moreover, the cessation of formal hostilities between England and France had not brought peace to much of France, as the many professional soldiers engendered by the long years of conflict formed themselves into the Free Companies, under commanders such as Hugh Calveley, Robert Knolles and Nicholas Dagworth. The victory of these Free Companies against a French royal army commanded by the count of Tancarville at Brignais in April 1362 seems to have brought about a new determination on the part of the French to eliminate this threat to order. The solution, which served multiple purposes, was to redirect the Free Companies into Spain under the guise of a crusade in 1365, while ultimately seeking to overthrow the English-supported Pedro 'the Cruel' of Castile, whose kingship was opposed by his half-brother, Enrique 'the Bastard' of Trastamára.

The primarily French force under Bertrand du Guesclin, which managed to overthrow Pedro, also contained a considerable number of English soldiers, some of them closely associated with the Black Prince. English diplomatic commitments, along with the threat posed to English shipping should the Castilian fleet now in Enrique's hands make common cause with the French, was enough to call for intervention. Nevertheless, the treaty of Libourne of September 1366 can only be characterized as a mistake. The prince agreed to advance the considerable sum of 56,000 florins (£9,333) toward Pedro's war effort, a debt that Pedro was never likely to repay. The cost of his own army was initially assessed at ten times this amount and would ultimately spiral to more than £250,000 before he ever left Gascony.

The campaign to reinstate Pedro was fraught with difficulties from the outset. Initially, the route to Castile was threatened by Charles of Navarre, who abandoned his alliance to Pedro and the prince, only to return after raids on his territory by Hugh Calveley demonstrated his vulnerability. The prince's army included his younger brother John of Gaunt, who had marched south from Brittany with Sir Robert Knolles and a force of some 500–600 men, primarily archers. Altogether, the prince's army was 6,000–8,500 men, many of them mercenaries drawn from the Free Companies. They assembled at Dax in January and crossed the Pyrenees through the famous pass at Roncevalles in mid-February. By the end of the month, the army was encamped outside Pamplona, but the next month was spent in a difficult and ultimately fruitless march west toward Burgos through difficult terrain in cold rain and wind with ever-dwindling supplies, only to find their route blocked by Castilian forces. Inexplicably, however, in early April, Trastamára abandoned his successful defensive strategy, despite the advice of his experienced French commanders Bertrand du Guesclin and Arnaud d'Audrehem. Apparently, the political repercussions of refusing to stand and fight outweighed military considerations and led the pretender to throw caution to the wind. Crossing the Najerilla River, he prepared to meet the prince's much larger army near the small town of Nájera.

The prince achieved complete tactical surprise when his army suddenly appeared on the left flank of Trastamára's army at dawn on 3 April, having approached from the north rather than from the east along the main road, as expected. Forced to reconfigure their lines and attack at once, the Castilian army faltered. An initial charge was pushed back by John of Gaunt and John Chandos in the centre of the prince's formation, and simultaneously the wings of the Anglo–Gascon army encircled the enemy. The battle was both short and one-sided, the prince achieving his last great victory. Some 5,000 Castilians lay dead on the field, although in an exaggeration of the chivalric ethos of the day, virtually none of the Castilian nobles were killed, being taken for ransom instead. The prince dissuaded Pedro the Cruel from taking his revenge by executing all of these 'traitorous' prisoners, but the greatest prize of all had eluded them, as Enrique of Trastamára had escaped the field of battle, first reaching Aragon and, ultimately, France.

Although he returned from Spain seemingly at the height of his reputation, the Black Prince was soon brought low by disease and confronted by revolt. He returned from Spain ill, perhaps with the dysentery that claimed the lives of many of his followers on the return journey to Aquitaine that began in August. The finances of the principality appear never to have been adequate to support the prince's administration, and Pedro's subsequent inability to reimburse the prince for the costs of the Nájera campaign compounded this problem. Although it has been commonplace to point to the extravagance of his court and his excessive demands for taxation, the situation was more complex. Wine exports in the 1360s, and the associated customs revenues, were only half of what they had been several decades earlier, and the transition from a war economy to a peace economy probably exacerbated the situation. Most importantly, the revolt of 1368 sparked by the collection of a hearth-tax, the *fouage*, must be seen as an Aquitainian revolt rather than a Gascon revolt: it reflects the artificial nature of the principality and its consequent fragility. While it is true that French administrative personnel – including most of the seneschals – had been replaced with English appointees, nonetheless French administrative practices seem to have been continued. The revolt was a rejection of Brétigny more broadly, fomented by the duke of Anjou and implicitly supported by Charles V. The refusal of the prince to attend the *parlement* in Paris in January 1369 justified the repudiation of the treaty and the resumption of war. The count of Armagnac announced his renunciation of fealty in the following month, and 900 towns and castles in Armagnac followed his lead within weeks. The remarkable speed with which the principality collapsed must have been both alarming and frustrating to the prince, but cannot be attributed solely to some failure on his part as an administrator as has sometimes been suggested. He himself was largely incapacitated and his commanders were unable to stem the tide of French troops that quickly overran the Rouerge, Quercy and the Agenais. The final military action undertaken by the prince has had a lasting effect on his image: this was the siege and sack of Limoges in September 1370. The siege lasted only 6 days before the town was taken and the population massacred. Authorities disagree as to how many died, with estimates ranging from 300 to 3,000. There is also disagreement as to the personal responsibility of the prince, who was now in a litter. The prince's reputation for chivalry, however, was badly damaged. Within a month, John of Gaunt was appointed lieutenant in Aquitaine and the prince returned to England.

In August 1372, the prince set out for France one last time, sailing for Calais with the king. An unfavourable wind prevented a successful crossing, and in the end the fleet returned to harbour in England. Thereupon, the prince resigned the principality of Aquitaine to his father, citing insufficient revenues to meet the expenses of government. The final 4 years of his life were spent in the shadows. Although a considerable number of the prince's retainers appear as members of parliament throughout the reign and especially in the last decade (when he was himself in England), his role in the affairs of state in general, and in particular in the Good Parliament of 1376, has almost certainly been overstated, and his political impact prior to his death was negligible.

The prince died on Trinity Sunday, 8 June 1376, his death being a great political and personal blow to his father. The Plantagenet inheritance had descended in unbroken succession from father to son since the crown had passed from John to Henry III. But what would happen now? The eldest son of the Black Prince, another Edward, had died in 1371 leaving the 9-year-old Richard of Bordeaux as his heir. Would the principle of representation be followed in order to allow a minor to succeed Edward III, or would the crown instead pass to an adult male in the royal line? And which one? John of Gaunt, the duke of Lancaster and third son of Edward III, was the obvious choice. But what if Richard himself died without heirs before the passing of his grandfather? Would the crown then go to Gaunt, or would it instead be conveyed through the line of Edward III's deceased second son, Lionel, Duke of Clarence, whose daughter Philippa, wife of Edmund Mortimer, earl of March, had given birth to a son, Roger? In these confusing circumstances, Edward III was forced to make specific provision for the succession to the throne, and although these provisions have only recently come to light in the form of a badly damaged copy of a draft, it is now possible to state unequivocally that Edward III did, in fact, designate Richard of Bordeaux as heir to the throne in late 1376. Moreover, and in contrast to the actions of Edward I in 1290, he limited the succession to the male line, even though this same policy had posed the primary barrier to his own claim to the crown of France.

As we have seen, the war with France had resumed in 1369. A resumption of hostilities had been inevitable since 1364, when Charles V had succeeded his father on the French throne. In a matter of years, Charles V had reshaped the diplomatic landscape of western Europe to the disadvantage of Edward III and the English cause, with Navarre, Flanders, Britanny and Castile all firmly now in the French camp. The Castilian fleet defeated an English fleet under the earl of Pembroke off La Rochelle in 1372, breaking the English grip that had existed for 30 years. With the English unable to reinforce Aquitaine, Charles V was able to overrun much of the duchy. As noted above, the king attempted to lead one last expedition himself, sailing from Southampton on 30 August 1372, but contrary winds prevented his crossing. The great warrior king had seen his last campaign.

The period after Brétigny also saw increasing domestic strife. Although unable to secure parliamentary consent, in 1363 the administration went ahead with the establishment of a new wool staple through which all English exports must flow. There was similar uncertainty over the administration of justice in the localities. In 1362, the powers of the recently created Justices of the Peace to pass judgements and pronounce sentences were confirmed, only to be withdrawn in 1364 and then reconfirmed yet again in 1368. The second half of the decade saw the Chief Baron of the Exchequer, the Chief Justice of the King's Bench, and the Steward of the King's Household all dismissed from office following allegations of corruption and abuse of their offices. Once the war in France recommenced, added financial pressures were brought to bear on the government and the king was obliged to seek subsidies in parliament.

In 1371, parliament agreed to an innovative tax to be levied on parishes rather than individuals, and this was projected to raise some £50,000. In order to secure this grant, Edward was forced to dismiss his Chancellor, Wykeham, the Treasurer, Thomas Brantingham, bishop of Exeter, and the Keeper of the Privy Seal, Peter Lacy. Another grant was made in 1373, but by 1376 this money was all spent and the king was in desperate financial straits once again, necessitating another parliament. The Good Parliament of April 1376 refused the king any direct taxes, agreeing only to an extension of the wool subsidy. Neither Edward III nor the Black Prince was in good enough health to attend this parliament, which was presided over by John of Gaunt. In their absence, the Speaker of the Commons,

Sir Peter de la Mare, launched an unprecedented attack on some of the king's closest associates: William Latimer, the King's Chamberlain; John Neville of Raby, Steward of the King's Household; and Richard Lyons, a prominent London banker. Lyons and Latimer, in particular, were accused of profiteering. Among others charged was Alice Perrers, the king's mistress. The charges were heard before the Lords, and the king was forced to dismiss Latimer and Neville, to imprison Lyons, and to banish Perrers.

Alice Perrers has often been taken to symbolize the corruption and decay in the last years of the reign of Edward III. She was previously married to a Lombard merchant named Janyn Perrers, but appears to have been widowed prior to the time that she became the king's mistress in the 1360s. Although the relationship did not become public knowledge until after Queen Philippa's death in 1370, she gave birth to John Southeray, the first of her three children with Edward III in 1364. During the final decade of the king's life, she received numerous and substantial grants of wardships and marriages, lands and even jewels that had previously belonged to the queen. More importantly, she was also at the nexus of the network of London merchant capitalists who financed – and greatly profited from – the king's war efforts in the 1370s. In 1375, she appeared at Smithfield at one of the last tournaments of the reign, dressed as the Lady of the Sun. Contemporaries such as William Langland were aghast. In *Piers Plowman*, he based the character of Lady Meed, the personification of venality, on Alice. Despite the attack on her at the Good Parliament in 1376, she was quickly restored to favour by the ailing king. She was probably at the king's bedside when he died, but Walsingham's account of her stripping the rings from his fingers before fleeing the scene appears to be caricature. After the king's death, she was tried in parliament before John of Gaunt, convicted and sentenced to banishment and forfeiture of all her lands and goods. In fact, she never left the realm, and was subsequently pardoned, although she spent the entirety of Richard II's reign in a largely unsuccessful struggle to recover her former property. She died at one of the few manors she managed to recover, at Gaines in Upminster in the winter of 1400–1401.

In the meantime, the king's health was continuing to fail. As early as 1369, the royal physician John de Glaston was absent from court for a number of days, preparing medicine for the king. By 1371–1372, Glaston was out of court for more than 2 months, seeing to the king's needs. In the mid-1370s, it seems that Edward suffered a series of strokes. His movements had become largely restricted to a handful of royal manors in the southeast. In June 1376, he was transported from

Havering to Kennington, where the Black Prince lay dying. In late September, the king himself fell ill, appointing trustees and writing a will in early October. He recovered sufficiently to move from Havering to Sheen in February, actually passing by Westminster as the Good Parliament was in session: the Lords are said to have come out and cheered his passage up the Thames. On 23 April, he was present at Windsor for the annual Garter feast, at which his grandsons Richard of Bordeaux and Henry Bolingbroke were knighted and admitted to the Order of the Garter, although neither boy had as yet any accomplishment in arms. The king returned to Sheen, where he died on 21 June 1377 in the fifty-first year of his reign.

The remarkable figure of £470 was distributed to paupers in Sheen prior to the departure of the funeral cortege. Edward's body, which had been embalmed at a cost of more than £20, was conveyed to London, where masses were said at St Paul's in the presence of Archbishop Sudbury on 28 June, and again on 4 July with John of Gaunt and Edmund of Langley in attendance. The wooden effigy that surmounted his coffin has survived, the face derived from a death mask of the king, providing us with a literal portrait. As he wished, he was interred among his Plantagenet ancestors in the chapel of Edward the Confessor in Westminster Abbey on 5 July 1377. His elaborate tomb was completed in 1386, and is adorned by a bronze effigy of the king, flanked by eight angels in prayer. Interestingly, although the earlier Plantagenet tombs of Edmund of Lancaster (brother of Edward I, d. 1298) and John of Eltham (brother of Edward III, d. 1336) had celebrated their Plantagenet ancestors, the tomb of Edward III celebrates the continuation of the dynasty. It was decorated with six niches on both the north and south side, which contained gilt-bronze miniature effigies of each of his beloved children, identified by their armorial shields. Both his achievements and his standing among contemporaries were captured in the epitaph inscribed on the tomb:

> Here lies the glory of the English, the flower of kings past, the pattern for kings to come, a merciful king, the bringer of peace to his people, Edward III, who attained his jubilee. The undefeated warrior, a second Maccabeus, who prospered while he lived, revived sound rule, and reigned valiantly; now may he attain his heavenly crown.

5

Richard II (1377–1399)

Richard of Bordeaux, the second son of the Black Prince and Joan of Kent, came to the throne at the age of 10 years old in June 1377. If he was not menaced by the presence of foreign troops faced by Henry III in 1216, he did still face a daunting diplomatic and military situation not unlike that which had confronted Edward III half a century earlier. For all these difficulties, however, he came to the throne already with a stronger sense of his own regality than any of his Plantagenet forebears. The fact of his having been born on the feast of the Epiphany (6 January 1367) seems to have shaped Richard's sense of self. By the time he was 4 years old, with the death of his elder brother Edward of Angoulême, he seemed assured of succession to the throne. With the passing of his father, the Black Prince, on 8 April 1376, he became his grandfather's heir. On 20 November 1376, the king, aged and infirm, invested his young grandson as prince of Wales, duke of Cornwall and earl of Chester. On Christmas Day of that year, Richard sat at the king's table, elevated above the king's own sons, his own uncles, John of Gaunt, Edmund of Langley and Thomas of Woodstock. In January 1377, he represented the king at the opening of the parliament that met in the Painted Chamber at Westminster. There, his elevation as prince of Wales was announced by the chancellor, Bishop Houghton of St David's. The chancellor sought to impress upon the elected members of parliament the honour and obedience owed to their future sovereign, following Matthew's gospel in stating, 'Here is my beloved Son, here is he who is wished for by all men'. He then went on to quote from Peter: 'your king is sent you from God, he is God's vicar or legate for you on earth'. A few months later, in April 1377, at the annual St George's Day celebrations, Richard was invested as a Knight of the Garter, as were his uncle, Thomas of Woodstock, earl of Buckingham, and his cousin, Henry Bolingbroke, earl of Derby. Meanwhile, preparations were being made for a campaign in France, of which Richard was to be nominal joint commander along with his eldest uncle John of Gaunt, duke of Lancaster. This campaign was not to be, however, as the old king's health was failing rapidly, and he died at Sheen on 21 June 1377.

Richard's coronation on Thursday, 16 July 1377, the first in a half-century, was a splendid affair. On the eve of the coronation, the king proceeded from the Tower to Westminster along a route thronged with onlookers, preceded by representatives of Bayeux, London and Gascony, followed in turn by his earls, barons and knights. The Great Conduit had been transformed into the 'Heavenly City', with angels surmounting the towers and wine flowing in place of water. Passing through Cheapside, Richard was offered wine from gilt cups by 'angels' who came forth from a 'castle' constructed along the way. The spectacle of the procession on 15 July was surpassed by the coronation ceremony on the following day. It must have filled Richard with a sense of his regal dignity. He duly took his coronation oath, and while he swore, like his great grandfather in 1307 and his grandfather in 1327, to uphold the laws made by his subjects, he did so only after the insertion of the qualifying phrase 'justly and reasonably' to describe those laws. If not the boy king himself, then certainly his advisors, led by Gaunt in his capacity as steward of England, were already jealously guarding the royal prerogative. After the coronation oath, Richard was ceremonially disrobed and then anointed with chrism. Then, last, but not least, Archbishop Sudbury of Canterbury crowned the new king, investing him with the other symbols of his royal office, the ring, sceptre and orb. Richard then sat enthroned before his subjects as their king for the first time. The ceremony was marred, however slightly, by the loss of one of the coronation shoes worn by the king as he was borne aloft from the church by his tutor, Simon Burley. The shoes were alleged to date back all the way to the reign of Alfred the Great, and later commentators would make much of the prophetic import of this accident, but at the time it seems to have had little impact.

There was no regency such as there had been in 1216, perhaps because, aside from Gaunt, who was too widely mistrusted to hold such an office, there was no obvious candidate of the stature of William Marshal. Instead, Richard's government over the next 3 years was directed by a series of 'continual councils' that came more and more to reflect the circle that had adhered to the Black Prince rather than the councilors of the recently deceased king. The first year of the reign proved particularly challenging, as within days of Richard's accession the truce with France expired, leading to a reopening of hostilities for which the English were little prepared. Although the French had engaged in a major naval build-up, the English fleet had deteriorated in Edward III's final years for want of money. So it was that, in the summer of 1377, the French admiral Jean de Vienne pillaged the Channel ports, landing with impunity and burning his way from Rye to Plymouth. A subsequent raid on the Isle of Wight found the residents there willing to pay a ransom of 1,000 marks in order to avoid the Frenchman's wrath. The situation on the continent was little better. A French siege of Calais finally foundered, but this had more to do with wet weather than English resistance. A heavier blow fell to the south, where the duke of Anjou marched down the Dordogne virtually unopposed. The great castles at Condat, Bergerac and Castillon all fell to the French, while the seneschal of Aquitaine was taken prisoner. Bordeaux, Richard's birthplace and the seat of his father's short-lived principality of Aquitaine, appeared dangerously vulnerable to siege. As at Calais, however, somewhat inexplicably, the French pulled back. Nevertheless, the English duchy was much reduced. An English counter-offensive in 1378, funded by the very generous parliamentary grant of a tax of a double tenth and fifteenth, which generated as much as £100,000, came to nothing. Hampered by the lack of adequate shipping, the campaign was poorly coordinated and culminated in an unsuccessful attack on Harfleur in Normandy by the earls of Arundel and Salisbury, followed by Gaunt's costly but equally ineffectual attempt to besiege St Mâlo.

The continuing need for military funding led to an innovative series of taxes, which was to have tragic consequences. The first of these 'poll taxes' had already been levied in 1377. The parliament that had met in February had agreed that a tax of one groat (4 d) should be assessed on all laypersons of either sex aged more than 14 years old; likewise, all beneficed clergy were to pay 12 d, and the unbeneficed, like the laity, 4 d. The revenues generated thereby had gone toward the construction of a new fleet in 1377–1378, but in the aftermath of the failures at Harfleur and St Mâlo the government was soon once again in desperate straits. In April 1379, therefore, another parliament 'granted a subsidy so wonderful that no one had ever seen or heard of the like'.[1] This second tax sought to address the issue of fairness, at least superficially, by introducing a sliding scale of liability. Once again, the laity, this time above the age of 16 years rather than 14 years, were to pay 4 d per person, but the elites in society were to pay higher rates based on their occupations or office. For instance, knights and sergeants of the law were to pay £1 (20 s), whereas mayors of great towns were to pay twice that. The mayor of the greatest town of all, London, was to pay £4 (the same rate as an earl); the royal justices were to pay £5 each, whereas the dukes of Lancaster and Brittany were to pay 10 marks (£6 13 s 4 d). A similar scale applied to the clergy as well, with the unbeneficed assessed at 4 d, bishops at 6 marks, and the two archbishops at the same 10 marks as the dukes.

Nevertheless, according to the chancellor, Richard, Lord Scrope, the second poll tax generated less than £22,000, not even one quarter of the amount expended on military activity in the previous year. Although a traditional tax of a tenth and fifteenth on movables was levied in early 1380, by later that year the government was still short of cash and sought yet another poll tax. This third poll tax in 4 years was granted in December by a parliament meeting in Northampton – it could not be held in Westminster due to popular discontent and fear of disorder in the capital. The third poll tax was set at a flat rate of 3 groats (12 d) per person on all individuals of either sex above the age of 14 years, with vague provision being made for the wealthy to assist the poor. The response to the tax was inevitable: widespread evasion. When the collectors set out to do their work, they discovered that roughly one-third of all those peasants who had paid the first poll tax in 1377 were now nowhere to be found. Some 458,356 individuals had apparently vanished, more than 100,000 of them in London and the southeast. Commissioners were appointed to seek out these tax evaders in various counties – and this proved to be efficient. By the end of May, some £37,000 had been collected, but not without widespread resentment and resistance. According to the *Anonimalle Chronicle*, it was these commissions that were responsible for provoking the Peasants' Revolt of 1381, specifically a hearing conducted at Brentwood by John de Bampton in late May that turned violent, and which was followed by an armed attack on the commission of trailbaston headed by the Chief Justice of the Common Bench, Sir Robert Bealknap, on 2 June. Once aroused, the chronicler claims, the peasants 'proposed to kill all the lawyers, jurors and royal servants they could find'.[2]

The Peasants' Revolt was long seen as a spontaneous outburst that was linked to the overall economic conditions in post-plague England and the oppression of the peasantry occasioned by a refusal of the political and economic elite to recognize their changed circumstances. There is probably some validity to this, especially in accounting for the wide geographic spread of disturbances in 1381, which ranged from London and the southeast, to East Anglia, west as far as Chester and Bridgewater, and north into Yorkshire. Nevertheless, recent studies have shown that there was a considerable level of coordination in the risings, particularly in the southeast, and that many of the participants in the uprising were not peasants in the old sense, but men of some standing in their local communities: stewards, bailiffs and jurymen. Two leaders, in particular, seem to have been able to energize the discontented populace and to articulate the basis of this discontent. John Ball, an itinerant radical preacher, perhaps at one time a chantry priest at St Mary's, York, and later Colchester, had been excommunicated and arrested repeatedly from the 1360s onward to no effect. He seems, in fact, to have been incarcerated in Maidstone gaol when the revolt broke out, being freed on 11 June when the prison was stormed by the other great figure of the revolt, Wat Tyler. On the following day at Blackheath, Ball preached a famous sermon to the rebels on the text:

> When Adam delved and Eve span,
> Who was then a Gentleman?

Although this proverb was already in wide circulation, Ball's exegesis was political dynamite, suggesting a complete overthrow of class structures, which certainly became central to the demands that would be made at Mile End and Smithfield. But if Ball gave the movement a slogan, the real practical leadership came from Wat Tyler.

Like Ball, Tyler remains a largely mysterious figure. He has most frequently been associated with Kent, but Essex has also been suggested as his place of origin. It has generally been accepted that he was indeed a tiler, although it has also been suggested that he was actually a member of the gentry of Kent, Walter Culpepper. This latter would perhaps explain his apparent use of an alias, Jack Straw, who has sometimes been taken to have been a real person, but is so enigmatic and illusory that his actual existence separate from Tyler must be doubted. In any case, Tyler led the revolt in the southeast. There is a story, probably apocryphal and reminiscent of similar stories associated with William Wallace's revolt against Edward I, that Tyler was driven to violence by an assault on his daughter by one of the tax collectors. Whether or not such abuse occurred, riots certainly did break out in Dartford on 4 and 5 June, and the violence soon spread to Maidstone. By 10 June, the rebels had reached Canterbury. Tyler is alleged to have seized the sheriff of Kent and forced him to produce and then burn all of his official records. By the next day, the rebels were back in Maidstone, where the gaol was opened and John Ball among others freed; but Maidstone was merely a stopping point on the route to London. On 12 June, the rebels assembled on Blackheath, where Ball preached to them about social justice. On the next day, a meeting was arranged between the king and representatives of the rebels. Richard travelled by boat to Rotherhithe, but fearing for his safety, the royal party chose not to disembark. This triggered a violent reaction, and the peasants now forced their way into London. The Savoy Palace of the unpopular John of Gaunt was sacked, and the Fleet prison was broken open. The New Temple was also ransacked, and at Temple Church the rebels 'seized all the books, rolls and remembrances kept in the cupboards of the apprentices of the law within the Temple, carried them into the high road and burnt them there'.[3] Yet, although written records, the proof of serfdom and other obligations, were widely destroyed, looting was largely avoided, suggesting some degree of discipline among the rebels. There was certainly bloodshed, much of it the blood of aliens, particularly Flemings. Froissart claims that Tyler himself killed the notorious Flemish financier Richard Lyons, but it is tempting to see the targeting of Flemings in the context of internal commercial rivalries within the city that had little to do with peasants from the surrounding countryside. As with any such popular rising, many longstanding personal grievances must have been settled under the guise of the present cause.

On 14 June, Richard II once again agreed to meet with the rebels, this time at Mile End. There, the king agreed to their demands as far as he was able, but meanwhile (rather than subsequently, as some chronicles report), another group of the rebels entered the Tower of London. The high officials whom they considered 'traitors' were seized and summarily executed. Both Archbishop Sudbury, the chancellor, and Sir Richard Hales, the treasurer, were brutally beheaded on Tower Hill: reputedly, it required eight imprecise strokes of the sword before Sudbury was finally decapitated. Beyond that, the queen mother's apartment was broken into. According to Froissart, 'these gluttons entered into the princess's chamber and brake her bed, whereby she was so sore affrayed that she swooned'.[4] Walsingham claims that 'they arrogantly lay and sat on the king's bed while joking; and several asked the king's mother to kiss them'.[5] Also present in the Tower during this chaotic disturbance was Richard's cousin (and future usurper as Henry IV), Henry Bolingbroke, son of John of Gaunt. How did he feel, one wonders, not to have accompanied the armed troop of his royal cousin, but rather to have been left behind, seemingly a lamb thrown to the wolves, lucky to escape with his life?[6]

On the night of 14 June, back in the Tower, Richard could view the smouldering ashes of manors and houses burned out across the city. Action was obviously needed, and a council was held, but it is unclear exactly what course of action was decided. The next day, Richard prayed at the shrine of St Edward the Confessor in Westminster Abbey before riding out to meet the peasants yet again, this time at Smithfield. This may very well have been the basis for a lifelong devotion to the saint and his church. At Smithfield, Richard and Wat Tyler met face to face. Tyler addressed the king with impudent informality as 'Brother', and went on to list his demands. These included the abolition of outlawry; the abolition of lordship except for that of the king himself; a division of all the goods of the church among the people; a single bishop for the realm of England; the abolition of villeinage and serfdom; and a universal annual land rent of 4 *d* per acre. To all these requests, the king gave his assent, 'saving the regality of the crown'.

The climax of this meeting remains controversial to this day, with different chronicles offering different interpretations of events. Tyler seems to have behaved uncouthly, asking for water and then rinsing his mouth in front of the king. He also showed disrespect for the king throughout their interview by leaving his head covered. Finally, insults were exchanged between Tyler and members of the royal party, perhaps spontaneously, perhaps by design in order to draw Tyler into a fight. Blows were struck. The Mayor of London, William Walworth, attempted to arrest Tyler, who slashed at Walworth with a dagger, which failed to pierce his armour. Tyler, however, had no armour, and Walworth wounded him in the neck. Tyler fell from his horse and was at once mortally wounded, perhaps by Ralph Standish, the king's sword-bearer. At this crucial moment, with the dying Tyler calling for his supporters to avenge his death, Richard II rose to the occasion, saying 'I am your leader, follow me',[7] and deliberately led the assembled rebels away from the field. Meanwhile, Walworth had raised the London militia, which now dispersed the remnant of the disorganized rebels. The young king cannot but have been struck by the rebels' sense of his power. He must also have learned, in part through Walworth's sudden attack on Wat Tyler, and equally through the eventual revocation of the promises made at Mile End and Smithfield, the politics of expediency. The other leader of the revolt in London, John Ball, fled after Tyler's death but proved unable to sustain the movement. He was arrested at Coventry and tried at St Albans before Sir Robert Tresilian, the most vindictive of Richard II's judges, on 12 July. Three days later, he was hanged, drawn and quartered, signalling the final collapse and failure of the revolt.

By 1381, Richard II was perhaps Europe's most eligible bachelor. In the 1370s, matches had been considered with daughters of a host of the crowned heads of Europe: Charles V of France, Charles of Navarre, Robert II of Scotland, and Bernabò Visconti, duke of Milan. But, in the end, the choice for Richard's bride fell upon Anne, eldest daughter of the Holy Roman Emperor Charles IV. This union had the advantage of detaching the house of Luxembourg from a traditional alliance with Valois France, and perhaps more immediately it served the purposes of Pope Urban VI who faced a papal rival in Avignon (Clement VII) following the outbreak of the Great Schism in 1378. The archbishop of Ravenna,

Pileo de Prata, had been sent to Prague by the pontiff to advance negotiations as early as spring 1379; there, he was soon joined by English envoys, Michael de la Pole and John Burley. In the following year, Richard's council agreed to the proposed match and began final negotiations, culminating in a treaty sealed in London on 2 May 1381 and ratified in Prague on 1 September.

Anne's passage to England was surprisingly slow, and she only reached Dover on 18 December. There, she was met by the king's eldest uncle, John of Gaunt, who conducted her to Leeds Castle where she spent her first English Christmas and New Year. On 18 January, she entered London with the king, to be treated to the same sort of spectacle as Richard had enjoyed 4 years earlier, London once again transforming itself into the 'City of Heaven' to receive her. On 20 January, Richard and Anne were wed in Westminster Abbey, and 2 days later the queen was crowned. The English chroniclers saw little value in an impoverished German princess who arrived with no dowry and an expensive following of aliens. Much like the Savoyard relatives of Eleanor of Provence, Anne's Bohemian kinsmen were awarded generous annuities and pensions, while her ladies in waiting married knights and esquires of the king's household, and her clerks were presented to valuable English benefices. Beyond this initial flurry of activity, however, Anne does not seem to have engaged deeply in politics. She did, of course, act as an intercessor, most famously with the Appellants at the trial of Simon Burley in 1388 (when she failed) and with her husband on behalf of the citizens of London in 1392 (when she succeeded).

Anne was born on 11 May 1366, and thus was of an age with her husband who was just 8 months her junior. Both were 15 years old at the time of their marriage and they seem to have developed a deep affective bond from the outset. Throughout the first decade of their marriage, Anne regularly accompanied Richard on his royal itineraries. She died very young, on 7 June 1394, at Sheen. The cause of death was not childbirth, as was so often the case with both royal and non-royal women in the middle ages, but possibly the plague. Richard, famously, ordered the palace at Sheen to be destroyed as he could no longer face the memories it contained. Both her funeral and the slightly later double tomb in Westminster that houses the remains of both Anne and Richard, were magnificent and speak to Richard's deep emotional bond to his first wife. That Anne produced no children has been a puzzlement for six centuries. Was she barren? Or was Richard himself infertile? Both are possibilities. But there is also another intriguing possibility that may shed light on both king and queen as well as their time. It is possible that the marriage was never consummated and that

Richard and Anne shared in a devout lay celibacy. Anne's piety is well attested, as is Richard's devotion to the cult of Edward the Confessor, whose chaste marriage to Edith was well known. Such chaste unions were not unknown in the late fourteenth century, but would be a remarkable commitment for a royal couple to enter upon. Without question, the lack of a male heir throughout his reign greatly exacerbated the difficulties that Richard faced in dealing with his political adversaries, leading most modern critics to doubt that his childlessness was a matter of choice.

It is difficult to know what to make of criticism of Richard's kingship in the early 1380s. John of Gaunt certainly thought that he had a natural right to advise his nephew, both as the eldest surviving son of Edward III, and also as hereditary steward of England. Other magnates, such as Richard Fitzalan, earl of Arundel, having been appointed by parliament in November 1381 'to advise and govern' the king, had a similar outlook. The king, however, in the aftermath of the Peasants' Revolt and with the recognition of his maturation embodied in his marriage, increasingly sought to develop his own circle of friends and advisors. These included associates of his father, the Black Prince, such as Simon Burley and Michael de la Pole (like Arundel, appointed to 'advise and govern' the king), but increasingly also younger men such as the chamber knights James Berners, John Beauchamp of Holt and John Salisbury, and most significantly of all, the young earl of Oxford, Robert de Vere. Richard was extraordinarily generous in his patronage to his intimates, and this, along with favour to the queen's Bohemian kinsmen, necessarily caused a reaction.

At the Salisbury parliament of 1384, the earl of Arundel criticized both the king's personal behaviour and the governance of the realm. Richard's response to Arundel's assault on his governance is recorded in the *Westminster Chronicle*, which states that the king turned white with anger and then turned to Arundel with the following challenge: 'If it is to my charge that you would lay this, and it is supposed to be my fault that there is misgovernment in the kingdom, you lie in your teeth. You can go to the Devil!'[8] He responded in a somewhat similar fashion in the following year when the archbishop of Canterbury admonished him about his insolence, and warned him of the need to seek better counsel. According to several chroniclers, Richard reached for his sword and would have struck at the primate if not for the physical restraint of his uncle, Thomas of Woodstock.

If Richard was increasingly drawn to a small inner circle of younger, less experienced courtiers, however, in some sense he was driven there by his uncles and other critics. The most notorious of his protégés, often compared to

Edward II's favourite Piers Gaveston, was Robert de Vere, who had succeeded his father as ninth earl of Oxford at 9 years of age in 1371. He was raised in the king's household, and his marriage was arranged with Philippa, daughter of Enguerrand de Coucy, earl of Bedford, and granddaughter of Edward III. The marriage duly took place in October 1376 when de Vere was 14 years old and his bride perhaps 9 or 10 years old. De Vere was another of those young men knighted by Edward III at the Garter celebrations of 1377 (along with Richard, and Henry Bolingbroke) and, early in the reign of Richard II, he was introduced into the king's court where he soon become Richard's dearest friend as well as a lightning-rod for criticism.

Although the early years of the reign had seen considerable military activity, virtually all of it had been both costly and fruitless. The so-called crusade into Flanders led by Henry Despenser, bishop of Norwich, in 1383 was only the most spectacular of these failures, leading to the bishop's impeachment before parliament later that same year. Nevertheless, the king himself had not yet led an army in person, a requisite of medieval kingship. Given latitude by a truce with France, in 1385 Richard II undertook a campaign of retribution against the Scots to punish them for recent incursions into northern England. The last feudal levy ever summoned in England provided the king with a substantial force that was estimated at some 14,000 men. Richard's army marched unopposed through Tweeddale, sacking Dryburgh and Melrose abbeys along the way, before reaching Edinburgh in mid-August. Although the campaign resulted in no major battle or important territorial acquisitions, Richard had demonstrated his military leadership and successfully reasserted English power within the territory of his northern neighbours. The king was pleased. He demonstrated his pleasure and new sense of power by granting a series of new titles and promotions. On the one hand, he rewarded members of the royal family: Edmund of Langley became duke of York and Thomas of Woodstock became duke of Gloucester. On the other hand, close associates of the king were also advanced: Sir Michael de la Pole became earl of Suffolk and Robert de Vere was elevated to the unprecedented title of Marquess of Dublin. It is possible that Richard also at this time expressed his intention to name Roger Mortimer as his heir, a move designed to weaken the strength of his uncles, and particularly the house of Lancaster.

Richard was beginning to develop his own style and his own vision. Throughout his life, the king was devoted to fashion and display, spending lavish sums on fine clothing and particularly on jewels. This was a characteristic he may well have inherited from his extravagant parents, but he seems also to have had a highly developed aesthetic and artistic sense in general. He was a patron of both visual and literary artists, and Richard also appreciated architecture: domestic, public and ecclesiastical. He is perhaps best known for his rebuilding of the Great Hall at Westminster Palace, where a magnificent hammer-beam ceiling was constructed to cover the massive central space. On a less grand scale, his interests are reminiscent of the uxorious pursuits of Henry III: at his wife's favourite manor of Sheen, he had a bath house constructed, as he did also at Eltham. Richard II is also famous for the invention of the pocket handkerchief, having ordered the production of small pieces of linen for 'the lord king to carry in his hand for wiping and cleaning his nose'.[9] The court culture developing around Richard II in the 1380s has been variously described as sophisticated, theatrical, 'civilianized', and even decadent. Perhaps all of these descriptions are apt, except the last; the intimation that Richard and de Vere shared an 'obscene familiarity', is little more than a cliché. The fact that de Vere repudiated his blue-blooded wife Philippa de Coucy in 1382 in favour of a Bohemian lady-in-waiting, Agnes Lanecrona, who had accompanied the queen to England, does not suggest a homosexual relationship. As had been the case with Gaveston, however, de Vere's familiarity was indeed obscene in the eyes of the nobility if only because it diverted away from them the royal patronage they considered their own by right of birth. This aspect of the court and its politics would prove particularly damaging to the king.

And yet, for all the facile comparisons of the reign of Richard II to that of his great-grandfather Edward II, there are stark differences in personality and temperament between the two. Richard was a devotee of the hunt, and a highly competent soldier. More importantly, he had a clear vision of kingship that was assertive and, quite unlike the spontaneous volatility of Edward II's reign. Clearly by the mid-1380s, Richard was developing an ever stronger sense of regality. This is illustrated in his distribution of badges bearing the sun, prior to his adoption of the White Hart. It can also be seen in his commemoration of his predecessors: not only his father, the Black Prince, but also his grandfather Edward III, whose marble tomb with its gilt bronze effigy was completed in about 1386; and perhaps most particularly in his later campaign for the canonization of his great-grandfather Edward II, whose tomb at Gloucester he embellished with his own emblem of the White Hart.

The first great period of crisis in the reign began at the 'Wonderful Parliament' at Westminster in October 1386. John of Gaunt and Richard II had had a falling out during the Scottish campaign of the previous summer when the duke had wished to press on beyond the Forth, but the king had refused. In July 1386, the duke had sailed for Spain, where he hoped to make good his claim to the throne of Castile in right of his second wife, Constanza, daughter of Pedro I. Although the duke and his nephew had not always seen eye to eye, Gaunt was a devoted royalist who provided Richard with tremendous support simply by virtue of his political and economic stature as duke of Lancaster and eldest surviving son of Edward III. The removal of this bulwark would prove devastating for the king.

Perhaps inspired by the absence abroad of Gaunt, the most experienced English commander, the summer of 1386 had seen an unprecedented French military build-up, and fear of invasion ran rampant across the country. In order to deal with this impending threat, the king's ministers, led by the chancellor, Michael de la Pole, requested an unheard-of quadruple subsidy from parliament. The commons' reply was to demand the dismissal of the chancellor, the treasurer, and various other government officials. Refusing to entertain such an encroachment on his royal prerogative, Richard is famously reported to have said that he would not dismiss a single scullion from his household at parliament's request.[10] Indeed, he demonstrated his utter disdain for the commons on 13 October, the feast of St Edward the Confessor, by promoting his favourite, de Vere, from Marquess of Dublin to duke of Ireland. He also refused to attend the parliament, which could not transact business in his absence. In order to end this stalemate, a delegation comprised of Richard's uncle, the duke of Gloucester, and Thomas Arundel, bishop of Ely, was dispatched to the king at Eltham to seek a reconciliation. Gloucester and Ely reminded the king that parliament would be dissolved after a period of 40 days if he failed to attend, removing any possibility of gaining the desired subsidy. In reply, the king appears to have threatened to seek French assistance in controlling his unruly subjects. This rather vague threat, altogether ludicrous in the circumstances of an impending French invasion, may have been an oblique reference to Henry III and his recourse to the mediation of Louis IX when his own prerogative rights had been attacked by Simon de Montfort and other baronial opponents a century earlier. According to the chronicler Henry Knighton, Bishop Arundel, perhaps alarmed by Richard's threat of French intervention, concluded this tense interview by reminding the king that ancient law provided for the removal of any king who was guided by evil council, and for his replacement by another of royal lineage.[11] This not very subtle reference to the fate of Edward II, with which Richard II was already quite familiar by the mid-1380s, cannot have been well received.

Returning to parliament, the king agreed to the dismissal of Chancellor de la Pole, who was immediately impeached by the commons. Other ministers, including the Treasurer and the Keeper of the Privy Seal, were also removed from office. A new continual council was appointed, including a number of outspoken critics of the king's governance, such as the new chancellor – Bishop Arundel himself – his brother, the earl of Arundel, and the Dukes of Gloucester and York. Richard did all that he could to distance himself from the tutelage of the council. He quickly arranged de la Pole's release from prison at Windsor, and later appointed de Vere as Justice of Chester. This was the region most loyal to the king, who was also earl there. Moreover, it was close to de Vere's primary holdings in the southwest, as well as his titular holdings and authority in Ireland. As such, the appointment was seen as provocative by the king's detractors. In the spring, Richard withdrew to the Midlands and Welsh marches, in no little part to inconvenience the officers of the council. During this so-called 'gyration', in August he summoned the Chief Justice of the King's Bench, Sir Robert Tresilian, along with his fellow justices, to a pair of meetings, the first in Shrewsbury, the second in Nottingham. There, the king addressed ten questions to the judges, all having to do with the king's prerogative and the regality of his person. The very first question posed was whether the appointment of the council was 'derogatory to the regality and prerogative of the lord king'. When the judges replied in the affirmative, the next two questions asked how those responsible for this derogation should be punished. The answer, chilling in its simplicity, was 'as traitors'. Other questions about the king's right to dissolve parliament, about parliament's authority to impeach royal ministers, and about parliament's right to seek a response to their own petitions prior to dealing with the king's business, were all answered to the king's satisfaction. So was the tenth and final question, asking how those should be treated who reminded the king of how Edward II had been bound by statute to the appointment of the Lords Ordainer. Again, they were to be treated as traitors. The king had the questions and their answers committed to writing and sealed. He also swore all those involved in these deliberations to silence, in order that he might use these new legal weapons only when the time was ripe. This was political dynamite. The violence that the ruling class had unleashed upon itself in the reign of Edward II had led directly to the promulgation of the Statute of Treason of 1352, which had very carefully limited the definition of treason. Richard II's questions to the judges redefined treason in the broadest possible context, essentially as any impediment to the king's exercise of his prerogative. The threat to the king's opponents, although implicit, was exceptionally clear.

Richard returned to London in November. By then, he had secured at least the superficial support of the city, whose leaders had undertaken an oath to uphold the king against any who supported or spoke treason. Armed with his new definition of treason, Richard summoned the duke of Gloucester and the earl of Arundel to come into his presence. These lords, with the earl of Warwick, mustered a considerable military following at Harringay Park and they submitted an appeal declaring Archbishop Neville of York, the duke of Ireland (de Vere), the earl of Suffolk (de la Pole), Chief Justice Tresilian, and the king's London agent, Mayor Nicholas Brembre, to be traitors. On 17 November, the three lords came before the king in Westminster Hall, accompanied by 300 men-at-arms, and laid their case against the king's inner circle. Completely out-manoeuvered, for the moment Richard referred the matter to parliament; but, ultimately, such a direct challenge to his authority could only be resolved by resort to arms.

Richard moved to Windsor, while the Appellants, as they became known, withdrew to Huntingdon, where they were joined not only by additional troops but also by two other lords, Henry Bolingbroke, earl of Derby, and Thomas Mowbray, earl of Nottingham. In the meantime, de Vere had travelled to the Ricardian stronghold of Cheshire where he raised a considerable force loyal to the king and began to move south. Unfortunately, the king, who had returned to London, was unable to place himself at the head of this army, and so the five Appellants were able to intercept and engage de Vere's force at Radcot Bridge in Oxfordshire on 20 December. De Vere appears to have demonstrated little skill as a commander and the Cheshiremen were cut to pieces and forced to flee the field. De Vere himself was able to escape only by urging his horse to swim across the Thames. He fled to the continent, but found himself unwelcome, first in Dordrecht and then in Paris; ultimately, he was allowed to settle in Louvain where he died, still in exile, in 1392. His companion-in-arms at Radcot Bridge, Sir Thomas Molyneux, Constable of Chester Castle, was even less fortunate. He was slain by Sir Thomas Mortimer. The king, in desperation, retreated to the fastness of the Tower.

A week after the battle at Radcot Bridge, the Appellants entered London and demanded the king's surrender. What happened next has long been a matter of speculation. The evidence is uncertain, but at the very least Richard seems to have been threatened with deposition. It is even possible that for a brief space of 2 or 3 days, he was actually deposed by the Appellants who could not then decide among themselves about a successor, and so in the end restored him. But the kingship to which Richard was restored at the outset of 1388 had very little relationship to the vision of kingship that he had formed over the previous several years.

As the New Year dawned, on 6 January 1388, the feast of Epiphany, Richard II attained his twenty-first birthday. Under the circumstances, there was no formal celebration of the king having reached the age of majority. A month later, on 3 February, the king opened parliament at Westminster, perhaps the most notorious session ever to meet in the Middle Ages: the Merciless Parliament. The proceedings began with the five Lords Appellant kneeling before the king and declaring that they had not 'countenanced, devised, or meditated the death of the king by any means,'[12] a remarkable declaration that would seem to indicate that public opinion thought otherwise. In any case, despite this humble profession of loyalty, they quickly brought a lengthy appeal of treason against an equal number of the king's closest associates: Archbishop Neville, de Vere, de la Pole, Tresilian and Brembre.

Not all of the Appellants' intended victims lay within their reach. De Vere, Suffolk and Archbishop Neville were safe on the continent, and Tresilian had taken sanctuary at Westminster. Of the five men initially appealed, only Nicholas Brembre appeared before parliament of his own volition, and gamely (but foolishly) attempted to defend himself. He was quickly convicted and hanged, on 20 February. Meanwhile, Tresilian had been forcibly removed from sanctuary in Westminster Abbey, his refusal to stand trial judged an admission of guilt. He too was hanged, at Tyburn, on 19 February. The Appellants were not yet satisfied, however, and after an Easter recess, parliament reconvened and took up the fate of the rest of the king's inner circle, his chamber knights. Beauchamp of Holt, Berners, Burley and Salisbury were all accused of treason, having accroached on the royal power. Richard made a personal plea for mercy for his former tutor, Burley, which, given his self-image, must have cost him dearly. Not only did he himself plead with the earl of Arundel in the newly built bath house behind the White Hall at Westminster, but the queen got down on her knees in her intercessory capacity. It was all for nothing, however. The only concession made was to spare Burley the ignominy of being hanged; he was beheaded on 5 May. A week later, the other chamber knights – Beauchamp, Salisbury and Berners – were hanged. At about the same time that Tresilian had been forcibly removed from sanctuary, his fellow justices Roger Bealknap, John Lockton, John Holt and William Burgh, along with John Carey, Chief Baron of the Exchequer, had been arrested and delivered to the Tower. They too were found guilty of treason, but their lives were spared and they were instead exiled to Ireland, where they were to languish until 1397. Meanwhile, the Appellants had seen to the appointment of men of their own: Robert Charleton was named as Chief Justice of the Common Pleas, where he was soon joined by Walter Clopton. Even relatively humble officials were liable to suffer for their association with the king's inner circle, as more than a dozen assorted serjeants-at-law, chancery clerks and exchequer clerks found themselves gaoled for as long as 2 years. It is also worth mentioning that if the Appellants could not physically punish de Vere, at least they could seek to humiliate both him and the king. This was achieved by his degradation from the Order of the Garter, an unprecedented act that was designed to mortify the king, whose election of de Vere as a Garter knight in 1385 had rankled with many more experienced soldiers who were passed over for the honour. All that said, however, the Appellants did little to consolidate their administrative authority, being satisfied with breaking that of the king.

One key player was missing from the Merciless Parliament – John of Gaunt, who was still abroad pursuing his claims in Castile. Nevertheless, his views on the events of the winter were probably communicated by his son-in-law, Sir John Holand, who returned from Spain in April. It may well be that Holand helped to moderate the actions of the parliament. Although he had begun to make a career as a soldier and supporter of the crown, Holand had fallen out of favour with his half-brother, the king (Holand was the second son of Joan of Kent by her marriage to Thomas Holland) for the killing of Richard's boyhood friend, Ralph Stafford, during the Scottish campaign of 1385. Now, however, as Gaunt's agent, he seems to have been reconciled with the king; in June 1388, he was elevated to the peerage as earl of Huntingdon, and would later be made Chamberlain of England, as well as duke of Exeter. He remained one of Richard's most steadfast supporters from this time forward.

Following the Merciless Parliament, Richard seems to have retreated into such traditional royal pastimes as the hunt, leaving the management of affairs to a continual council appointed by parliament. Although we do not know the exact membership of this council, it seems likely that the earls of Arundel and Gloucester dominated its activities. Their primary objective – aside from destroying the king's inner circle – appears to have been a renewal of the war with France, and they embarked upon a diplomatic campaign that was aimed at constructing a grand military coalition involving Brittany, the Low Countries and Aquitaine. In the end, only the duke of Brittany agreed to participate, but even he ultimately withdrew and made his peace with Charles VI after learning that Gaunt, now in Aquitaine, would not join this proposed expedition. Undaunted, the earl of

Arundel led a naval expedition to the area of La Rochelle, but lacking allies, achieved little. Meanwhile, the truce with Scotland had expired and the Scots launched a major invasion into the north of England. One of the two Scottish forces in the field, commanded by the earl of Douglas, delivered a humiliating defeat to an English army under Henry (Hotspur) Percy at Otterburn on 5 August 1388. Although attacks on Carlisle and Berwick were repulsed, these deep penetrations into English territory and the concomitant looting and destruction, coupled with a costly expedition to France, did little to raise the stature of the Appellants in the eyes of the public. Moreover, although the Appellants had thought that they could carry out their military plans with ordinary royal revenues – especially the profits from the forfeited estates of their victims, such as de Vere and de la Pole – such was not the case and, by September 1388, at Cambridge, they were forced to ask a reluctant parliament to make a grant of the traditional tenth and fifteenth. The commons were much more concerned with domestic questions of law and order, specifically the issue of livery and maintenance, through which retainers of the great men of the realm appeared to flaunt the law at will. When the Appellants balked at the proposal that all badges of livery be abolished, Richard himself stepped into the breach offering to take the lead by putting aside his own badges of livery. His statesmanlike willingness to negotiate a compromise (finalized in the parliament of January 1390) indicates a remarkable new maturity, and began a surprisingly quick recovery of royal authority.

On 3 May 1389, Richard II declared himself of age before his council in the Marcolf chamber at Westminster. On the following day, he replaced Bishop Arundel as chancellor, appointing William Wykeham, the aged bishop of Winchester and longtime servant of Edward III. He also replaced the treasurer and dismissed the earls of Arundel and Gloucester from the council. Later in the month, he appears to have performed a crown-wearing, a powerful symbolic gesture. Perhaps he even considered a second coronation to mark the beginning of his personal rule. He certainly had a new pair of slippers made to replace a part of the regalia lost in 1377. Interestingly, he also presented a set of vestments to Westminster Abbey, which included a chasuble that was adorned with the coats of arms of the king and queen, but perhaps more significantly, also depicting figures of the Virgin, St Edward the Confessor, St Edmund King and Martyr and John the Baptist, the same quartet that was so powerfully presented on the Wilton Diptych a few years later. Another interesting insight into the mindset of the king in 1389 is the production for him of a volume of English statutes. Although the compilation contains the Magna Carta and the *Articuli super Cartas*, there is certainly a concentration on the reign of Edward II, with which Richard seems more and more to have associated himself. Richard was profoundly interested in the history of English kingship, and would remain so until his final days.

Soon after Richard's reassertion of power, a new truce was agreed between England and France in May 1389. The absence of war allowed Richard to forego the second instalment of the subsidy that was promised at the Cambridge parliament. Stability was further enhanced by the king's apparent reconciliation with the Appellants. No attempt was made to recall de Vere or others from exile, and no acts of retaliation were aimed at the Appellants or their supporters. Even more importantly, in the autumn of 1389, John of Gaunt returned from Spain. Richard rode out to meet his uncle before Reading, where he was holding a council, and the two exchanged a kiss of peace. It was Gaunt who, in December 1389, formally reconciled the king with the five Lords Appellant.

During the early 1390s, Richard attempted to expand the base on which his restored power rested. In part, he did this by retaining knights and squires from throughout the kingdom, building links with the leaders of the county communities, which had been lacking before. In another way, he expanded his base by elevating the sense of regality. It was during the early 1390s that terms such as 'royal majesty' and 'highness' came to replace the more mundane 'my lord' in royal address. Richard also extended his patronage during these years. The royal court continued to be a centre of literary culture, and it has been convincingly argued that the virtual explosion of vernacular literature during his reign must, in part, reflect Richard's patronage. Although there is no evidence that the king ever patronized or rewarded the royal clerk, Geoffrey Chaucer *qua* poet, Chaucer clearly wrote *Troilus and Criseyde* with the court in mind. Another writer with court connections, Thomas Usk, produced his *Testament of Love* in the 1380s. Two of Richard's chamber knights, Sir John Clanvow and Sir John Montagu, were well-regarded writers. Clanvow, although best known today for his Lollard sympathies, wrote *The Boke of Cupid*, whereas Montagu's works have not survived, but were commented upon favorably by Christine de Pisan. The best known case of Richard's literary patronage is his commission of John Gower to write a poem about love. Gower had offered advice to the young king in his earlier *Vox clamantis*, and Gower famously dedicated the *Confessio amantis* to Richard II – even if he later followed the shifting political winds and rededicated it to England and added praise for Bolinbroke. He had been commissioned by the king himself after meeting the royal barge while rowing on the Thames. Finally, the great chivalric chronicler Froissart visited the court in 1395 and presented the king with a book of his poems.

Work was also undertaken to convey majesty visually. This is best exemplified in the Coronation Portrait and the Wilton Diptych, both of which embody Richard's image of kingship. The Coronation Portrait, which was probably painted in about 1395, shows the youthful king enthroned, facing forward wearing his crown. In his right hand, he bears an orb, in his left the royal sceptre. Enveloped in an ermine trimmed red robe, he wears a blue tunic decorated with the crowned initial 'R'. The pose is suggestive not only of the king as dispenser of justice, as found on royal seals, but also of the divine judge, as frequently depicted similarly in sculpture. The Wilton Diptych, probably dating to around 1397, is an even more complex statement of royal majesty. As a portable altarpiece, the Diptych was highly personal, more for Richard's self-absorption than for any public audience. On the left-hand panel of the Diptych, Richard kneels, wearing a crown, his hands extended upward as if to receive some gift. He is flanked by the royal saints, Edmund and Edward the Confessor, along with John the Baptist. Opposite the king and saints, on the right-hand panel, are the Virgin and Child surrounded by 11 angels. Mary appears to present the infant Christ to Richard, and Christ in turn appears both to reach forward toward Richard and to bless the king. It has been argued that the Diptych embodies Richard's commitment to the crusading movement and thus the banner he receives from the Christ child stands for his patrimony, the Holy Land. Even more suggestive, however, is the argument that the painting represents the king surrendering and receiving back England (or, indeed, all of Britain) from the Virgin as her dowry. A detailed miniature painting of an island was discovered on the upper orb of Christ's banner during cleaning in the 1990s and this supports this new interpretation. The iconography is entirely consistent with Richard's vision of his kingship in the 1390s.

Architecture was also used to convey Richard's vision. Westminster, both the abbey and the palace, had always held a special place in Richard's conception of kingship, and this became increasingly clear in the 1390s. Although he had initiated funding for the rebuilding of the abbey with an annual grant of £100 in 1386, in the aftermath of Radcot Bridge and the Appellant crisis it is unlikely that this money ever reached the abbey. Nevertheless, in 1390–1391, he arranged for the abbey to draw £120 from the revenues of alien priories, and he supplemented this with occasional cash gifts, such as one for £106 13 s 4 d immediately after Queen Anne's death, and with licenses to facilitate the acquisition of sufficient labour both to quarry the Purbeck marble in Dorset required for the columns in the nave, and for general construction.

Even before this decade of increasing royal power began, indeed at the very depth of his kingship, Richard signalled his commitment to Westminster as a royal centre. Following the hanging of the chamber knights, Sir John Salisbury and Sir James Berners by the Merciless Parliament, he had them both interred in the chapel of St John the Baptist in Westminster Abbey. In this, he may have been following the French lead as, in 1380, Charles V had honoured his great marshal, Bertrand du Guesclin, with burial in the Capetian royal mausoleum at St Denis. Whatever his inspiration, this was a pattern that the English king would develop further throughout the 1390s. In 1395, Richard ordered the burial of John Waltham, bishop of Salisbury, who had specified his final resting place as his own cathedral, not just in Westminster, but in the very heart of the abbey in the Confessor's chapel. The bishop, said Richard, was 'deserving of burial among kings'. Later in the year, Sir Bernard Brocas, the queen's chamberlain, was buried in St Edmund's chapel, to be followed by another chamber knight, Sir John Golafre, in 1396, and by Archbishop Robert Waldeby of York in 1398. The royal mausoleum of Henry III's imagination was being transformed into the resting place not only for the royal family, but for the broader *familia*, which was comprised of those who served the king with steadfast devotion.

In the same years, Richard's personal predisposition toward peace with France and the concomitant possibility of renewing the crusading movement became increasingly clear. Although such a policy was unpopular with many of the magnates, particularly Gloucester and Arundel, and may have been at the heart of popular disturbances in Cheshire in 1393, as the local economy depended heavily on the provision of archers for military service, by 1392 Richard was in communication with the French court regarding the prospects of peace, initially in the broadest sense. He had received letters carried to him by a Norman knight named Robert le Mennot who, following a conversion experience in the Holy Land, had become a vocal exponent of peace, earning the nickname 'the Hermit'. Le Mennot was associated with Philippe de Mézières, the best-known exponent of Christian cooperation. As early as 1385, Richard may have been moved by conversations with the exiled King Leo of Armenia, who made repeated attempts at Anglo–French mediation. The peace process was brought to a sudden and unanticipated halt, however, in August 1392, when Charles VI was stricken with the first of the seizures that would leave him increasingly incompetent to rule over the remaining 30 years of his reign. Nevertheless, in May and June 1393,

Richard was in Canterbury, anticipating a crossing to Calais in order to seal the peace with France. The draft treaty, however, included a provision by which Richard would perform liege homage for Aquitaine, recognizing the overlordship of the king of France. This proved unacceptable to public opinion both in England and in Gascony, as vocally attested in the parliament of January 1394, and the treaty had to be shelved. Be that as it may, neither the French nor the English were anxious to resume hostilities and negotiations continued.

The summer of 1394 was defined by the death of Queen Anne, an event that deeply moved the king. The extravagance of Richard's mourning is best – if not most accurately – remembered in his decision to have destroyed the site of her death, Anne's favourite manor of Sheen: this was not, in fact, ordered until the following year, when Richard wished to use the building stone elsewhere. Nonetheless, he did spend massive sums on funeral arrangements, not least on the magnificent double tomb that was designed to hold his own remains, as well as Anne's. The emotional outpouring and physical legacy of Richard's grief can only be compared to the memorial crosses that Edward I left behind to mark the final passage of his own beloved Queen Eleanor a century earlier. Although he has often been criticized for his outburst of violence against the earl of Arundel at Westminster at the actual funeral service on 3 August – spilling blood and causing a delay to the service while the abbey was cleansed of this pollution – the earl's late arrival and early departure from the obsequies was contemptible in every way, and in Richard's mind must have been unforgivable. It is worth noting that, while he was in Ireland on campaign in 1394, Richard had a certain small chest moved to Westminster Abbey for safekeeping. The chest contained various papal bulls and other papers relating to the marriage of his parents (and his own legitimacy), but perhaps more interestingly, it also contained an obligation from the earl of Arundel, presumably the debt of £40,000 that the king had imposed upon him in return for his release from the Tower following the fracas at the funeral. This would not be lightly dismissed.

Soon after the queen's death, Richard resolved to go in person to Ireland. No English king had crossed the Irish Sea since John, and the English grip on lordship there had grown tenuous since the invasion of Edward Bruce in 1315. That Ireland had been on the king's mind for some time is clear from his appointment of his favourite Robert de Vere first as Marquess of Dublin in 1385 and then as duke of Ireland a year later. In the aftermath of the Merciless Parliament and Richard's recovery of power, the earl of Gloucester was appointed king's lieutenant in Ireland in October 1391, but the commission was subsequently cancelled. Instead, the young earl of March, Roger Mortimer, was appointed. The appointment was complicated, however, by the fact that, at 19 years of age, he was still a minor: and it would be 2 years before he would actually cross to Ireland, and by then it would be in company with the king.

Richard assembled a sizable force of no fewer than 7,000 men for this first Irish expedition. He landed at Waterford on 1 October. He quickly achieved his initial goal of subduing the Irish chieftain Art MacMurrough who called himself king of Leinster. MacMurrough, following a 3-month campaign of harassment came into the king's peace on 7 January. Soon thereafter, the head of the O'Neill clan performed homage and fealty to Richard in person at Drogheda, and other chieftains followed suit. By early spring 1395, Richard had seemingly restored English lordship throughout all the areas to which it had ever extended. Returning to England in May, Richard had enhanced his military reputation and provided, in the language of his settlements with the Irish chieftains, another glimpse into his vision of kingship. Unfortunately, the Irish settlement would not prove lasting and would draw Richard back to the island, with fateful consequences in 1399.

On his return from Ireland, the king once again turned to the subject of peace with France. But his expedition to Ireland may also have inspired him to search for a broader peace, extending beyond the realm of international relations and warfare. It was particularly after his return from Ireland, where a number of Irish kings had performed oaths of obedience to him, that the language of kingship associated with Richard II began to exhibit a marked difference. No longer addressed merely in terms of lordship, both letters addressed to the king and letters sent out in the king's name increasingly made use of the language of majesty, which hitherto had been largely unknown, or at least unused, in England. Perhaps this is another instance of Richard adopting some of the cultural elements of French kingship, and it may also reflect his increasing interest in the imperial crown. In the end, however, it seems to have had as much to do with domestic politics and Richard's own essential vision of kingship as with anything else. Scholars have pointed to Richard's correspondence with other European rulers, such as the count of Holland, to whom, in 1398, Richard described how the Appellants 'had rebelled against the royal will . . . leaving to him little but the royal name'. The king's response had been to adjudge them 'to a natural or civil death, bringing to the lives of his subjects a peace that would last for ever'. This vision of royal peace may well be the key to unlock the 'tyranny' of Richard II. Instead of a peace, a lengthy truce of 28 years was agreed to in 1396, to be accompanied by a diplomatic wedding between Richard II and the 7-year-old daughter of Charles VI, Isabella, the first Anglo–French royal marriage in nearly a century. The truce allowed both England and France to maintain honour, and realize practical benefits, while sacrificing next to nothing. It was confirmed during a series of personal meetings between Richard II and Charles VI in October 1396 at Ardres, near Calais. The truce itself spoke of the possibility of healing the papal schism and of renewing crusading activity against the Turks, both of which may have been dearer to the king's heart than war with France. There is much contemporary evidence, albeit indirect, to support such a view. Richard's chamber knight, Sir John Clanvow, wrote pointedly of the difference between the justice of crusading warfare and the evil of internecine fighting between Christian kings. Similarly, Philippe de Mézières, who served as go-between in the negotiations between Richard II and Charles VI, in his *Letter to King Richard II*, urged an Anglo–French crusade. As well as Richard himself, many leading members of the court embraced de Mézières' crusading vision. Richard, along with Charles VI, sponsored the little-known crusading Order of the Passion, and a presentation copy of de Mézières' *De la Chevallerie de la Passion de Jhesu Crist* made for Richard is the only known extant text. The king's uncles, John of Gaunt and Edmund of York, as well as his cousin the earl of Rutland and his half-brother the earl of Huntingdon, were all members of the order.

The culmination of Richard's peace policy came in the meetings at Ardres with Charles VI. On Friday, 27 October 1396, Richard was resplendent in a robe of red velvet and a gold collar that had previously been given to him by the king of France. Interestingly, his companions wore the livery of Queen Anne. A second, formal, meeting was held on the following day, and treated not only Anglo–French relations, but also the Great Schism, which Charles VI was anxious to heal. On Monday, 30 October, Isabella was formally presented to the English king by her father, and on the following Saturday the royal couple were wed in the church of St Nicholas, Calais. Three days later, Richard II and Queen Isabella sailed from Calais for England, enjoying a smooth crossing of just 3 hours. On 23 November, the queen made a ceremonial entry into London. She was crowned on 5 January by Thomas Arundel, now archbishop-elect of Canterbury. The coronation, and the king's birthday on the next day, were celebrated by a fortnight of tournaments and other entertainments.

As 1396 drew to a close, Richard seemed to stand at the head of a united Christian Europe. Armed with a 28-year truce with France, a sizable dowry in his royal coffers, and at least the appearance of restored relations with his magnates, he was in a position to pursue his dreams. Unfortunately, that they were just dreams soon became apparent. To realize the vision of a triumphant crusade of the Christian powers was one of Richard's central ambitions. In anticipation of peace with France and an end to the Schism, a multi-national expedition led by Sigismund of Hungary had already been dispatched in 1396 to begin the rollback of the Turks. Many of the crusaders were Burgundian, but the army included such prominent French knights as Marshal Boucicaut, Jean de Vienne and Enguerrand de Coucy, as well as an English contingent under the king's cousin, Sir John Beaufort, eldest son of John of Gaunt by his mistress (and later third wife), Kathryn Swynford. By Christmas, or New Year's at the latest, however, word had reached Paris and London of the massive defeat of the Crusaders by the Turks at Nicopolis on 25 September 1396. The death or capture of so much of the flower of European chivalry spelled the end of the crusading movement as heretofore envisioned.

As an expression of the new Anglo–French friendship, Richard had agreed to support the planned French expedition against Milan, and for this he needed money. The January parliament of 1397 at Westminster started well enough, with Bishop Stafford of Exeter extolling the present well-being of both church and state. The commons, however, were less pleased with the proposal to fund a French expedition into Italy; had the matter not collapsed under its own weight when the French called off the expedition, it might well have led to a showdown. Richard had gone before the commons in person to make the case for the campaign, but all the commons would concede was that this was a private undertaking of the king and so not a matter for their consideration or funding. Tensions were raised further on 1 February when the commons sent forward a set of grievances. These included complaints about the qualifications of sheriffs and escheators, the state of the defence of the Scottish Marches, the continuing abuse of badges of livery and finally the excessive cost of maintaining the royal household. The king responded to the first three grievances in a conciliatory fashion, but vehemently refused to consider the fourth, which impinged upon his prerogative. He demanded to know the author of this attack on his regality, and the unfortunate clerk, Thomas Haxey, was brought before him and sentenced as a traitor, although later pardoned. The king made very clear that he would not countenance a repeat of the assaults made on his prerogative during the ascendancy of the Appellants.

In the spring of 1397, another of Richard's grand schemes seemed to be coming to fruition. In pursuing a Plantagenet dream that stretched back to the reign of Henry III, Richard II seems to have had a very genuine desire to obtain the imperial crown. In the spring of 1397, the Archdeacon of Cologne visited England, and an English delegation was sent to Cologne in July bearing costly gifts not only for the archbishops of Cologne and Trier, but also for the dukes of Bavaria and Saxony, all imperial electors. Richard's agents had received the homage of Rupert of Bavaria, Count Palatine of the Rhine in May, and in return for an annual pension of £1,000 the archbishop of Cologne likewise performed homage to Richard on 7 July. Meanwhile, on 10 July, payment was made to another imperial elector, the count of Guelders. Perhaps it was this seeming international diplomatic success that emboldened Richard to strike at his enemies with sudden force.

On the very same day that payment was made to the count of Guelders, 10 July 1397, the earl of Warwick was arrested after dining with the king and taken to the Tower. At the same time, Archbishop Arundel, given considerable assurances for his brother's safety, was convinced to persuade the earl to surrender himself. He too was quickly dispatched; not to London, however, but to the Isle of Wight. In the meantime, the king himself rode through the night to Pleshy to beard his uncle Gloucester in person. Gloucester was sent on to Calais, whence he would never return alive. Richard sent letters to the sheriffs announcing the arrests, made on the advice of the earls of Rutland, Kent, Huntingdon, Somerset and Salisbury, along with Lord Despenser and Sir William Scrope. The king sent out supplementary letters, stating that the arrests had nothing to do with the events of 1387, but rather were for other offences against the king's majesty. It is, in fact, possible, if not likely, that this was true. At least some of the contemporary chronicles, particularly those written in France, allege that there was a conspiracy against Richard in 1397. The English chroniclers, and most subsequent historians, have seen the coup as an act of revenge, 10 years in the making. Walsingham, however, provides an intriguing explanation, which might not be so far-fetched as it initially sounds. In his account, Walsingham states that, in July 1397, Richard was informed by an embassy from Cologne that he had secured a majority of the votes to be elected emperor, but that some electors would not ratify the decision because of his seeming inability to rule the lords of his own kingdom. This was the provocation that led to a drastic demonstration of his control over his lords.

The conspirators were to be tried in parliament. Meanwhile, Richard set about strengthening his position. He already had retainers spread throughout the counties, and now he acted to place trusted men in charge of strategic castles. The Sheriff of Cheshire, for instance, was ordered to raise some 2,000 archers. The king also sought to raise cash through loans from throughout the kingdom. At Nottingham on 5 August, a formal appeal of treason was made against Gloucester, Arundel and Warwick. The New Appellants, as they are sometimes called, were the same individuals that Richard had named in his letters of 13 July (the earls of Rutland, Kent, Huntingdon and Salisbury, Thomas, Lord Despenser and Sir William Scrope), with one significant addition – that of Thomas Mowbray, earl of Nottingham.

When parliament opened on 21 September, the assembly was overawed by the deployment of some 200 Cheshire archers, whose presence foreshadowed the eventual outcome of the proceedings. After an opening speech by the chancellor, Bishop Stafford, stressing the intrinsic and indivisible nature of royal power, a familiar group of courtiers, the earls of Rutland, Huntingdon, Kent, Nottingham, Somerset and Salisbury, along with Lord Despenser and Sir William Scrope, presented their appeal of treason against the duke of Gloucester, the earls of Arundel and Warwick, and Sir Thomas Mortimer, for their actions in 1387–1388. John of Gaunt, firmly in Richard's corner, presided over the trial as steward of England, a trial that included several bitter exchanges. In one of these, the king reminded the earl of Arundel, the first to be tried, of his refusal to grant mercy to Simon Burley a decade earlier. Arundel, despite protests that the king had previously pardoned him for his actions in 1387–1388, was quickly convicted and sentenced to a traitor's death. Like Burley, however, he was spared drawing, hanging and quartering, condemned only to beheading. On Monday 24 September, it was the duke of Gloucester's turn. Thomas Mowbray, as Captain of Calais, now announced that the duke was, in fact, already dead and unable to stand trial. Nonetheless, his confession, extracted during his imprisonment in Calais, was copied into the parliamentary record.

On the same day, Archbishop Arundel was also found guilty of treason, stripped of his temporalities and banished from the realm for life. Finally, on Friday 28 September, the earl of Warwick was tried. He admitted his guilt and begged for mercy. The earl of Salisbury pleaded on Warwick's behalf and the king relented and spared the earl's life, stripping him of his lands and sentencing him to exile in the Isle of Man, where he remained for the rest of the reign. In the aftermath of the Revenge Parliament, the king took steps to prevent any sort of political cult arising around his vanquished foes. The earl of Arundel was reburied in a plain, unmarked grave. Gloucester's corpse was returned to England, but he was given burial not in Westminster as had been originally planned and which fitted his royal blood, but rather in Bermondsey Priory. Only

Archbishop Arundel survived to trouble the king. The archbishop had been given 6 weeks to leave the realm and made the most of that time. Significantly, and perhaps with a sense of irony, he seems to have left London on 13 October, the feast day of St Edward the Confessor that was so important to the king himself and the Plantagenet dynasty. Yet even after he finally departed the realm, he proved troublesome to Richard. Although the king wrote in thanks to the men of Ghent for receiving the archbishop, in fact Arundel made his way to Rome to lay his case before Pope Boniface IX and await his chance to return.

The king's enemies having been punished, it was time to reward his followers and recast the nobility of England. Henry Bolingbroke, earl of Derby, now became duke of Hereford; Edward, earl of Rutland, duke of Aumale; Thomas Holand, earl of Kent, duke of Surrey; John Holand, earl of Huntingdon, duke of Exeter; and Thomas Mowbray, earl of Nottingham, duke of Norfolk. John Beaufort, who had survived the disaster at Nicopolis was elevated from earl of Somerset to Marquis of Dorset. With the elevation of all these new 'duketti', as the chroniclers derisively termed them, there was also room for the creation of new earls. Ralph Neville became earl of Westmorland; Thomas Despenser was granted the earldom of Gloucester that his great-grandfather had so desired; Thomas Percy became earl of Worcester; and William Scrope became earl of Wiltshire. As parliament moved toward adjournment, the question was raised of the status of the other two Appellants of 1387, Bolingbroke and Mowbray. They were members of the newly elevated 'duketti', it is true, but Richard sought to allay any lingering fears of further reprisals by stating publicly that he considered both to be his 'loyal liegemen'.

By the end of September 1397, Richard stood triumphant. His greatest enemies had been destroyed and his most trusted friends rewarded. Not only had he elevated his inner circle to the highest levels of the aristocracy, he had further rewarded them in a striking way, both visually and symbolically, by allowing them to quarter their arms – as he had done himself – with those of St Edward the Confessor. At the same time, Richard had increased the size and strength of his bodyguard of Cheshire archers, and a great many Cheshire knights and squires were awarded the livery of the White Hart and attached to the king's affinity. This retinue was to become greatly feared and loathed throughout the realm, and yet they developed a remarkable familiarity with the king. A famous quotation attributed to these Cheshire archers enjoins the king: 'Dycun sleep quietly while we guard you.'[13] It has been suggested that Richard's most prominent and influential character trait was not some complex psychosis, or even the narcissism that he surely possessed in some degree, but rather a simple sense of inferiority, or perhaps more accurately, insecurity. Throughout the reign, there had been good reason for Richard to be insecure. But, in 1397, his position was virtually unassailable. His continuing sense of insecurity, manifested in the Cheshire affinity and the relentless grinding down of his beaten enemies, became self-fulfilling. At the same time, Richard appears to have taken an interest in arranging the appointment of members of his household as sheriffs, rather than using local gentry, perhaps again pointing to his continuing insecurity.

Sometime in December 1397, on the road between Windsor and London, Thomas Mowbray, duke of Norfolk, joined the travelling party of Henry Bolingbroke, duke of Hereford. The exact details of their conversation will never be known, as each subsequently presented a version more favourable to himself, but the consequences of their exchange were to prove momentous for themselves, the king and the realm. Essentially, Mowbray warned Bolingbroke that both were in extreme danger for the part that they had played at Radcot Bridge and the subsequent events of 1387–1388. When Bolingbroke dismissed such alarming rumours by noting that both men had been repeatedly pardoned by the king, Mowbray questioned the value of the king's word. After all, Arundel had argued at his recent trial that he too had been pardoned for his actions as an Appellant. More than that, however, Mowbray alluded to conspiracies against John of Gaunt and his sons, and he apparently struck a nerve when he informed Bolingbroke of a plot at court to destroy the very foundation upon which the house of Lancaster rested by restoring the 1322 verdict of treason and disinheritance against Thomas of Lancaster. Long doubted by historians, this latter part of Mowbray's allegations has recently been taken more seriously. If the plot to destroy the house of Lancaster has never been proven, its plausibility has nonetheless been enhanced by the fact that, at the ensuing Shrewsbury parliament, the new earl of Gloucester, Thomas Despenser, achieved the annulment of the verdict of treason against his own grandfather and great-grandfather, the elder and younger Hugh Despensers. Whether Bolingbroke himself believed Mowbray, or perhaps suspected a plot designed to entrap him, after consultation with his father Gaunt, he chose to bring this dangerous conversation to the attention of the king.

The royal court spent the Christmas season in 1397 at Coventry. The king was at nearby Great Haywood in Staffordshire on 20 January when he summoned Bolingbroke to rehearse his conversation with Mowbray. He then commanded his cousin to repeat the story yet again before the impending session of parliament. Parliament opened in Shrewsbury on 28 January 1398. At first sight, this would seem a curious location for a parliament, particularly in winter, but certainly it sent an interesting signal. Aside from the matter of geographic isolation, Shrewsbury lay close to the king's stronghold in the principality of Chester. It was too small easily to accommodate and feed the various contingents who would attend, perhaps magnifying the splendour of the court. It was also in Shrewsbury that, 10 years earlier, Richard had posed his notorious questions to the judges.

The Shrewsbury parliament formally annulled all of the acts of the Merciless Parliament of 1388, although the duke of Norfolk, ominously perhaps, did not subscribe his name to this measure. The parliament also arraigned several of the king's remaining adversaries, including Sir Thomas Mortimer, who had been responsible for the death of Thomas Molineux at Radcot Bridge. At the same time, it ratified a new definition of treason that was consistent with Richard's own sense of his regality. Finally, the king's finances were given a substantial boost as he was granted the customs duties on both wool and leather for life. The only failure of the session, from the king's point of view, was the inability to settle the dispute between Mowbray and Bolingbroke, which was delegated to a parliamentary committee for reference back to the king.

Despite the annulment of the verdict against the Despensers, on 20 February Richard issued a statement reaffirming the rights to all the lands of Thomas of Lancaster to John of Gaunt and Henry Bolingbroke, 'that might fall to the crown by reason of Lancaster's treason against Edward II'. Three days later, Bolingbroke and Mowbray made their appearance before the king and the parliamentary committee at Oswestry. The case was adjourned to be heard at Windsor in April, with Mowbray in the meantime to be held in custody. A further meeting of the parliamentary committee at Bristol on 19 March tentatively agreed that the dispute between the dukes of Norfolk and Hereford should be settled by combat unless proof of guilt or innocence in the case should be found. The two opponents appeared before the king again on 28 April at Windsor, where no settlement was reached. Indeed, matters were further complicated when the duke of Hereford added new accusations to the charges against Norfolk, including the murder of the duke of Gloucester. Bolingbroke threw down his gage, which Mowbray picked up. The king, who may have genuinely sought reconciliation between the two dukes, now commanded that the dispute be settled by combat at Coventry in August, the date subsequently being moved to 16 September.

The duel between Bolingbroke and Mowbray was an international sensation. The duke of Milan, Giangaleazzo Visconti, sent Bolinbroke a fine suit of armour, while Mowbray received similar gifts from various German supporters. There were interested observers from Portugal, the Low Countries and, most of all, France. Charles VI sent a series of representatives to Richard urging him to extend the truce with France and to work with his father-in-law to end the papal schism. Division within the political community in England could further neither of these goals, and in the end Charles sent the count of St Pol personally to request of Richard that he call off the duel. Nevertheless, on Monday 16 September, the duke of Aumale and duke of Surrey, the Constable and Marshal of England, respectively, prepared the lists at Coventry for combat. The Herald of the duke of Brittany, with whom the king had recently entered into a diplomatic understanding that would ultimately lead to a firm alliance, directed the proceedings. Bolingbroke and Mowbray entered the lists, but at this point, at the king's command, the herald of Brittany suddenly ended the contest before it truly began. Bolingbroke was banished for 10 years and Mowbray for life. The king's judgment was a legitimate exercise of his authority in the court of chivalry, but it struck contemporaries as unjust, particularly in the case of Bolingbroke. The king himself acknowledged that the judgment against Bolingbroke was not indicative of any offence that his cousin had committed, but necessary nonetheless in order 'to bring peace and tranquility to the realm'.[14] The king further softened the blow somewhat, when he specifically reserved Henry's right to 'sue for livery of any inheritances that may descend to him' – that is to say, the duchy of Lancaster.[15]

Soon after the departure of Mowbray for Bohemia and Bolingbroke for France, the king arrived in Westminster to celebrate the Feast of St Edward the Confessor on 13 October. This was always a special occasion in the royal calendar, but perhaps never more than in 1398. The last of his major opponents had been dispatched into exile. Furthermore, he had the validity of all that had transpired confirmed by a papal legate. Still, the stability of the new dispensation was questionable. Even as the king celebrated his triumph at Westminster, he was confronted by the Countess of Warwick who sought to intercede on her husband's behalf. Richard, we are told, in an episode reminiscent of his confrontation with the archbishop of Canterbury in 1384, displayed the Plantagenet temper by seizing a sword and swearing that, were she not a woman, he would put her to death instantly. Richard's apparent supremacy in England may have led him to reconsider his relationships outside the realm. He certainly focused his attention on preparations for the duke of Surrey's impending expedition to Ireland. He was also much involved with France, but not all of his dealings with the Valois court were as harmonious as in previous years. Not only did he delay until the last moment before confirming the extension of the truce, but he openly expressed his opposition to French intervention in Italy. Both his alliance with the duke of Brittany and his diplomatic contacts with Giangaleazzo Visconti of Milan (albeit the latter had a cordial relationship with Bolingbroke as well) must have appeared threatening to the French. On a more personal level, his decision to take Sir Pierre de Craon into his service (with the grant of an annuity of £500) must have raised eyebrows in Paris. De Craon had attempted to assassinate the Constable of France some years earlier, and his welcome presence in Westminster must have been as unpalatable to Charles VI as Bolingbroke's reception in Paris was to Richard. Finally, Richard continued to drag his feet with regard to a settlement of the papal schism. France had already unilaterally embarked upon the so-called 'way of cession', withdrawing obedience from Pope Benedict XIII of Avignon. Meanwhile, Richard maintained his support of Pope Boniface IX in Rome, perhaps in the hope of obtaining the imperial crown. In any case, in the autumn of 1398, he was rewarded by Boniface with a concordat stating that the pope would confirm episcopal elections in England only after receiving the king's concurrence.

Richard held what proved to be his final Christmas court at Lichfield. Attended by the papal legate Peter de Bosc, as well as an ambassador from Constantinople, the emperor's uncle Hilario Doria, it was a glittering affair. Gifts came from the dukes of Burgundy and Berry, and jousts were held throughout the period that ran from the celebrations of the birth of the Lord to the birth of the king on Epiphany. And yet, the New Year began ominously, both literally and figuratively. A comet appeared in the sky, leading the French chronicler known as the *Religieux de St Denis* to prophesy revolution and the fall of kings. Meanwhile, John of Gaunt lay dying in Leicester. It is not clear whether the king actually visited his uncle on his deathbed. Although his death – or at least his funeral – was announced as early as 8 January, in fact the earl of Lancaster did not pass away until 3 February. In accordance with his will, he was buried at St Paul's, alongside his first wife, Blanche of Lancaster.

The death of John of Gaunt presented Richard with a momentous choice. Should he allow his cousin Henry Bolinbroke to return to enter his inheritance? He had committed himself to this less than 6 months previously, and nothing resonated more fully with the aristocracy as a whole than the sanctity of landed tenure and rights of inheritance. Nevertheless, faced with the prospect of a popular, and now perhaps implacably hostile, adversary in his cousin Henry, on 18 March 1399 the king revoked his letters confirming Bolingbroke's right to his inheritance and had his exile extended from a term of 10 years to life. Even so, he acted with some discretion. It is true that he parcelled out the great honours that comprised the heart of the duchy – Leicester, Pontefract and Bolingbroke going to the duke of Aumale; Lancaster itself and Tutbury to the duke of Surrey – as well as lesser lordships, but these grants were all made with the interesting provision that they would stand only until such time as Bolingbroke 'or his heir, shall have sued the same out of the king's hands according to the law of the land'. Perhaps Richard envisioned the reestablishment of a less powerful house of Lancaster not under Bolingbroke, but rather his young son, Henry of Monmouth. Although he can hardly have imagined that Bolingbroke would sit idly by and accept his disinheritance, he did believe that his strong relationship with Charles VI and the duke of Burgundy would ensure that Bolingbroke would remain in Paris, a prisoner in a gilded cage.

So it was that, in the spring of 1399, Richard II felt secure in committing himself to campaign in Ireland in person. The settlement of 1395 was, by this time, at the point of collapse and in need of immediate attention. Richard may also have thought that a military success in Ireland would be instructive for his English subjects. He sought huge sums of money in support of this effort, and he induced his newly created aristocracy to participate fully in this exercise. A dozen magnates and half a dozen bishops accompanied the royal army when it finally departed from Haverford on about 29 May, probably arriving in Waterford a couple of days later on 1 June. Initially, at least, the campaign seemed to show promise. Soon, however, it became clear that the king's former adversary Art MacMurrough would not submit to him for a second time. The king moved north to Dublin, where the lack of progress in the lordship paled into insignificance against the news freshly received from England. Bolingbroke had escaped from France and landed on the coast of Yorkshire.

Before we pass to the final challenge to Richard's throne in 1399, it is necessary to consider an issue that had been of great concern, although in the background, during much of the reign: the succession. Richard had been confronted by questions of succession since before his own accession to the throne. His grandfather, Edward III, had thought it necessary to issue an order of succession, providing for descent of the crown in the male line and thus to Richard in 1376; even so, the king's legitimacy was, at times, impugned with allusions to the promiscuity of his mother, Joan of Kent. Of greater moment, however, was Richard's inability to produce an heir of the body. As noted earlier, various explanations have been offered to account for this: that Queen Anne, whom Richard deeply loved, was barren; that Richard was infertile; that Richard and Anne, following current religious fashion, had entered into a chaste marriage. A hint in the direction of voluntary celibacy is provided by Richard's association with the cult of St Edward the Confessor. The king had campaigned under the saint's banner in Ireland in 1395, but more significantly, in the autumn of 1395 – probably on 13 October, the feast day of the Confessor – he unveiled a new royal coat of arms in which the saint's arms were impaled with his own. This symbol of his heraldic 'marriage' to St Edward seems to allude to a spiritual rather than a physical lineage. Richard's marriage to a 7-year-old French princess in 1396 is far more comprehensible if we assume that Richard had no expectation of producing an heir of the body.

Regardless, however, whether the source of royal sterility was biological or voluntary, the fact remains that throughout his reign, Richard was able to manipulate the issue of succession for his own political purposes. According to Walsingham, in 1399 Sir William Bagot recalled an earlier conversation in which Richard had indicated that he was considering resigning his crown in favour of his cousin, the duke of Aumale. To this, Mowbray himself had objected that Hereford was more closely related and a more appropriate choice for an heir. Certainly, based upon the entail of 1376, Henry Bolingbroke was Richard's heir in 1399. This made his attempted recovery of the Lancastrian inheritance a matter of urgent importance to both men.

Henry Bolingbroke had passed his banishment in Paris, lodging at the Hôtel de Clisson. He was well known to the French royal court, although pressure from England led to a foreclosure of negotiations for a marriage between Henry and a daughter of the duke of Berry. He received sympathy from the French court when news of Gaunt's death arrived, but this was tempered by the news that his inheritance had been sequestered and his banishment prolonged into a life sentence. It is unlikely that either Charles VI or the duke of Burgundy, effective ruler of France at the time, would favour any dramatic confrontation that might further diminish the hopes for peace with England and an end to the papal schism. Bolingbroke did, however, find support from the duke of Orléans, who entered into a treaty of friendship with the 'duke of Lancaster' in June.

Bolingbroke obviously had widespread support among the Lancastrian affinity, and very likely among the landholding classes more broadly. If Ralph Neville, earl of Westmorland, joined him because the two were brothers-in-law, the commitment of another northern lord, Henry Percy, earl of Northumberland, seems to have been based solely on the justice of Bolingbroke's cause. The addition of Archbishop Arundel and his nephew, Thomas, putative earl of Arundel, like Bolingbroke in exile on the continent, is not as obvious as it might seem; animosities between the FitzAlans and the house of Lancaster stretched back across several generations. Their support of Henry's cause thus gave considerable weight to Bolingbroke's stance.

The Lancastrian invasion was quickly accomplished. Henry is known to have been in Paris as late as 17 June but, by about 4 July, he landed on the Humber at Ravenspur. Henry moved north into the Lancastrian heartland, securing the surrender first of Pickering and then turning west to Knaresborough. From here, he moved south to Pontefract, at the epicentre of Lancastrian power, and also symbolically important as the cult centre of that earlier opponent of royal tyranny, Thomas of Lancaster. At nearby Doncaster, the northern lords flocked to Bolingbroke's banner, and he swore an oath that he sought only his rightful inheritance to the duchy of Lancaster. Nonetheless, he also initiated a letter-writing campaign in which he portrayed himself not only as seeking justice for himself, but as the champion of all those who had suffered under Richard's misrule. If the Kirkstall abbey chronicler exaggerates the size of Henry's army at 30,000, it was nonetheless a substantial force.

Edmund of Langley, duke of York and keeper of the realm during Richard's absence in Ireland, acted with all speed. In late June, he ordered the sheriffs to muster whatever troops they could at Ware, and he initially raised a substantial force. On 4 July, he wrote to his nephew, the king, informing him of Bolingbroke's landing. Two weeks later, he wrote to the Mayor of London, forbidding the sale of weapons or armour to any but those who were loyal to the king. Richard's inner circle, including the infamous Sir John Bushy, Sir William Bagot and Sir Henry Green, worried about the potential disruption of their lines of communication with the king, immediately proceeded to Bristol. This city also appears to have been Bolingbroke's objective. By 20 July, he had moved south from Doncaster to Leicester, moving on to Coventry 3 days later and then to Warwick on 24 July. Henry's army continued to grow, reaching an estimated size of 100,000 men, actually leading him to dismiss some of his would-be followers as he could not provide for such numbers. On 27 July, Henry met his uncle, the duke of York, at Berkeley. Although the exact details of their discussion are unknown, it is clear that York declared his nephew's cause to be just and threw in his lot with Bolingbroke. Loyalists – such as Bishop Despenser, Sir William Elmham and Sir Walter Burley – were arrested and the combined forces of Lancaster and York marched on Bristol on 28 July. The constable of Bristol Castle, Sir Peter Courtenay, faced with overwhelming numbers, surrendered after a perfunctory show of resistance. Richard's unpopular councilors, William Scrope, earl of Wiltshire, Bushy and Green, were surrendered as well. Another of Richard's despised counselors, Bagot, had already sailed from Bristol to join the king in Ireland.

What Bagot must have found was disheartening. Confronted by a lack of shipping, the king was unable to make a rapid return to England. Richard does not appear to have left Dublin any earlier than 17 July, and probably landed at Milford Haven only on 24 July when Bolingbroke's army was at Warwick. In the meantime, he had sent the earl of Salisbury ahead with a small force and orders to raise a royal army in north Wales and Cheshire. Once he had landed, Richard probably spent a week in south Wales before recognizing that his only hope was to reach the army being raised by the earl of Salisbury at Chester. They met at Conway by 12 August, but the news was not encouraging. Salisbury reported that he had raised an army of 40,000 men, but had been unable to maintain it. The forces he had left behind in the south under Aumale and Worcester had also evaporated, either by accident or design. Along with the defection of York, and the executions at Bristol, the tide was very clearly turning against the king.

Henry tarried in Bristol only long enough to see to the executions of Scrope, Bushy and Green, perhaps acting under his authority as steward of England. In any case, by 2 August, he had reached Hereford, and by way of Leominster and Ludlow he reached Shrewsbury on 5 August. On that very day, a delegation led by the sheriff of Chester, Sir Robert Legh, sought out the duke. The supposed heartland of Ricardian loyalty and power had surrendered without offering any resistance, and Henry (for his part) proclaimed that the men of Cheshire should be spared from any looting or pillage by his own forces, although in the event this was not to be the case. On 9 August, Henry advanced to Chester itself, but although he drew up his forces in battle formation, there was no need, as the city surrendered at once. Similarly, Richard's stronghold at Holt, where he had stored considerable treasure, capitulated without a fight.

The rapid collapse of all resistance left Richard in a quandary at Conwy. A military option no longer being realistic, he decided to negotiate. He dispatched the duke of Exeter, accompanied by the duke of Surrey, to offer terms under which Bolingbroke might be allowed to enter his inheritance. Having heard what the two emissaries had to say, Henry took them both into custody. Henry's response to Richard's embassy, was to dispatch one of his own, headed by the earl of Northumberland who now travelled to Conwy, securing Flint and Rhuddlan along the way. Although he had been accompanied by a large force, he left these troops at some distance and approached Conwy with only a small escort. When they met, Northumberland swore an oath to the king that the duke sought only to recover his Lancastrian inheritance, as was his legal right. Beyond this, according to Jean Creton, the terms offered to Richard were that he be directed by parliament, at which, with Bolingbroke sitting as chief judge (again perhaps in reference to his office as steward of England) Exeter, Surrey and Salisbury, the bishop of Carlisle and Richard Maudeleyn would be tried for treason. These terms, a virtual return to the conditions of the Merciless Parliament, were obviously unacceptable to Richard, but he decided to play for time. Indeed, again according to Creton, he swore that in the fullness of time he would have his revenge for this outrage, and that he would flay his enemies alive. For now, however, he agreed to accompany Northumberland – following his swearing of an oath to his good faith in the terms he conveyed – to Chester for a meeting with his cousin of Lancaster.

Once the king discovered the true size of Northumberland's retinue, he reportedly requested his return to Conwy, but Northumberland refused to accede to his sovereign's wishes. Richard discovered en route that Rhuddlan, where they stopped to dine, and Flint were both held by Bolingbroke's men. He had been hoodwinked, and was now effectively a prisoner. Upon reaching Flint, the king heard mass and then from the ramparts he watched the arrival of the Lancastrian army. He was not only confronted by Archbishop Arundel, who with considerable irony assured him that 'no harm should happen to his person', he was also faced with the fact that his erstwhile companions Albemarle and Worcester were in the very midst of his foes. Then Bolingbroke arrived. With courtesy, he waited outside until after the king had dined, and when he entered the courtyard and the king came down to him, Bolingbroke bowed low before him. However, he did not mince words. His first statement to the king said nothing about his Lancastrian inheritance, but addressed the 22 years of misgovernance that England had suffered under Richard, and offered his assistance to the king in correcting this state of affairs. The king, having expressed his satisfaction with this arrangement, Bolingbroke called for horses for the king, and a pair of nags was produced for Richard and Salisbury to ride to Chester.

Once at Chester, Richard was placed in the highest tower in the castle, to be guarded by the sons of his dead nemeses, the earls of Gloucester and Arundel. That evening at dinner, the earl of Worcester, as Steward of the Household, broke his rod of office, thereby releasing the king's household from service to him. According to Creton, all of Richard's companions were separated from him and could not henceforth converse with him. By 19 August, essentially ruling England in Richard's name, Henry sent out summonses for a parliament to meet at Westminster at the end of September. On 20 August, the king and his captor departed Chester and made for Coventry and from there to Lichfield. There, it would seem, a rescue was attempted by the king's loyal Cheshiremen, and Richard attempted a dramatic escape, climbing down from his tower at night, only to be spotted and placed under a heavier guard thereafter. Humiliation after humiliation were heaped upon the king. Beyond the pathetic nag that he had been given to ride, throughout their progress from the West Country to London, Richard was allowed no change of clothing. A few miles outside London, a delegation from the city rode out to the royal party. Creton presents Bolingbroke as another Pilate, who in presenting the king to 'his people' saw a means to encompass his death without any blame. Entering London, Bolingbroke went directly to St Paul's and the tomb of his father, where he wept copiously, perhaps as much from joy as from grief.

The end-game to this struggle was far from clear. A return to rule by continual council may have been envisioned, but given the king's documented capacity for dissimulation followed by long-deferred vengeance, it cannot have been considered safe to have Bolingbroke 'rule' England while Richard still 'reigned'. There is an indication that the decision to depose Richard had been taken 3 weeks before parliament opened on 30 September, as reference to the king's regnal year is omitted from documents issued by 'royal' clerks after 10 September.

In some ways, defeating Richard militarily had been the easy part for Bolingbroke. In searching for a precedent for the removal of a king, the events of the reign of Edward II must have come to mind. That reign had been a constant undercurrent for most of Richard's reign in any case. But the deposition of 1326–1327 was viewed officially, and had been since early in the reign of Edward III, as an abdication. Despite any pressure that might be brought to bear, it was highly unlikely that Richard would abdicate in public. Resignation was more feasible. But even here there were problems, for unlike the situation in 1327, in 1399 the question of Richard's heir remained uncertain. Moreover, resignation being voluntary, potentially the act could subsequently be rescinded. So it was deposition after all. But the deposition of Richard II was not modelled on the case of Edward II. Rather, the Lancastrian advisors turned to the example of the deposition of the Holy Roman Emperor Frederick II at the Council of Lyons in 1245. But again, there were difficulties, as there was no desire to involve the pope or a church council in English constitutional practice.

According to the official Lancastrian version of events, the 'Record and Process', on Michaelmas 1399 a delegation was sent to meet with the king at the Tower to seek his renunciation. There, the earl of Northumberland swore that Richard had pledged his willingness to renounce the throne of his own free will before himself and Archbishop Arundel while at Conway. After some discussion, Richard is reported to have agreed to the terms of the renunciation 'with a cheerful countenance', and then signed the declaration with his own hand. Indeed, he is said to have added his wish that Henry should succeed him, which he further signified by placing his signet ring on his cousin's finger. Very little, if any, of this account should be taken at face value. Almost certainly, Richard refused to renounce his throne. The Dieulacres chronicle may come closest to the truth when it states that he 'placed [the crown] on the ground and resigned his right to God'. To whom else could an anointed king turn?

On 30 September 1399, in Westminster Hall, the renunciation was read out before parliament and then accepted. The articles of deposition are long and detailed, but their essence is captured in the first article, which states that 'the king is indicted on account of his evil rule'. The bishop of St Asaph pronounced the sentence of deposition. Henry Bolingbroke now rose and addressed the assembly, and asserted his right, by descent, to the throne. The lords, spiritual and temporal, one by one gave their assent. A date for the coronation of Henry IV was quickly established – 13 October, the feast of St Edward the Confessor. Perhaps Henry Bolingbroke was trying to associate himself with his namesake, King Henry III, but the irony of such a choice of date cannot have been lost on Richard or the wider contemporary audience.

But what about Richard II? As had been the case in 1327, the presence of a former king was an extremely awkward reminder of the usurpation that had taken place. Initially, there was talk in the commons of trying Richard, along with his former henchmen, but on 21 October, the Lords announced a resolution that Richard should be 'kept in safe and secret ward'. A week later, Henry IV announced a sentence of perpetual imprisonment against his cousin and erstwhile sovereign. On 29 October, Richard was transported down river to Gravesend, beginning a northward journey into the heart of Lancastrian power, finally being confined at Pontefract. Again, the irony of the association with Thomas of Lancaster and Edward II is difficult to overlook.

A plot to seize King Henry and his sons at Epiphany 1400, Richard's thirty-third birthday, was exposed and came to nothing. Indeed, less than nothing. The earls of Huntingdon, Kent and Salisbury, along with Sir Thomas Despenser, were unable to keep their conspiracy secret, and they were themselves seized by townspeople in various parts of the country – Bristol, Cirencester and Pleshy – and summarily executed. Most likely, this abortive rising sealed Richard's fate. By mid-January, rumours of Richard's death were widespread; by month's end, they had reached Paris. Perhaps even Henry was not entirely sure of the situation. A discussion in the king's council on 8 February 1400 concluded that, if Richard were still alive, he should be kept under the tightest possible security, whereas if he were indeed dead, then his body should be publicly displayed. Within 10 days, the answer – to the prayer obliquely raised in Henry's council – was known: Richard was dead and his corpse, face exposed, was en route from Pontefract to London. The body was displayed to public view in St Paul's for 2 days before burial, not with Anne in the purpose-built double tomb in Westminster, but in the Dominican friary in Langley, ironically the resting place of another Lancastrian victim, Piers Gaveston. There, Richard would remain, very likely in the tomb in which Edmund, duke of York, and his wife were later interred, for 13 years until Henry V provided for his reinterment in the Plantagenet mausoleum in Westminster Abbey.

Perhaps a final word can be said about both Richard and the Plantagenets through a consideration of Richard's Westminster tomb. The figures are decorated not only with the initials 'A' and 'R', but also with various heraldic devices. The queen is portrayed with knots and chained and collared ostriches as befits her Bohemian ancestry, whereas Richard's robes are adorned with his emblem of the White Hart, and also with the sunburst. Less regal, but in the end more poignant for this last Plantagenet ruler, the king's tomb is also decorated with the broom pod, the *planta genesta* from which the family had derived its name some two and a half centuries earlier. Richard II would be the last Plantagenet king laid to rest in Westminster Abbey, and it is still his portrait, seated in majesty, that greets every pilgrim who enters this everlasting shrine to the Plantagenet dynasty.

Conclusion

What did the idea of 'dynasty' mean to the Plantagenet kings of England? At a basic level, it pointed to a sense of lineage; an awareness of ancestry and the past were powerful forces at all levels of medieval society, but particularly among the aristocracy and royal family. This awareness of ancestry was physically manifested and reinforced in numerous ways: the accounts of chroniclers; the elaboration of genealogies; the decoration of royal residences, along with the construction of memorials; and the ritual celebration of important dates. The Plantagenets engaged in all of these activities through patronage or direct participation, celebrating and proclaiming the legitimacy and permanence of their dynasty.

England was unique in the early medieval period in having produced a single royal dynasty, the West Saxon house of Alfred. These kings of Wessex who became the kings of England did not have to compete with rival princely houses as was so often the case on the continent, particularly in France. The Normans and Angevins sought to associate themselves with the house of Wessex through marriages in order to legitimate their rule, but this was no longer the case for the Plantagenets, who sought their brides abroad. Still, from Henry III to Richard II, all of the Plantagenet kings venerated the last 'English' king, Edward the Confessor, and his shrine at Westminster was transformed into the quintessential Plantagenet shrine, linking the English past, present and future under their rule.

The Plantagenet sense of dynasty can be seen in a number of manifestations, but nowhere more than in the development of Westminster Abbey as a dynastic church. Neither the Normans nor the Angevins had developed such a dynastic centre. Although they were crowned at Westminster, they were all buried elsewhere, in various personally selected locations ranging from Caen to Fontevrault and Rouen in France, and from Winchester to Faversham to Reading and Worcester in England. There is very little evidence of any sense of dynasty in these burials. The individual is commemorated, not the ruling family. This was dramatically changed by the Plantagenets. Henry III, Edward I, Edward III and

Richard II all lie in the semi-circle surrounding the magnificent tomb of Edward the Confessor that was dedicated late in the reign of Henry III. The placement of the tombs alone establishes the Plantagenet sense of dynasty in this royal mausoleum, but one can go considerably further in discussing the decoration of these public memorials.

Henry III was buried before the high altar in the original resting place of Edward the Confessor. His gilt bronze effigy shows Henry wearing his crown and coronation robes, his headrest adorned with English leopards. Although Edward I was interred in a plain marble tomb, he arranged splendid memorials for both his wife, Eleanor of Castile, and his brother, Edmund of Lancaster. Eleanor's tomb is decorated with heraldic shields representing England, Leon, Castile and Ponthieu, celebrating the union of her ancestry with the Plantagenet dynasty. Edmund's tomb, to the north of the high altar, similarly conveys the dynastic awareness of the Plantagenets. There are ten niches each on the north and south side of his tomb, which once contained sculptural figures depicting Edmund himself, his brother Edward I and father Henry III, as well as other members of the royal family and members of the house of Lacy, into which his son Thomas had recently married. This theme is further developed and extended in the tombs of Edward III and Philippa, both of which also contained 'weepers' mourning the dead. In this case, the 32 figures that were represented in the niches on Philippa's tomb represented her ancestors, siblings, children and the spouses of her children. Likewise, the king's tomb depicted each of his 12 children and no-one else. This is a statement of dynasty.

The ultimate test of any dynasty is longevity: the ability to produce male heirs and transmit the succession from father to son without challenge is of paramount importance. The rival Capetian house of France had needed two centuries to establish itself on the throne. From Hugh Capet to Philip II, every Capetian king of France crowned his own son and heir as king during his own lifetime. Only in the thirteenth century did Philip II feel confident enough to allow his son Louis VIII to remain uncrowned. In England, the situation was very different. Henry III came to the throne as a boy of 9 years old in 1216, with the rules of succession not having been thoroughly established. Under both the Norman and Angevin kings, the crown had passed from brother to brother as often as from father to son, nor was it always clear that the eldest son stood as heir to the throne. Although Henry III's claim to the throne was not challenged from within the royal family, he did for a time face the all-too-real threat of being supplanted by a Capetian claimant in the person of the future Louis VIII. Nonetheless, after a long and tumultuous reign in which the authority of the king to rule was severely challenged, the right of the Plantagenet dynasty to rule was confirmed. Not only would Henry be succeeded by his son, Edward I, without incident, but Edward I felt so secure in his succession that he could take 2 years in returning from his Crusade before finally arriving in England in 1274. Edward II likewise succeeded his father without controversy, having been publicly presented to the people of England as his father's heir as early as 1297. Despite his overthrow by Queen Isabella in 1326/1327, Edward II passed his crown on to his eldest son, Edward III. Perhaps based on his own difficult youth, Edward III drew up a will, which was only recently rediscovered by historians, in which he limited the succession to the male line. By now, however, the sense of succession from father to son was so well established by the Plantagenets that, when Edward III died in 1377, the throne went without question to his 10-year-old grandson Richard, as son and heir of Edward of Woodstock, eldest son of the late king. The end of the Plantagenet dynasty came only with Richard II's failure to produce an heir of his body. Had Richard produced a son and heir, it is difficult to imagine the successful usurpation of the throne by Henry IV.

What then is the legacy of this dynasty that ruled England for nearly all of the thirteenth and fourteenth centuries? First of all, the Plantagenet dynasty should be seen as the first English, or perhaps more accurately British, dynasty of the late middle ages. Despite the imperial dreams of Henry III and Richard II, the Plantagenet dynasty found itself increasingly more English. If Henry still thought of himself as French in cultural terms, nonetheless the resources available to him, both economic and human, were derived from his English holdings. His failure to recognize the changing nature of his kingdom was an important reason for the challenge to his authority led by Simon de Montfort, which had such far-reaching consequences. Edward I seems to have better understood his position, and while he did continue to involve himself in continental affairs, particularly in defending English rule in Gascony, his legacy is clearly British. His impact on the development of the common law, divergent from a continental civil law tradition, is of great significance, but it is his military legacy that remains most familiar. The conquest of Wales and his repeated attempts to establish English rule in Scotland point to a British vision that could not have been conceived by his father. Edward II, for all his other shortcomings, held onto this vision of English hegemony in the British Isles, despite such catastrophic setbacks as Bannockburn. He refused to recognize the legitimacy of Robert Bruce and continued to plan Scottish campaigns throughout his reign. Edward III, it is true, revived English claims to the ancestral Plantagenet holdings in France, but at the same time his reign saw the development of an increasingly conscious English identity, expressed in the use of the English language in both official government documents and the growing vernacular literature of the day. Richard II, although born in Bordeaux and associated with French cultural models and an international aesthetic, was nonetheless British. His only personal military campaigns were to Scotland and Ireland, and if the most recent interpretation of the Wilton Diptych is correct, he is depicted offering Britain to the Virgin as her dowry. This is a magnificent assertion of the divine right of the Plantagenet dynasty to rule, but to rule the British Isles.

Another crucial legacy of the Plantagenet era is the development of parliament. Neither the name nor the institution had existed in 1216 when Henry III came to the throne: the first use of the term *parliamentum* appears in 1236, but the new representative body became a permanent part of the English political landscape by the end of the reign. The Provisions of Oxford in 1258 called for a radical reordering of government, much of whose business was to be conducted – and personnel appointed – in parliament. If the king was successful in avoiding the most restrictive elements of the provisions, the centrality of parliament as an institution became increasingly clear. In 1265, when Simon de Montfort summoned burgesses and knights of the shire to attend parliament in London, this was a novelty designed to shore up his support. After 1327, however, an assembly not containing these representatives would no longer be considered a true parliament. During the later years of the thirteenth century and the first half of the fourteenth century, parliament took on increasingly significant functions not only as a court of law, but also as a legislative body, and most importantly as the only legitimate source of grants of taxation. By the end of the reign of Edward III, the commons had found their voice, literally, in the person of the Speaker of the House of Commons. The office was first held during the Good Parliament of 1376 by Sir Peter de la Mare, who led a spirited attack on the king's favourites and officials. In the reign of Richard II, the most dramatic events were all played out in parliament, with the Wonderful Parliament of 1386, the Merciless Parliament of 1388 and the Revenge Parliament of 1397. By the turn of the fifteenth century, parliament had become inseparable from the governance of England, and this is perhaps the greatest aspect of the Plantagenet legacy, not only for England, but for the world.

Notes

Notes to Introduction

1 The duchy of Aquitaine is frequently referred to as Gascony in medieval English sources, and as Guyenne in French sources. Although there are technical differences between the three terms, they were used interchangeably in medieval sources, and will be considered synonymous throughout this book.

Notes to Chapter 1: Henry III (1216–1272)

1 *L'Histoire de Guillaume le Marechal*, in *English Historical Documents*, Volume II, 1042–189, eds D. C. Douglas and G. W. Greenaway (London, 1953), p. 84.
2 F. M. Powicke, *The Thirteenth Century* (Oxford, 1953), p. 61.
3 At the Painted Chamber at Westminster, the inscription was in French and read 'Ke ne dune ke ne tine ne prent ke desire,' 'He who does not give what he holds, does not receive what he desires.'
4 D. A. Carpenter, *The Minority of Henry III* (Berkeley and Los Angeles, 1990), p. 390.
5 *Calendar of the Close Rolls 1254–1256*, p. 326.
6 D.A. Carpenter, 'King Henry III and the Tower of London', *London Journal*, 19, (1995), 95–107, reprinted in D. A. Carpenter, *The Reign of Henry III* (1996), pp. 199–218.
7 'Largesce' was the open-handed generosity expected of kings and so necessarily opposed to 'covetousness'. 'Debonereté' is less easily translated, but might be rendered as 'nobility of spirit', or more simply as goodness, kindness or meekness; it is therefore opposed to ire.
8 P. Binski, *Westminster Abbey and the Plantagenets: Kingship and the Representation of Power, 1200–1400* (London and New Haven, 1995), p. 7.
9 *Calendar of the Close Rolls 1237–1242*, p. 258.

10 Quoted in M. Howell, *Eleanor of Provence: Queenship in Thirteenth-Century England* (Oxford, 1998), p. 23.

11 *Calendar of the Patent Rolls 1247–1258*, p. 217.

12 Presumably, like the money of Bordeaux, this was worth £87.50 sterling.

13 J. R. Maddicott, *Simon de Montfort* (Cambridge, 1994), p. 117.

14 Matthew Paris, *Historia Anglorum*, ed. F. Madden (RS, 1866–69), iii. 99, 320.

15 Matthew Paris, *Chronica Majora*, 6 vols., ed. H. R. Luard (RS, 1884–1889), vol. 5., p. 706.

16 Ibid., pp. 697–8.

17 J. R. Maddicott, op. cit., p. 188.

18 *The Song of Lewes*, ed. C.L. Kingsford (Oxford, 1890), p. 38.

19 *Flores Historiarum*, ed. H.R. Luard (RS, 1890), iii, p. 262.

20 *De Antiquis Legibus Liber. Chronica Maiorum et Vicecomitum Londoniarum*, ed. T. Stapleton (1846) p. 73.

21 Quoted in J. R. Maddicott, op. cit., p. 295.

22 *The Chronicle of Walter of Guisborough*, ed. H. Rothwell (London: Camden, vol. 89, 1957), p. 200.

Notes to Chapter 2: Edward I (1272–1307)

1 J. C. Parsons, *Eleanor of Castile: Queen and Society in Thirteenth-Century England* (New York, 1995), p. 14.

2 *Foedera*, 7 vols (London, 1816–69), I, i, p. 189.

3 *Thomas Wright's Political Songs of England*, ed. P. Coss (Cambridge, 1996), pp. 130–1.

4 *The Chronicle of William de Rishanger*, ed. J. O. Halliwell (1840), p. 78. John Marshal remarked that 'he still had the hammer and anvils to make more and better sons'.

5 *The Chronicle of Walter of Guisborough*, ed. H. Rothwell (London: Camden vol. 89, 1957), pp. 210–12.

6 F. M. Powicke, *The Thirteenth Century 1216–1307*, (2nd edn) (Oxford, 1962), p. 280.

7 *Le Livre des Hommages D'Aquitaine*, ed. Jean-Paul Trabut-Cussac (Bordeaux, 1959).

8 Quoted in M. Biddle, *King Arthur's Round Table* (Woodbridge, 2000), p. 393.

9 *The Chronicle of Walter of Guisborough*, op. cit., pp. 358–9. Interestingly, a similar story is told of Archbishop Winchelsey, who is reputed to have prompted a fatal heart attack in the Abbot of Oseney in 1297 – see *The Chronicle of Lanercost*, ed. H. Maxwell (London, 1913), pp. 162–3.

10 *The Chronicle of Walter of Guisborough*, op. cit., p. 216.

11 Ibid., pp. 220–1.

12 *The Chronicle of Bury St. Edmunds 1212–1301*, ed. A. Gransden (London, 1964), pp. 78–9.

13 M. Prestwich, *Edward I* (Berkeley, 1988), p. 200.

14 *The Chronicle of Bury St. Edmunds 1212–1301*, op. cit., pp. 113–14.

15 J. P. Trabut-Cussac, *L'Administration Anglais een Gascogne Sous Henry III et Edouard I de 1254 a 1307* (Geneva, 1972), p. 211.

16 *The Chronicle of Lanercost*, op. cit., p. 55.

17 *The Chronicle of Bury St. Edmunds 1212–1301*, op. cit., p. 117.

18 *The Chronicle of Walter of Guisborough*, op. cit., pp. 289–90.

19 Cited in *Edward I*, op. cit., p. 471.

20 *The Chronicle of Lanercost*, op. cit., p. 86.

21 *The Chronicle of Walter of Guisborough*, op. cit., pp. 382–3.

Notes to Chapter 3: Edward II (1307–1327)

1 *The Chronicle of Walter of Guisborough*, ed. H. Rothwell (Camden, third series, 89 1957), p. 291.

2 G. L. Haskins, 'A Chronicle of the Civil Wars of Edward II', *Speculum*, 14 (1939), 75.

3 *The Chronicle of Bury St Edmunds, 1212–1301*, ed. A. Gransden (London, 1964), p. 158.

4 *Roll of the Princes, Barons and Knights who Attended Edward I at the Siege of Caerlaverock*, ed. T. Wright (1864), p. 18.

5 *The Letters of Edward Prince of Wales, 1304–1305*, ed. H. Johnstone (Cambridge, 1931), p. 11.

6 *The Chronicle of Walter of Guisborough*, op. cit., pp. 382–3.

7 *Annales Paulini*, in *Chronicles of the Reigns of Edward I and Edward II*, ed. W. Stubbs (RS, London, 1882) i, p. 259.

8 Ibid., p. 262; *Flores Historiarum*, ed. H. R. Luard (RS, London, 1890), iii, p. 331.

9 Westminster Abbey Muniments, no. 5460.

10 J. R. Maddicott, *Thomas of Lancaster 1307–1322: A Study in the Reign of Edward II* (Oxford, 1970), p. 325; J. R. S. Phillips, *Aymer de Valence, earl of Pembroke 1307–1324* (Oxford, 1972), p. 31.

11 *Thomas of Lancaster 1307–1322: A Study in the Reign of Edward II*, op. cit., p. 124.

12 *Annales Londonienses*, in *Chronicles of the Reigns of Edward I and Edward II*, ed. W. Stubbs, 2 vols (London, 1882), p. 221.

13 *Flores Historiarum*, op. cit., iii, p. 229.

14 Thomas W. Ross, ed. 'On the Evil Times of Edward II: A New Version from MS Bodley 48', *Anglia*, 75 (1957), 173–93.

Notes to Chapter 4: Edward III (1327–1377)

1 *Calendar of the Close Rolls 1323–1327*, p. 577.
2 *Chronicle of Lanercost*, ed. H. Maxwell (London, 1913), p. 258.
3 *Scalachronica*, ed. H. Maxwell (Glasgow, 1907), p. 157.
4 P. Chaplais, *English Medieval Diplomatic Practice* (London, 1982), p. 436.
5 *Chronicle of Lanercost*, op. cit., p. 310. All of his subsidies in 1337 add up to £225,000.
6 *Chronica Adae Murimuth et Roberti de Avesbury*, ed. E. M. Thompson (RS, London, 1889), p. 311.
7 *Foedera*, 7 vols (London, 1816–69), II, ii, p. 1131.
8 *Annales Londonienses*, in *Chronicles of the Reigns of Edward I and Edward II*, ed. W. Stubbs, 2 vols (London, 1882), vol. 1, pp. 132–3.
9 *Calendar of the Patent Rolls 1367–1370*, p. 341.
10 *Chronica Johannis de Reading et Anonymi Cantuariensis, 1346–1367*, ed. J. Tait (Manchester, 1914), pp. 132–3.
11 *Chronicles of Jean Froissart*, ed. G. Brereton (Harmondsworth, 1968), p. 69.
12 *Calendar of the Patent Rolls 1330–1334*, p. 74.
13 *Chronicles of Jean Froissart*, op. cit., p. 92.
14 *Parliament Rolls of Medieval England*, ed. G. Given-Wilson *et al.* (Woodbrige, 2005).
15 *Chroniques de Jean le Bel*, eds J. Viard and E. Déprez (Paris, 1904–1905), vol. 2, p. 111.
16 *Chronica Adae Murimuth et Roberti de Avesbury*, op. cit., p. 386.
17 *Chronicle of Lanercost*, op. cit., p. 333.
18 *Chronicle of Lanercost*, op. cit., p. 337.
19 Menteith was executed as a traitor for having previously sworn an oath of homage to Edward III.
20 *Polychronicon Ranulphi Higden*, ed. J. R. Lumby (RS, London, 1883), vol. 8, p. 344.
21 R. Horrox, *The Black Death*, (Manchester, 1994), p. 84.
22 Quoted in R. Horrox, *The Black Death*, (Manchester, 1994), p. 250.
23 *The Life and Campaigns of the Black Prince*, ed. R. Barber (New York, 1986), p. 58.
24 *The Life and Campaigns of the Black Prince*, ed. R. Barber (London, p. 1979), p. 105.

Notes to Chapter 5: Richard II (1377–1399)

1 *Anonimalle Chronicle 1333–1381*, ed. V. H. Galbraith (Manchester, 1927), p. 127

2 Ibid., p. 135.

3 Ibid., p. 141.

4 *Chronicles of Froissart*, trans. Lord Berners, ed. G. C. Macauley (London, 1924), p. 256.

5 Thomas Walsingham, *Historia Anglicana*, ed. H. T. Riley (RS, London, 1863), vol I, p. 459.

6 How near run a thing this was is revealed by Henry IV's later pardon to John Ferrour of Southwark who saved him in the Tower 'in a wonderful and kind manner'.

7 *Historiae Vita et Regni Ricardi Secundi*, ed. G. B. Stow, Jr. (Philadelphia, 1977), p. 66.

8 *The Westminster Chronicle 1381–1394*, ed. L. C. Hector and B. F. Harvey (Oxford, 1982), p. 69.

9 TNA, E 101/401/5, f. 1.

10 *Knighton's Chronicle 1337–1396*, ed. G. H. Martin (Oxford, 1995), p. 215.

11 Ibid., pp. 354–62.

12 *The Westminster Chronicle 1381–1394*, op. cit., pp. 234–5. The parliament roll assigns a similar profession of innocence only to Gloucester.

13 *Kenilworth Chronicle* (British Library Add. MS 35295), cited in M. V. Clarke, *Fourteenth Century Studies* (Oxford, reprint, 1969), p. 98.

14 *Chronicles of the Revolution 1397–1400*, ed. C. Given-Wilson (Manchester, 1993) p. 90.

15 *Calendar of the Fine Rolls, 1391–1397*, p. 293.

Select Bibliography

This bibliography is in no way meant to be comprehensive. The primary sources listed below are those cited at various points in the book and are gathered here for the sake of convenience. The list of secondary sources concentrates almost exclusively on monographs and general studies. The extensive literature available in scholarly articles has not been included, but can be pursued through the bibliographies contained within the works listed here. Place of publication is London unless otherwise specified.

PRINTED PRIMARY SOURCES

Annales Londonienses, in *Chronicles of the Reigns of Edward I and Edward II*, ed. W. Stubbs, 2 vols (1882).

Annales Paulini, in *Chronicles of the Reigns of Edward I and Edward II*, ed. W. Stubbs, 2 vols (1882).

Anonimalle Chronicle 1333–1381, ed. V. H. Galbraith (Manchester, 1927).

Calendar of the Close Rolls, 45 vols (1892–1954).

Calendar of the Fine Rolls, 22 vols (1911–1963).

Calendar of the Patent Rolls, 70 vols (1891–1982).

Chronica Adae Murimuth et Roberti de Avesbury, ed. E. M. Thompson (1889).

Chronica Johannis de Reading et Anonymi Cantuariensis 1346–1367, ed. J. Tait (Manchester, 1914).

Chronica Majora of Matthew Paris, ed. H. R. Luard, 7 vols (1884–1889).

Chronicle of Bury St Edmunds 1212–1301, ed. A. Gransden (1964).

Chronicle of Lanercost, ed. H. Maxwell (1913).

Chronicle of Walter of Guisborough, ed. H. Rothwell (1957).

Chronicle of William de Rishanger, ed. J. O. Halliwell (1840).

Chronicles of Froissart, trans. Lord Berners, ed. G. C. Macauley (1924).

Chronicles of Jean Froissart, ed. G. Brereton (Harmondsworth, 1968).

Chronicles of the Revolution 1397–1400, ed. C. Given-Wilson (Manchester, 1993).

Chroniques de Jean le Bel, eds J. Viard and E. Déprez, 2 vols (Paris, 1904–1905).

De Antiquis Legibus Liber. Cronica Maiorum et Vicecomitum Londoniarum, ed. T. Stapleton (1846).

Flores Historiarum, ed. H. R. Luard, 3 vols (1890).

Foedera, conventiones, literae et acta publica, ed. T. Rymer, 7 vols (1816–1869).

Haskins, G. L., 'A Chronicle of the Civil Wars of Edward II', *Speculum* 14 (1939).

Historia Anglicana of Thomas Walsingham, ed. H. T. Riley (1863).

Historia Anglorum of Matthew Paris, ed. F. Madden (1866–1869).

Historiae Vitae et Regni Ricardi Secundi, ed. G. B. Stow (Philadelphia, 1977).

Knighton's Chronicle 1337–1396, ed. G. H. Martin (Oxford, 1995).

Letters of Edward Prince of Wales, 1304–1305, ed. H. Johnstone (Cambridge, 1931).

L'Administration Anglais en Gascogne Sous Henry III et Edouard I de 1254 a 1307, ed. J.-P. Trabut-Cussac (Geneva, 1972).

L'Histoire de Guillaume le Maréchal, ed. P. Meyer, 3 vols (Paris, 1891–1901).

Le Livre des Hommages d'Aquitaine, ed. J.-P. Tabut-Cussac (Bordeaux, 1959).

The Life and Campaigns of the Black Prince, ed. R. Barber (New York, 1986).

Parliament Rolls of Medieval England, ed. C. Given-Wilson *et al.*, 16 vols (2005).

The Peasants' Revolt of 1381, ed. R. B. Dobson (1970).

Polychronicon Ranulphi Higden, ed. J. R. Lumby (London, 1883).

Roll of the Princes, Barons and Knights who Attended Edward I at the Siege of Caerlaverock, ed. T. Wright (1864).

Scalachronica, ed. H. Maxwell (Glasgow, 1907).

Song of Lewes, ed. C. L. Kingsford (Oxford, 1890).

Statutes of the Realm, eds A. Luders, T. E. Tomlin *et al.*, 11 vols (1810–1828).

Thomas Wright's Political Songs of England, ed. P. Coss (Cambridge, 1996).

Westminster Chronicle 1381–1394, eds L. C. Hector and B. F. Harvey (Oxford, 1982).

SECONDARY SOURCES

Allmand, C., *The Hundred Years War: England and France at War, c.1300–c.1450* (1976).

Barber, R., *Edward Prince of Wales and Aquitaine: A Biography of the Black Prince* (Woodbridge, 1978).

Bennett, M., *Richard II and the Revolution of 1399* (Stroud, 1999).

Biddle, M., *King Arthur's Round Table* (Woodbridge, 2000).

Binski, P., *Westminster Abbey and the Plantagenets: Kingship and the Representation of Power, 1200–1400* (London and New Haven, 1995).

Brown, M., *The Wars of Scotland 1214–1371* (Edinburgh, 2004).

Buck, M. C., *Politics, Finance and the Church in the Reign of Edward II* (Cambridge, 1983).

Carpenter, D. A., *The Minority of Henry III* (Berkeley, 1990).

Carpenter, D. A., *The Reign of Henry III* (1996).

Chaplais, P., *English Medieval Diplomatic Practice* (1982).

Given-Wilson, C., *The Royal Household and the King's Affinity: Service, Politics and Finance in England 1360–1413* (1986).

Goodman, A., *The Loyal Conspiracy: The Lords Appellant under Richard II* (1971).

Goodman, A., *John of Gaunt* (1992).

Goodman, A. and J. L. Gillespie, eds, *Richard II: The Art of Kingship* (Oxford, 1999).

Green, D., *Edward the Black Prince* (2007).

Haines, R. M., *King Edward II: His Life, His Reign, and Its Aftermath, 1284–1330* (2003).

Hamilton, J. S., *Piers Gaveston, earl of Cornwall 1307–1312* (1988).

Holmes, G. A., *The Good Parliament* (1975).

Horrox, R. *The Black Death* (Manchester, 1994).

Howell, M., *Eleanor of Provence: Queenship in Thirteenth-Century England* (Oxford, 1998).

Johnstone, H., *Edward of Carnarvon 1284–1307* (Manchester, 1946).

Kenilworth Chronicle (British Library Add. MS 35295), cited in M. V. Clarke, *Fourteenth Century Studies* (Oxford, reprint, 1969).

Maddicott, J. R., *Thomas of Lancaster 1307–1322: A Study in the Reign of Edward II* (Oxford, 1970).

Maddicott, J. R., *Simon de Montfort* (Cambridge, 1994).

Mortimer, I., *The Perfect King: The Life of Edward III, Father of the English Nation* (2006).

McNamee, C., *The Wars of the Bruces: Scotland, England and Ireland 1306–1328* (East Linton, 1997).

Ormrod, W. M., *The Reign of Edward III: Crown and Political Society in England 1327–1377* (1990).

Oxford Dictionary of National Biography, 60 vols (2004).

Palmer, J. J. N., *England, France and Christendom, 1377–1399* (1972).

Parsons, J. C., *Eleanor of Castile: Queen and Society in Thirteenth-Century England* (New York, 1995).

Perroy, E., *The Hundred Years War*, trans. W. B. Wells (1945).

Powicke, F. M., *King Henry III and the Lord Edward: The Community of the Realm in the Thirteenth Century*, 2 vols. (Oxford, 1947).

Powicke, F. M., *The Thirteenth Century 1216–1307*, 2nd edn (Oxford, 1962).

Phillips, J. R. S., *Aymer de Valence, earl of Pembroke 1307–1324* (Oxford, 1972).

Prestwich, M., *Edward I* (1988).

Rogers, C. J., *The Wars of Edward III* (Woodbridge, 1999).

Rogers, C. J., *War Cruel and Sharp: English Strategy Under Edward III, 1327–1360* (Woodbridge, 2000).

Ross, T. W. ed. 'On the Evil Times of Edward II: A New Version from MS Bodley 48', *Anglia*, 75 (1957).

Saul, N., *Richard II* (1994).

Stones, E. L. G. and Grant G. Simpson, *Edward I and the Throne of Scotland 1290–1296*, 2 vols. (Oxford, 1978).

Sumption, J., *The Hundred Years War I: Trial by Battle* (1990).

Sumption, J., *The Hundred Years War II: Trial by Fire* (1999).

Sumption, J., *The Hundred Years War III: Divided Houses* (2009).

Tuck, A., *Richard II and the English Nobility* (1973).

Vincent, N., *Peter des Roches, An Alien in English Politics 1205–1238* (Cambridge, 1996).

Vincent, N., *The Holy Blood: King Henry III and the Westminster Blood Relic* (Cambridge, 2001).

Watson, F., *Under the Hammer: Edward I and Scotland, 1286–1307* (East Linton, 1998).

Waugh, S., *England in the Reign of Edward III* (Cambridge, 1991).

Index